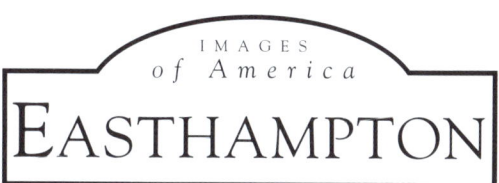

IMAGES
of America

EASTHAMPTON

To Jeanette Zywah
Best Regards
Ed Dwyer

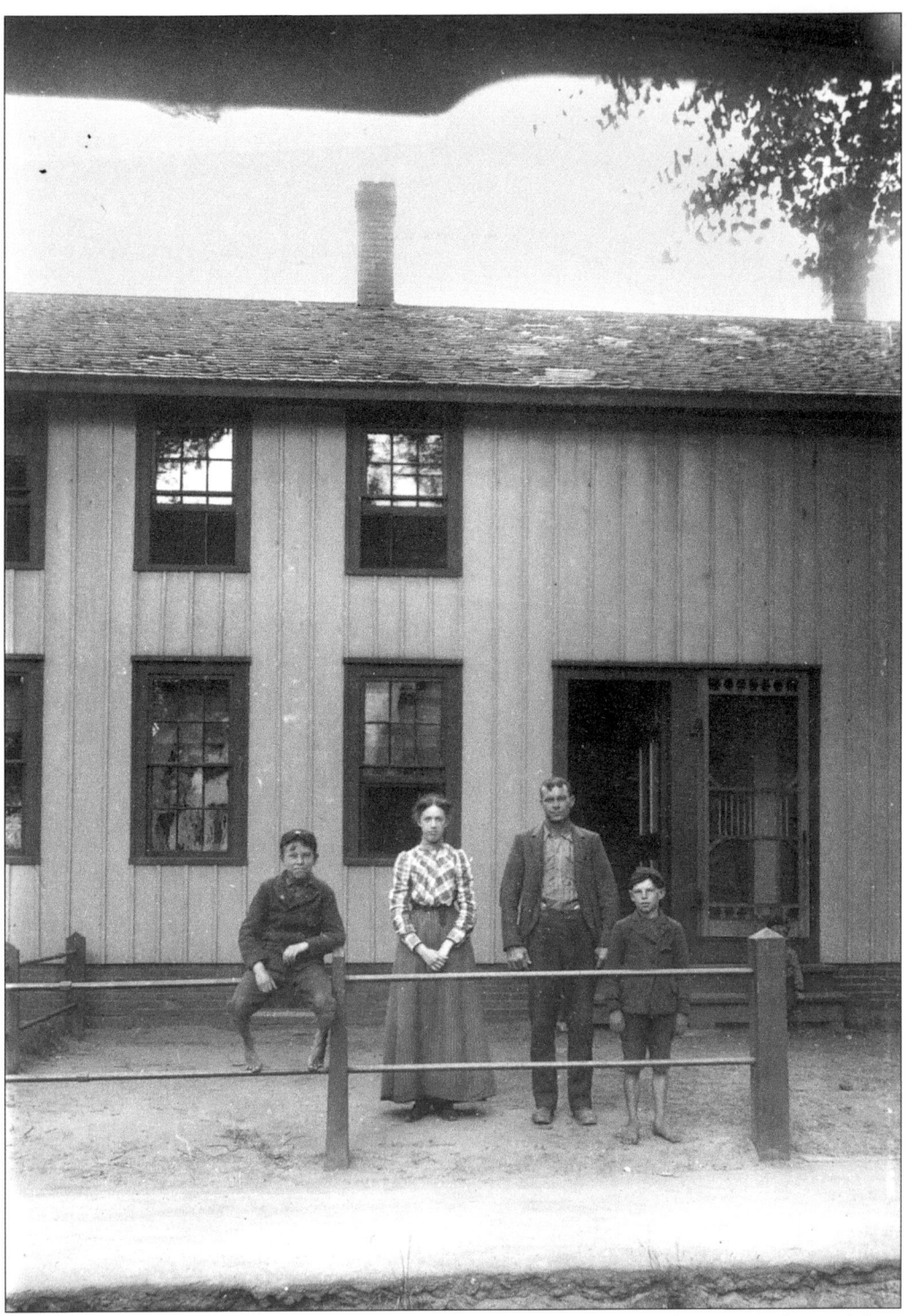

In this Howes Brothers photograph from the late 19th century, a family poses in front of their 19 Maple Street row house. This dwelling was rented to them from the Nashawannuck Manufacturing Company, which owned several dwellings along Maple Street.

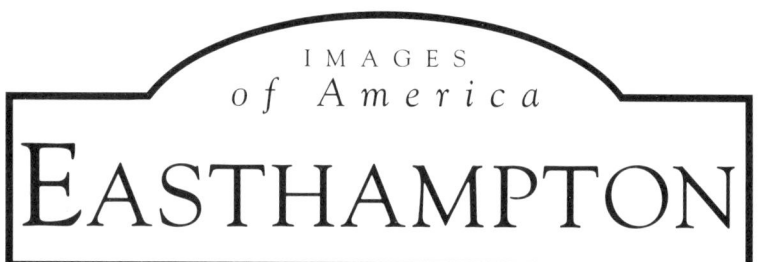

IMAGES
of America

EASTHAMPTON

Edward Dwyer

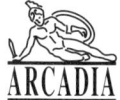

ARCADIA

Copyright © 2000 by Edward Dwyer.
ISBN 0-7385-0418-1

First published in 2000.

Published by Arcadia Publishing,
an imprint of Tempus Publishing, Inc.
2 Cumberland Street
Charleston, SC 29401

Printed in Great Britain.

Library of Congress Catalog Card Number: Applied for.

For all general information contact Arcadia Publishing at:
Telephone 843-853-2070
Fax 843-853-0044
E-Mail sales@arcadiapublishing.com

For customer service and orders:
Toll-Free 1-888-313-2665

Visit us on the internet at http://www.arcadiapublishing.com

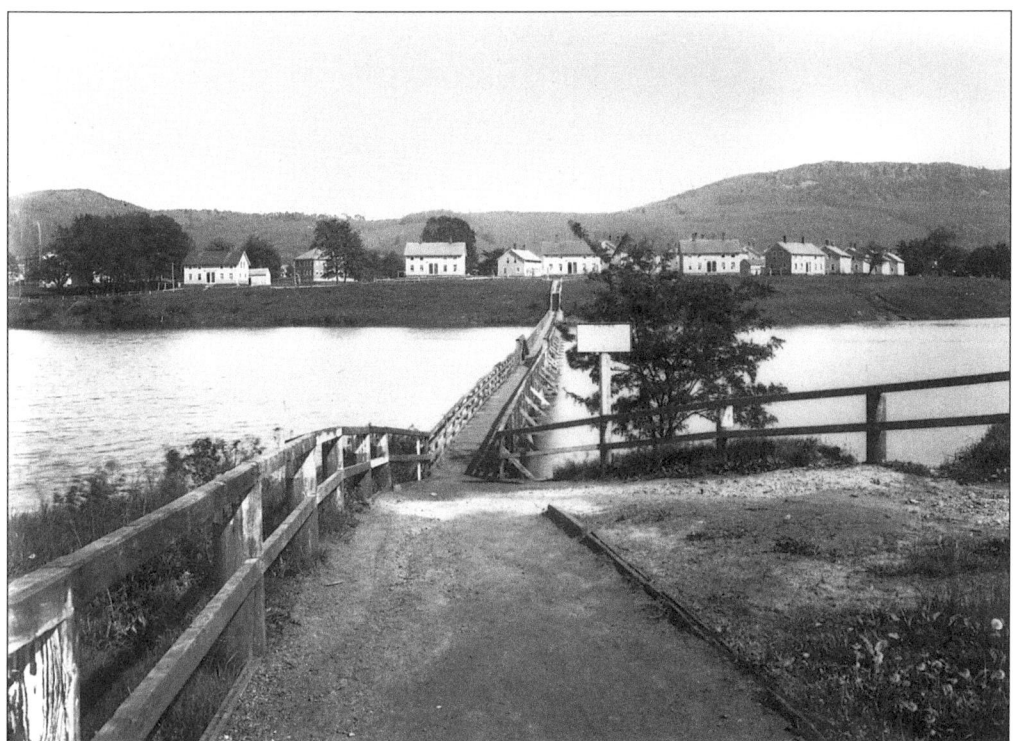

The New City village was owned by the West Boylston Manufacturing Company, which rented apartments to its employees. This footbridge crossing the Lower Mill Pond provided a quick path to the mills. Today, the pilings still stand in the water as the only reminder of that bridge.

CONTENTS

INTRODUCTION

On June 17, 1785, Easthampton became a separate political entity of Massachusetts. The actual beginning of the community had occurred a century earlier, when Easthampton was still a village of Northampton. On December 13, 1664, land was granted to John Webb, the first settler of European heritage. The next year, Webb began the slow process of establishing a community. This community grew as various farmers and sawmill operators took residence near the Manhan River and the village of Pascommuck. (Pascommuck is a Nipmuck word translating to "where it bends," referring to the Oxbow area of the Connecticut River).

The European community was under constant fear of attack from Native Americans. On May 24, 1704, the village of Pascommuck was attacked by a war party of some 72 Native Americans, killing 19 of the 38 villagers. Gradually, however, settlers returned and reestablished Pascommuck, and the settlement along the Manhan River continued to grow. Eventually, there were enough settlers to form a district—an independent political entity separate from Northampton. In those days, a town was formed in order to hire a minister and to maintain a meetinghouse, what we would call a Congregational church today. In 1789, the first minister of the town was ordained. He was the Yale-educated Rev. Payson Williston. By 1809, Easthampton was able to change its charter and formally become a town, giving the town a formal presence in the Massachusetts House of Representatives.

Throughout the first half of the 19th century, Easthampton remained an agrarian community. The town was a close community of just a few families. One of the highlights of this era was the establishment of Williston Seminary in 1841. The seminary is now the Williston-Northampton School, a prep school.

A major change in the town's economy occurred in 1847. Samuel Williston, son of the town's first minister, established a new company: the Williston-Knight Button Company. This signaled the beginning of the first phase of Easthampton's industrial development. Following the success of this venture, several new industrial operations were created near Nashawannuck Pond. In 1848, the Nashawannuck Manufacturing Company, an elastic-making company, opened. After that, the Glendale Company (another elastic maker) was established, first in the village of Glendale and then in Easthampton. The Easthampton Rubber Thread Company was created to manufacture narrow rubber strips for the elastic industry. The George Colton Elastic Mills became the third elastic maker. At the lower millpond, the Williston Mills were incorporated to manufacture cloth from cotton.

Many new residents, seeking employment at the mills, ushered in changes to the town. The first high school was established in 1864. The First National Bank began the same year, with the Easthampton Savings Bank starting in 1869. That year, a modern town hall was dedicated, the same building serving as the seat of government today. By 1871, the railroads began to make regular scheduled runs through town. The public library was established in 1881. Streetcars began operating in 1895, the same year a telephone system began. More importantly, new churches were established, as the second Congregational Church was followed by the Methodist, Episcopalian, Lutheran, and Catholic Churches.

By 1899, the economic and social fabric of the town underwent major changes. Two major employers moved to Easthampton. The West Boylston Manufacturing Company produced cloth from cotton, while the Hampton Company processed cloth by dying, mercerizing, or bleaching cloth. These companies recruited many new residents to town, including French-Canadian and Polish workers. The West Boylston Manufacturing Company built three model mill villages for their employees. Another major change occurred in 1912, when the Glendale Company purchased the Nashawannuck Manufacturing Company. During World War I, all the local mills were able to secure federal war contracts and they prospered.

However, the economy following the war posed difficulties to the town. The West Boylston Manufacturing Company lost contracts, laid off many employees, and, by 1927, began looking for a buyer for their mills. They also began a branch in Montgomery, Alabama, and closed the Easthampton division in 1931. The Nashawannuck Pond industries also faced uncertainty. The Williston-Knight Button Company, then known as the United Button Company, closed in 1922. In 1927, the Glendale Company and the Colton Elastic Mills, after years of competition, decided to merge. These companies, together with the Conant-Houghton mills of Littleton and Lowell, formed the United Elastic Corporation. The Easthampton Rubber Thread Company became a subsidiary of United Elastic.

The post-WWI depression hit Easthampton early and hard. Many left town at that time to seek employment elsewhere, as several mills (especially the former West Boylston mill) stood empty for years.

A third economic boom came with WWII, as defense contracts were awarded to several local industries. Cardanic, General Electric, Textron, and the Campagna Corporation (a maker of prefabricated housing for the European theater of war) all set up mills in Easthampton. The United Elastic Corporation and the Hampton Company also obtained war contracts. This boom continued after the war. Stanley Home Products arrived in 1947 and, with their "Stanley Home Parties," offered many jobs for local employees. (The company would sell products to dealers, who would sell them at parties held in the customers' homes). A new trend was beginning at that time, as many began using their cars to take out-of-town jobs. The end of this economic prosperity began in 1962, when the Hampton Company closed. By 1971, the Glendale division of the United Elastic Corporation closed. In 1995, Stanley Home Products also closed.

Yet the town continues to adapt and grow. In the early 1970s, a major subdivision was built off Plain Street, in the section of town called the Plains. In the industrial park on O'Neil Street, Tubed Products constructed a major mill, employing several hundred workers today. In 1996, the town of Easthampton took the first step to becoming a city, as a new charter was passed and a mayor became the chief executive. Three years later, Easthampton officially became a city and now looks towards the 21st century with renewed optimism.

One

SETTLEMENT

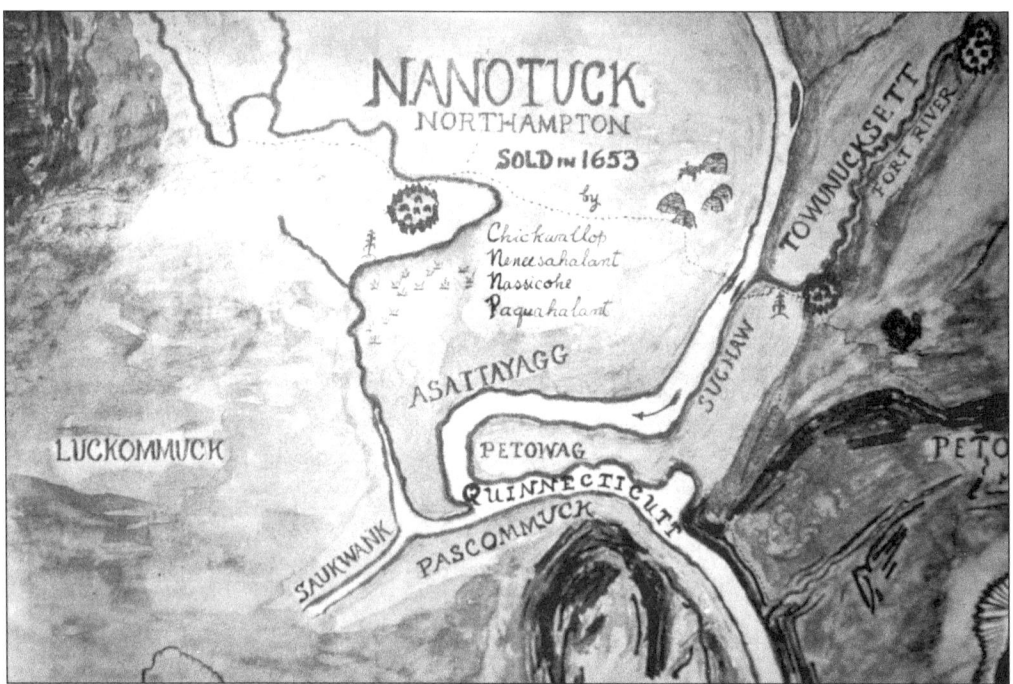

Present-day Easthampton was originally part of Nonotuck, which was part of the Algonquin nation. The first Europeans settled this area in 1633. In 1635, William Pynchon received permission to move to the Connecticut Valley, settling Springfield the next year. In 1653, Pynchon purchased the entire area north of Springfield, including all of present-day Hampshire County. The land, which is comprised of today's Easthampton, was called Pascommuck, a Nipmuck word translating to "where it [the Connecticut River] bends."

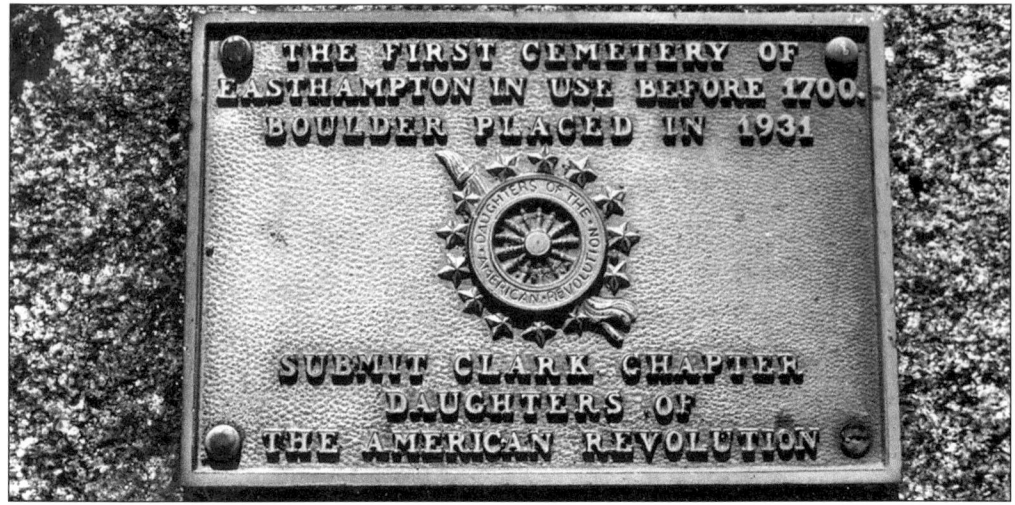

In 1653, John Webb settled in today's Northampton and was granted land in Pascommuck, probably near present-day Fort Hill Road. After Webb's death in 1670, a second attempt at settlement was made. In 1699, a party of five families established homes in the area near Fort Hill Road and East Street. Fearful of Native Americans, settlers used an unmarked area on Fort Hill Road as a cemetery. This marker commemorates that site. The Daughters of the American Revolution dedicated this stone in 1931.

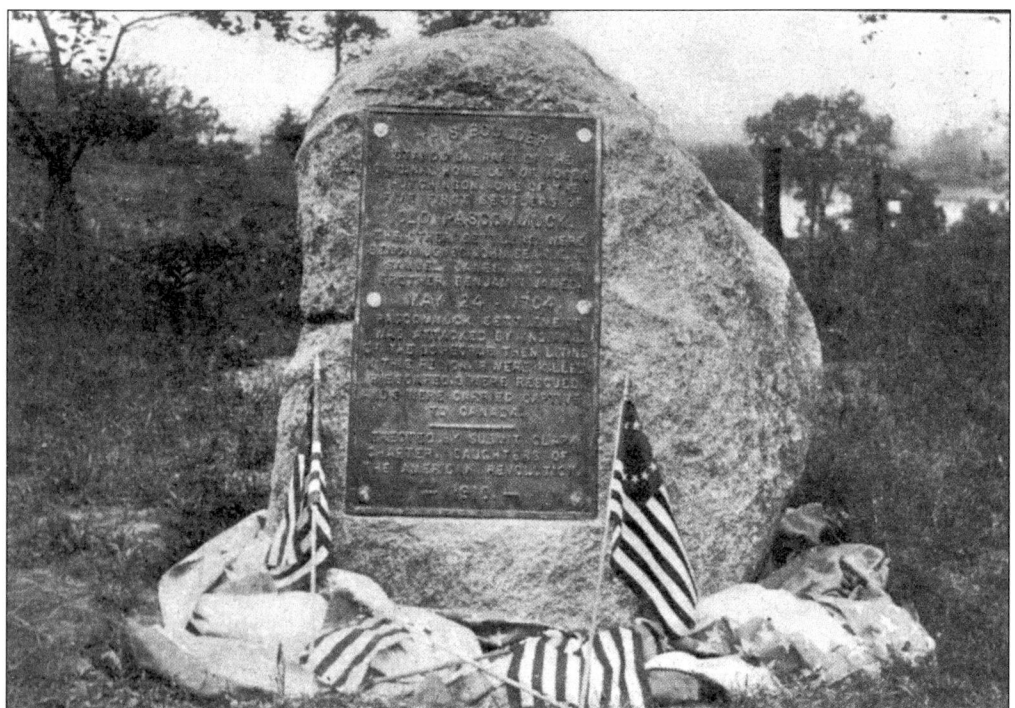

On May 24, 1704, the village of Pascommuck was attacked by a group of Native Americans allied with the Quebec colony of France. This boulder stands on the site of the home of Moses Hutchinson. Other settlers included the families of Benoni Janes, John Searle Jr., Samuel Janes, and Benjamin Janes. Of the 33 inhabitants of the village, 19 were killed and eight escaped during the attack. Of the six taken captive, three escaped.

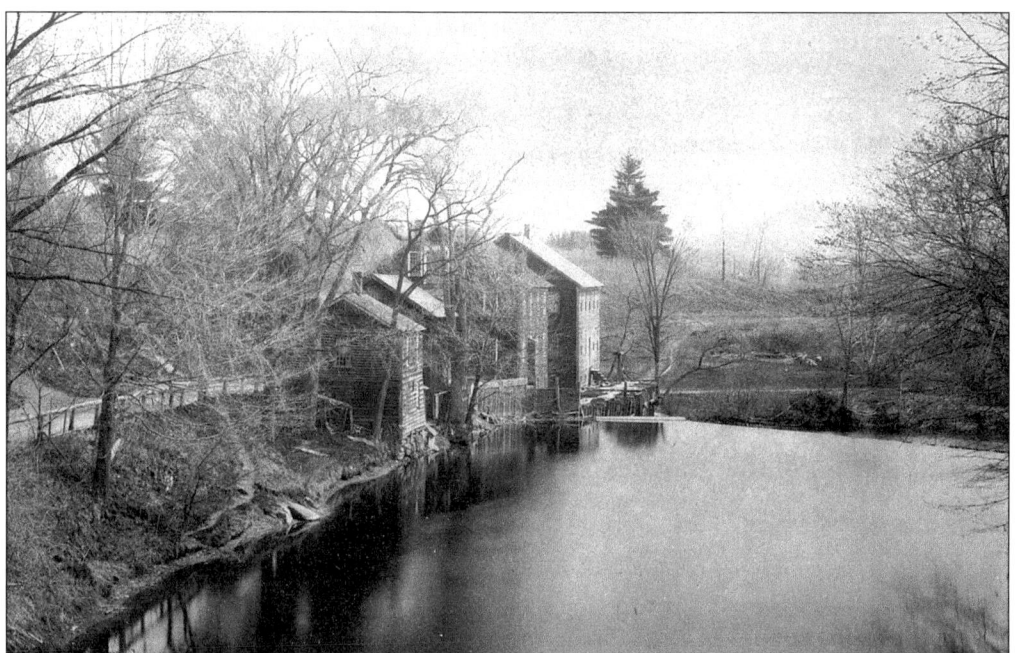

While Pascommuck was being settled, the land near the Manhan River looked attractive to other settlers. In 1644, David Wilton, Medad Pomeroy, and Joseph Taylor established a sawmill near West Street. Twelve years later, Samuel Bartlett opened a gristmill on the Manhan River. This 19th-century photograph shows a later mill in use.

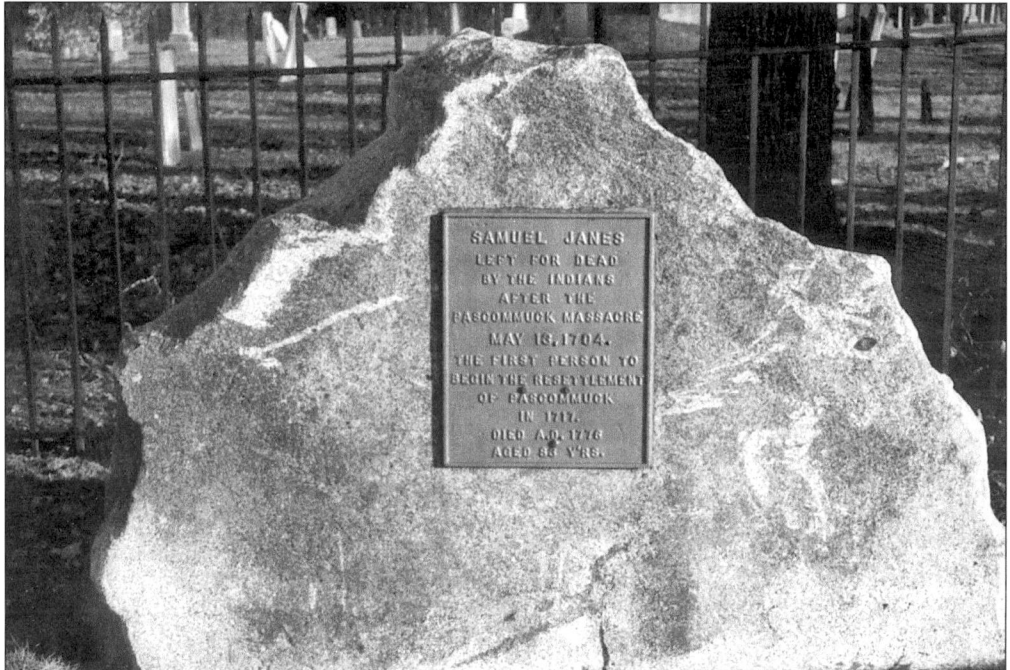

Pascommuck Village was settled for a third time in 1717, when Samuel Janes, a survivor of the 1704 attack, resettled on his dead father's land. This plaque is located at the East Street Cemetery, where Janes and his family are buried.

11

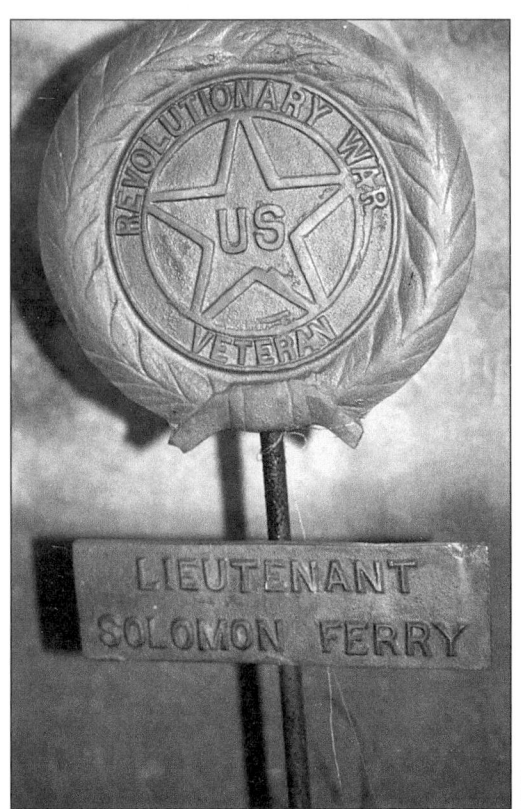

Although it was only a village of Northampton at the time, the future Easthampton saw some 43 residents enlist for the Revolutionary War. One who saw action in the war was Lt. Solomon Ferry. He is buried in the East Street Cemetery, where this marker commemorates his service.

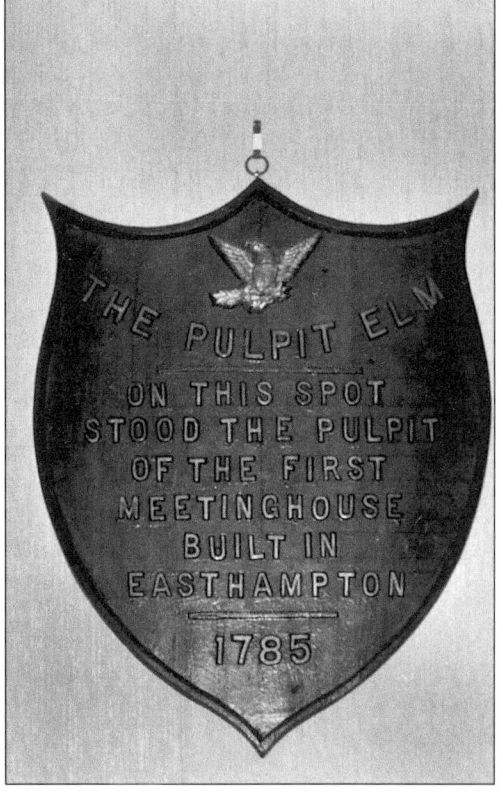

In 1785, Governor Bowdoin signed a proclamation creating the district of Easthampton. Although not recognized as a town until 1809, the residents were able to hire a minister and construct a meetinghouse. The name Easthampton was chosen since the other points of the compass—Northampton, Southampton, and Westhampton—were already taken. The site of the first meetinghouse is commemorated with this plaque on its former site at the town common, Pulaski Park.

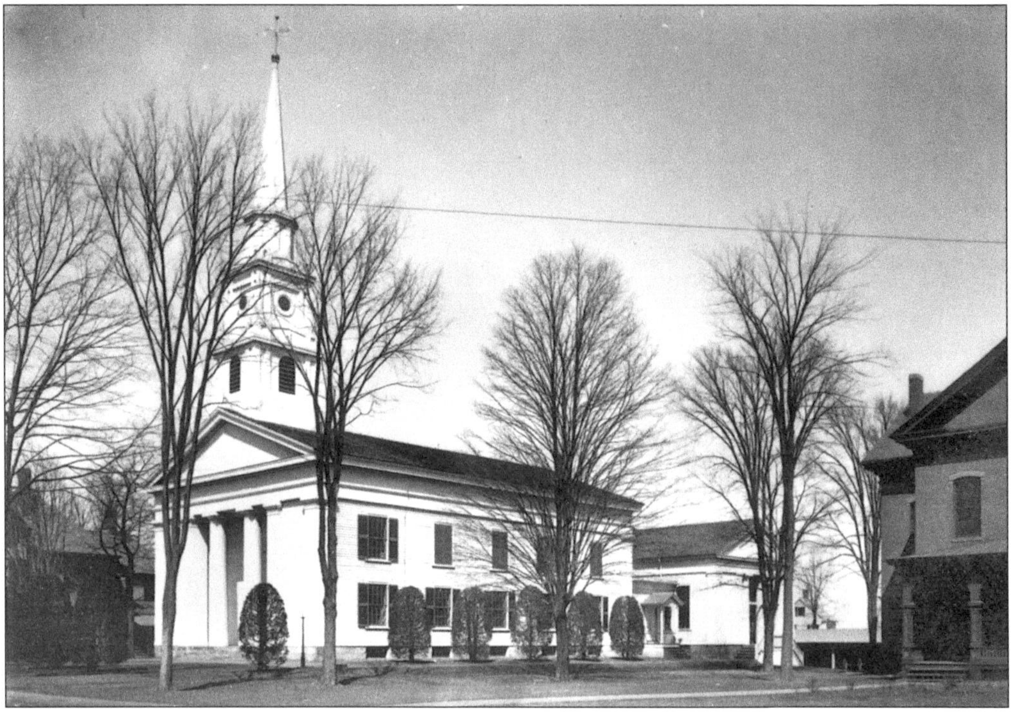

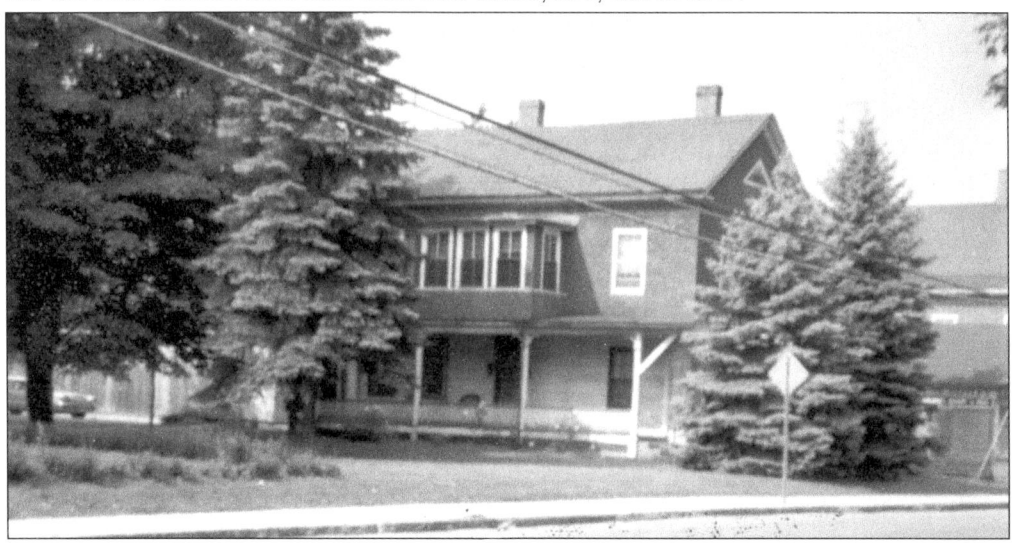

Initially, the town and church were closely associated. The town, made up of just a few families, did not have a regular minister during the first four years as a district. On August 13, 1789, Payson Williston was ordained as minister. His pastorate continued until his retirement in 1833. This new church was constructed in 1836. It was relocated to the north side of Main Street in 1866, the year this photograph was taken. The small building in the rear of the church was the town's second town hall. Both were destroyed by fire in 1929.

Following Rev. Payson Williston's retirement, the first town hall was constructed in 1833. The town developed a town meeting system to govern itself, with a board of selectmen to run daily affairs. In 1842, this building was moved from Main Street to Pleasant Street and refurbished. As this recent photograph shows, it is still in use as a private residence.

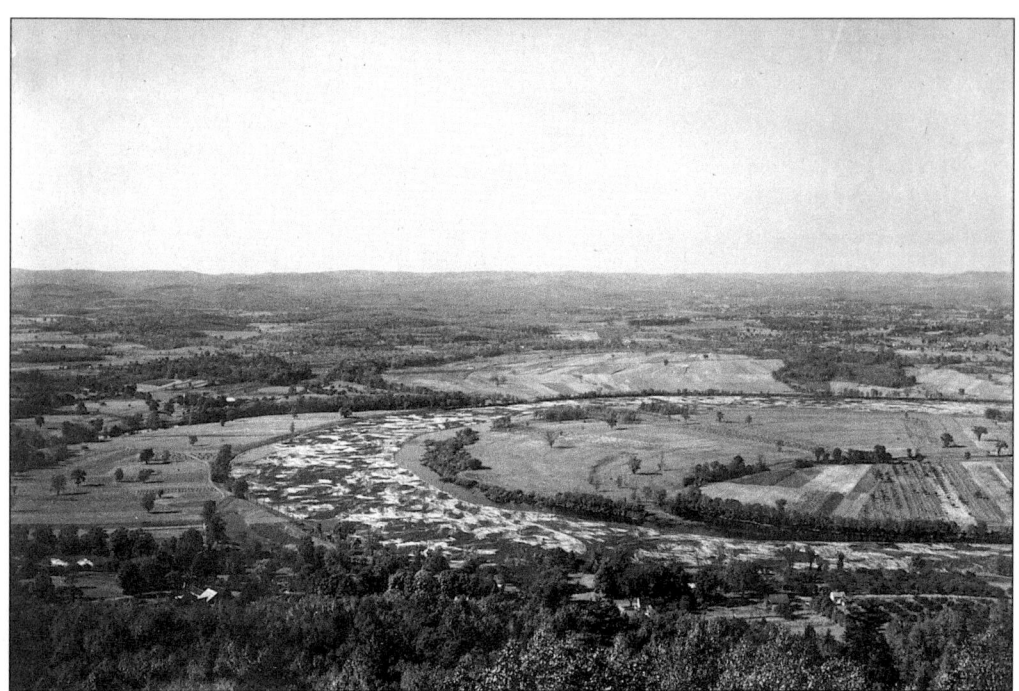

The Oxbow emerged as the town's best-known geographic feature. The Connecticut River flowed through the bend until 1840, when an ice floe created a new and straight path for the river to follow. In this 1899 photograph, logs wait in storage for a Mount Tom sawmill or the paper industry of Holyoke.

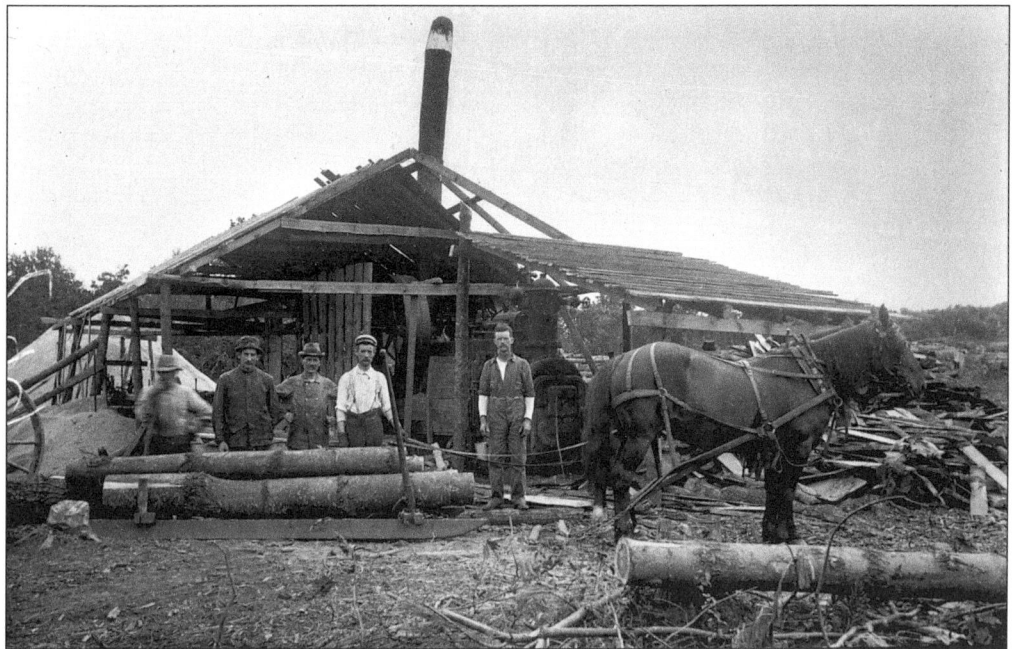

By 1674, the first sawmill began in Easthampton. Several more sprung up near the Manhan River or along Broad Brook. This 1890s Howes Brothers photograph shows one of the many sawmills, which used to be active in Easthampton.

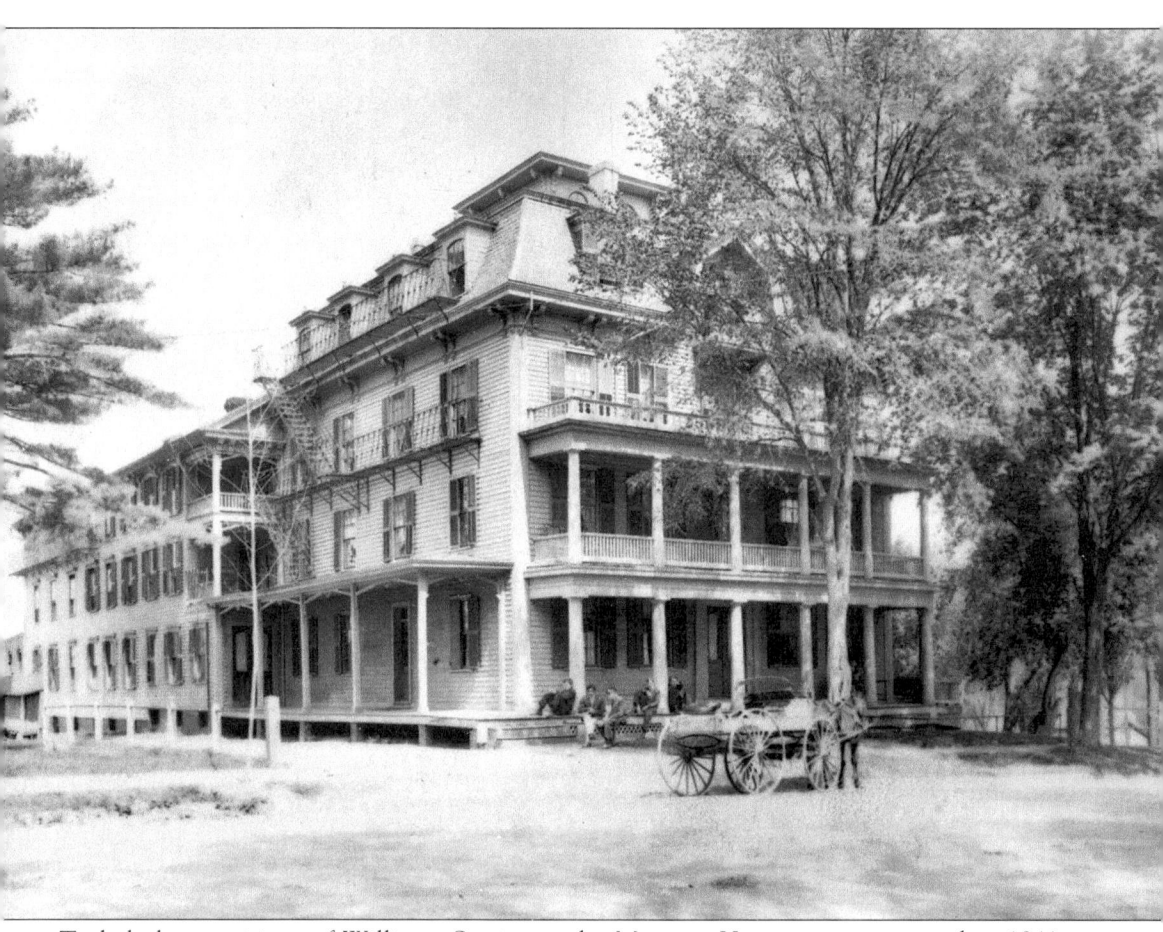

To help house visitors of Williston Seminary, the Mansion House was constructed in 1841. This building was used as a hotel until Williston Seminary purchased it in 1916. The school used it as a dining hall for their students and as a dormitory for their seventh- and eighth-grade students. In 1949, it was sold to new owners who converted the interior to apartments. It was torn down in 1969.

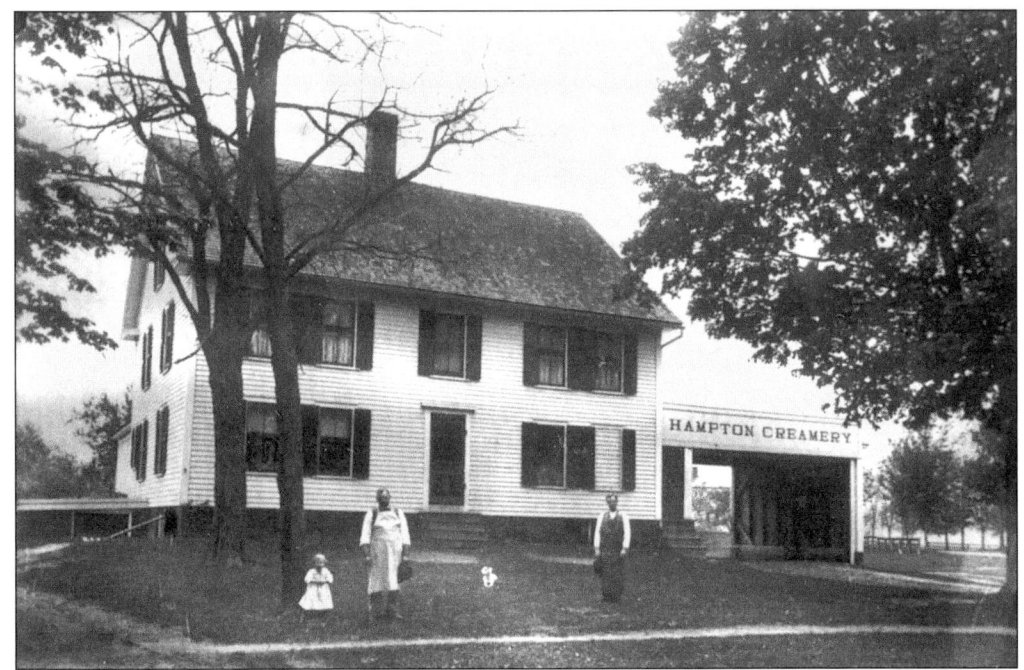

Constructed in the 1750s, the Stage Coach Tavern was constructed on Main Street and was used as an inn for many years. This picture was taken in the late 19th century, when it was used to house a dairy, the Hampton Creamery. In 1935, the house was taken down and is now the site of an apartment building and a liquor store.

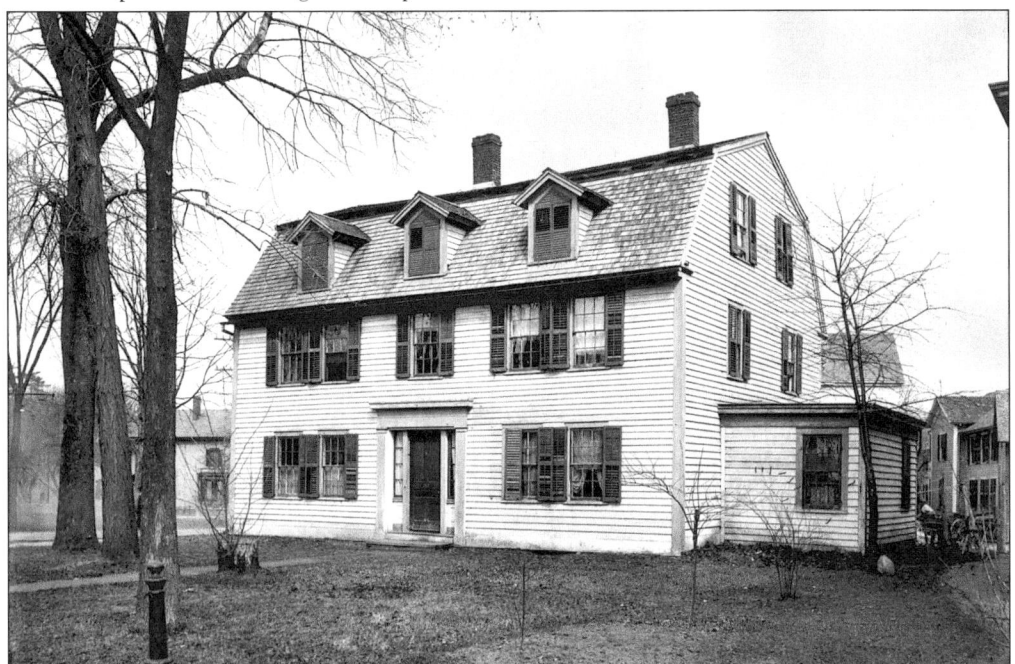

Still located on Main Street, the Seth Janes house was a farm from its construction in the 1700s until 1841, when Williston Seminary purchased it in order to build its campus on adjoining land. This house, now used as apartments, has lost its Dutch Colonial design due to alterations.

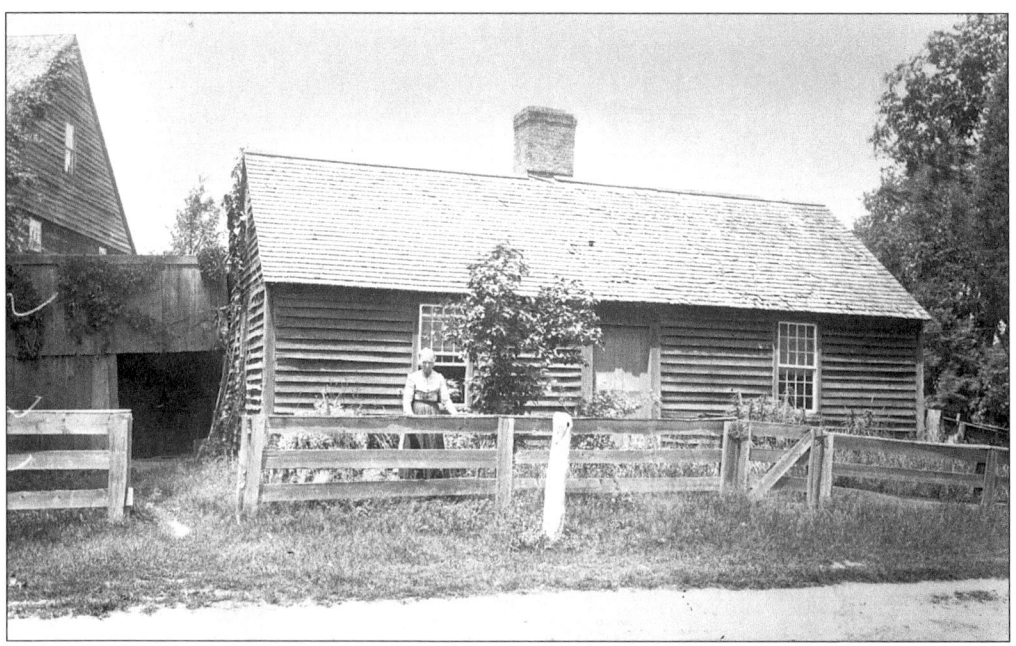

The Alpress House was built on East Street in the mid-1700s. The two-room, one-story building was constructed around a center chimney. The house has not only been damaged by time, but also by a truck that veered into it from East Street in 1931. The building was taken down in 1934.

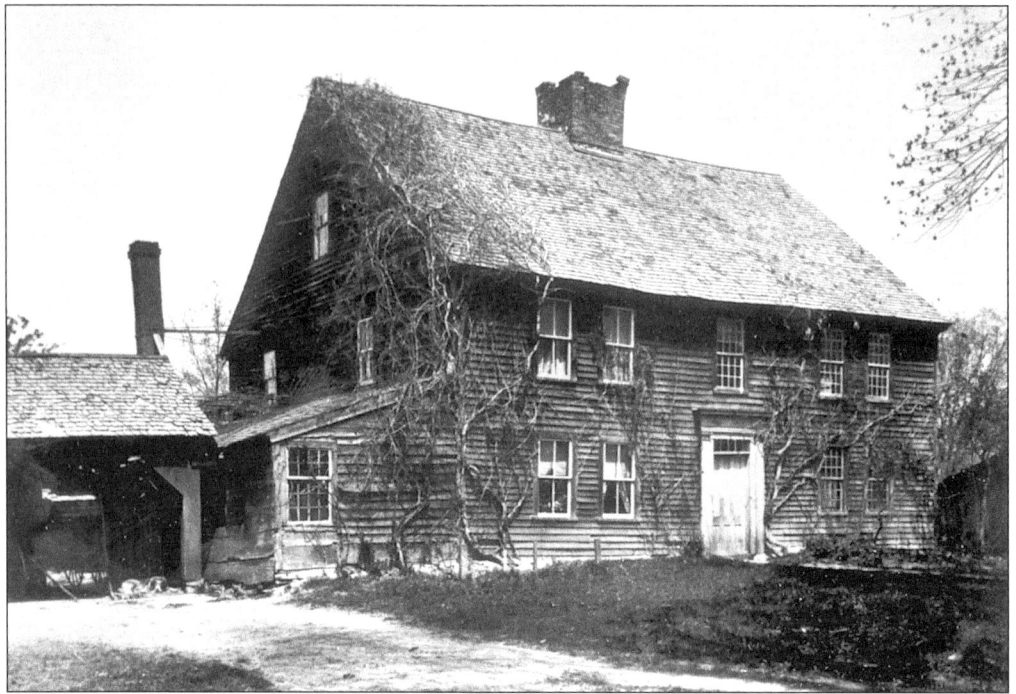

Next to the Alpress house was the Janes Parsons house. The Parsons family built this house in 1750. It was the third house built at the location and was taken down in 1905. The first house was destroyed during the 1704 attack (see page 10) and the second one was consumed by fire.

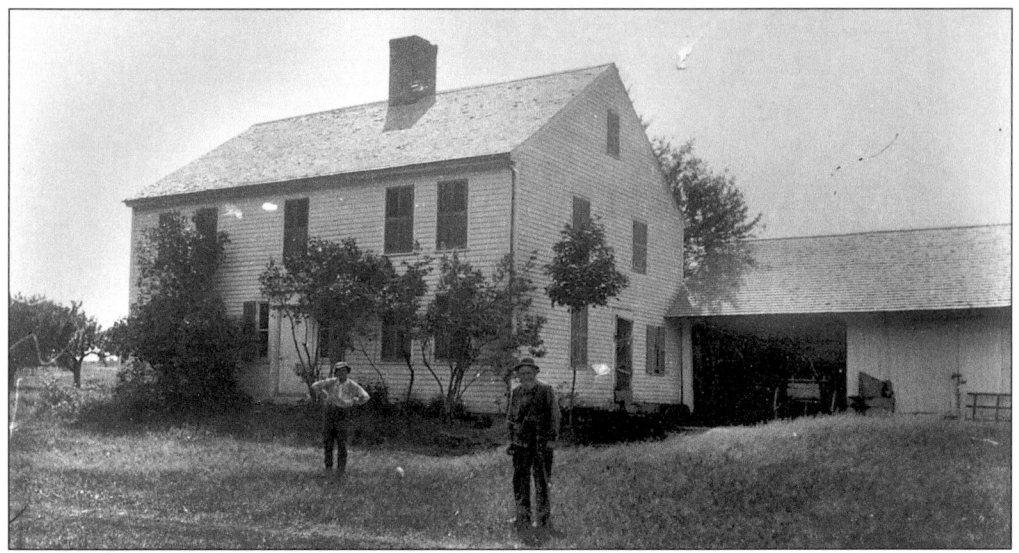

Israel Hendrick was the first to settle in the southeastern part of town when he built his first house in 1774. Replacing that house was this one, constructed in 1820. Joseph Hendrick was the owner when the Howes Brothers took this photograph in 1900. Wright Root became its owner in 1907. His family held it until it was taken down in 1990.

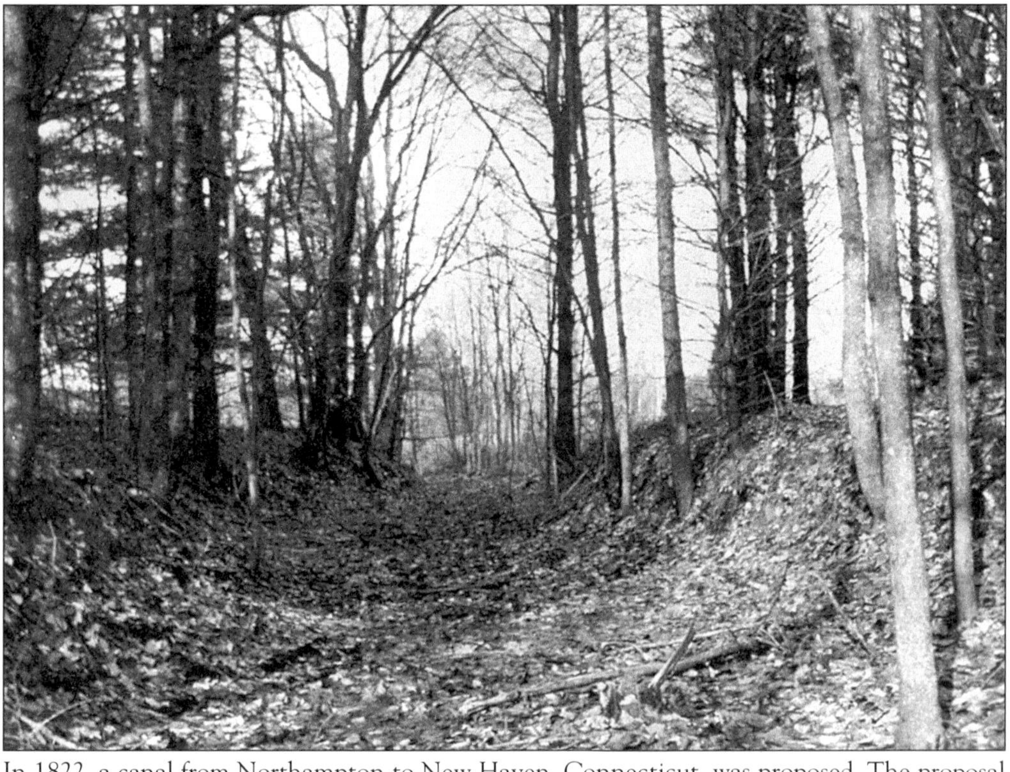

In 1822, a canal from Northampton to New Haven, Connecticut, was proposed. The proposal hoped to compete with New York City's monopoly of western trade given to them by the Erie Canal and the Hudson River. In 1835, the first canal boat finally passed through Easthampton. This photograph shows the remains of the canal in the late 19th century.

18

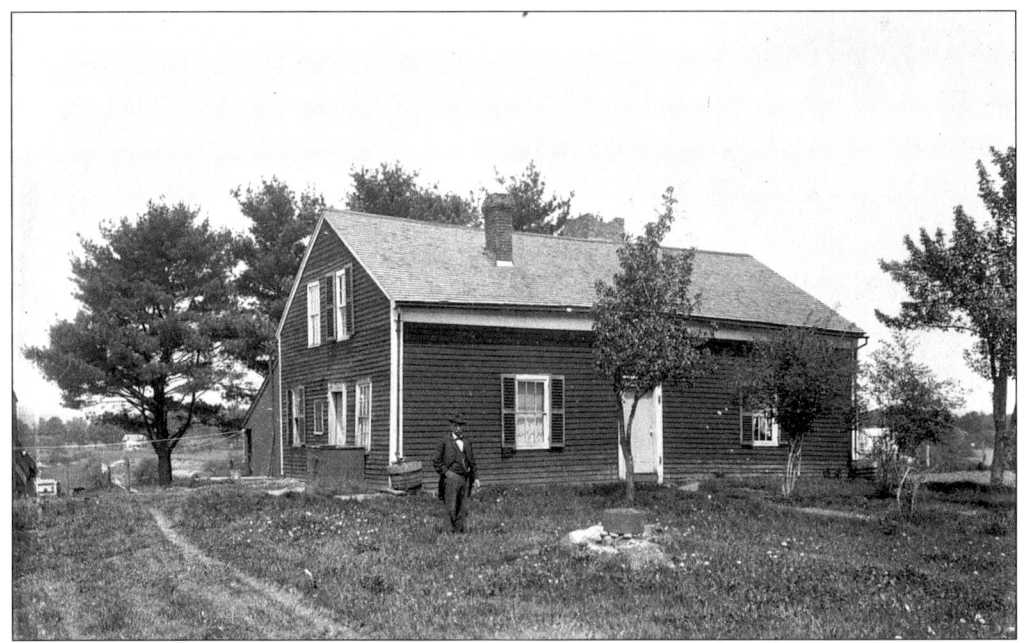

This farm was located at 45 Park Street and was built in the mid-1700s. Later, the adjoining land for this farm was purchased. By 1900, Garfield Avenue was built near it. This two-story farmhouse has been rebuilt and is still a residence.

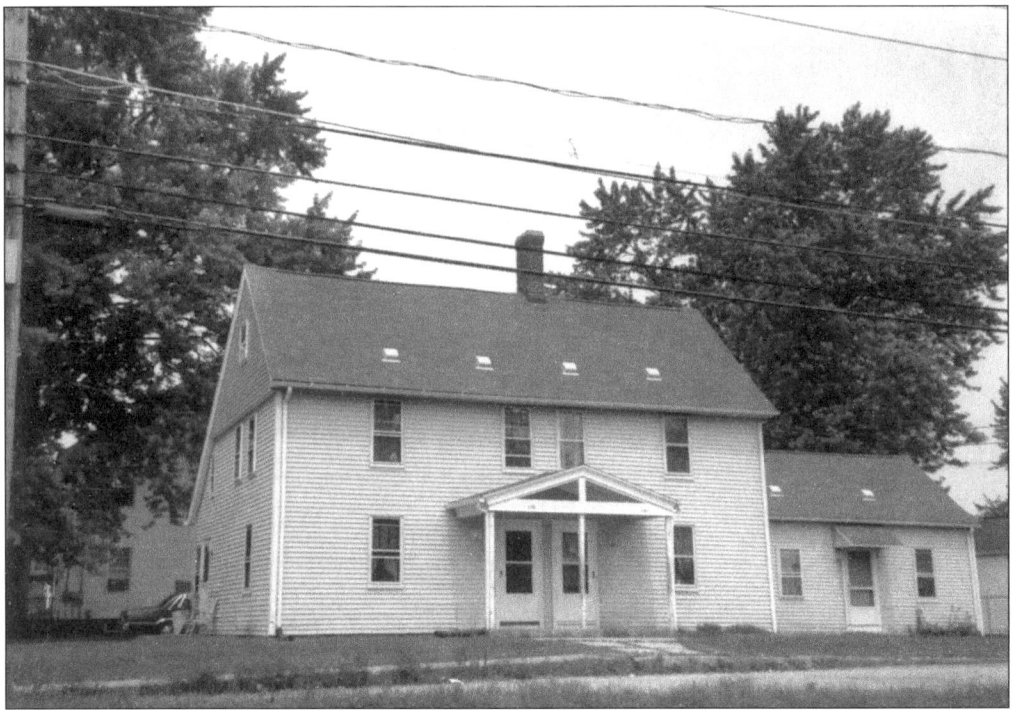

Built in the mid-18th century, this saltbox-style building has been a farm, a mill house, and a private residence. Owned by the Clark and Ferry families, it was sold in 1860 to the Williston Mills, which used the adjoining farmland to construct employee housing.

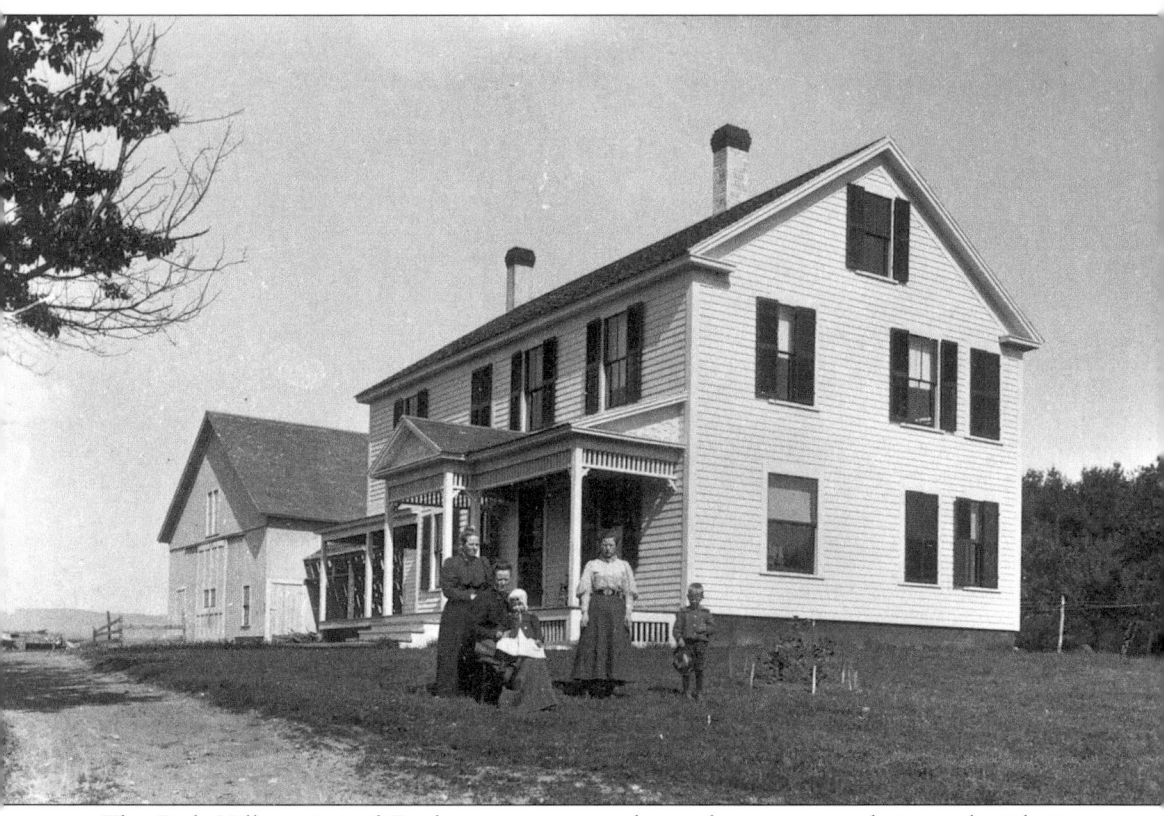

The Park Hill section of Easthampton was used as a hunting spot during colonial times. Beginning in 1800, three farms were built on Park Hill. Regarded as some of the best farmland in the city, this farm is now owned by the Micka family and is used as an orchard.

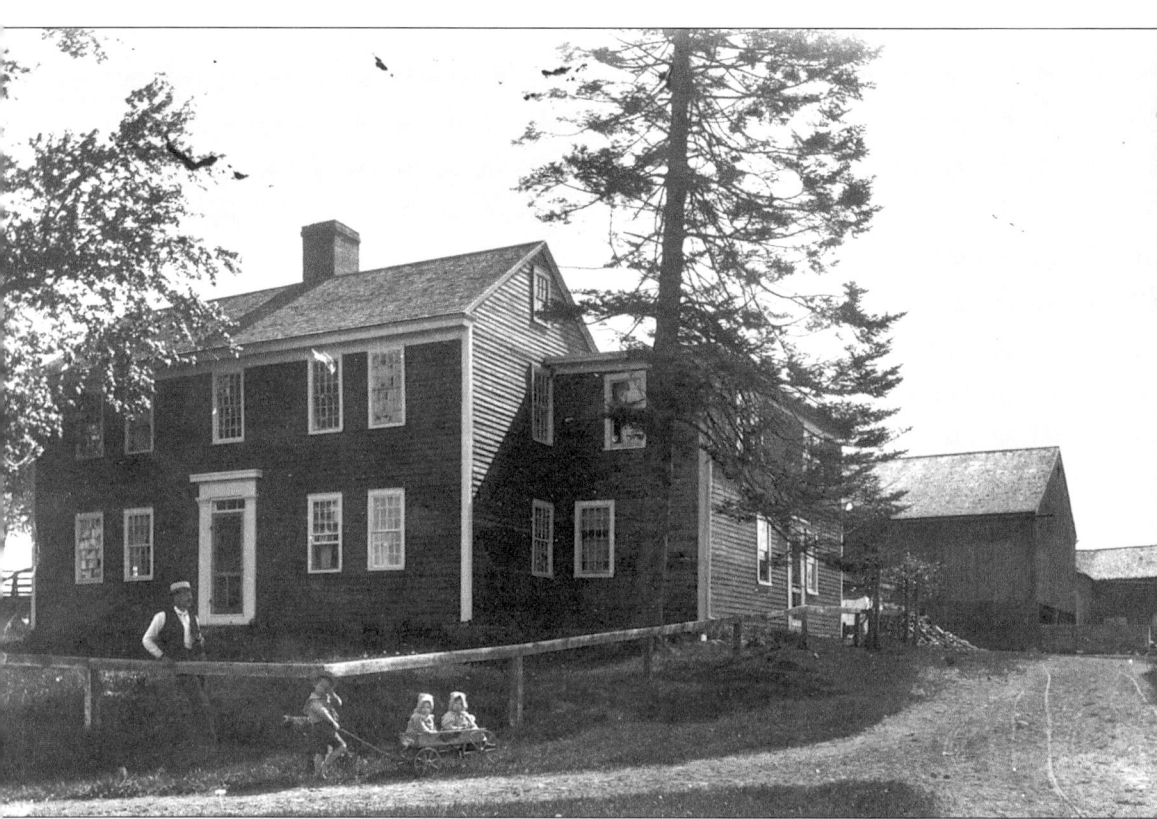

Daniel Lyman settled in Park Hill in the early 19th century. Three generations farmed here, while a fourth generation lived here and moved on when reaching adulthood. A member of that fourth generation, Lauren Lyman, was awarded the Pulitzer Prize in 1934 for his exclusive story on Charles Lindbergh's decision to leave the United States and move to England. This house at 45 Park Hill Road is still a farm.

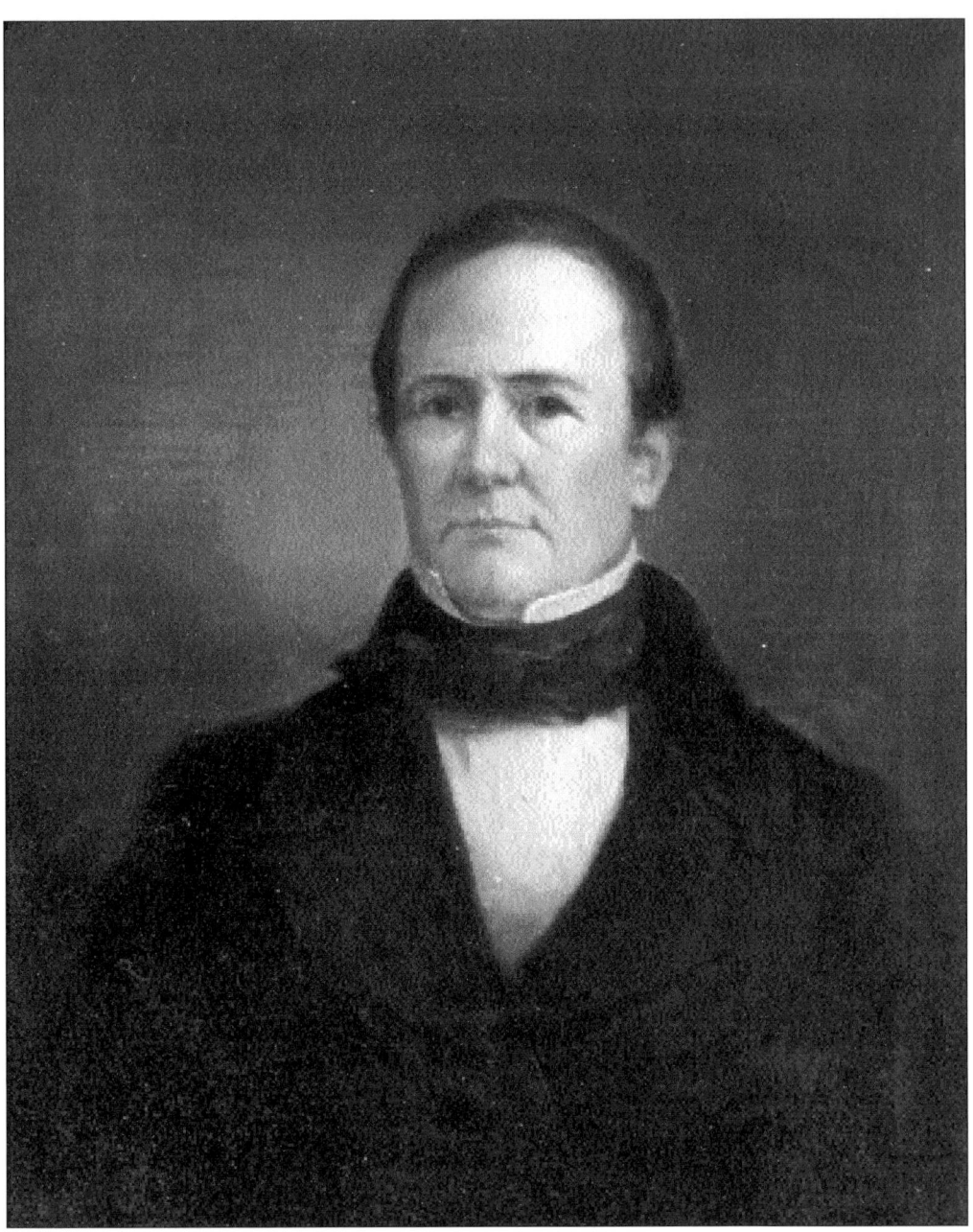

Samuel Williston, the eldest son of Rev. Payson Williston, began a covered button business in Haydenville. At first, local farm women hand-sewed buttons at home. Eventually, Williston hired Francis Sydney, a Creole who was familiar with English button-making, while his business partners, the Hayden Brothers, perfected a technique to make buttons by machine. In 1847, Williston had a dam built to impound the flow of Broad Brook, thus creating Nashawannuck Pond and beginning industrialism in Easthampton.

Two

UPPER MILL POND INDUSTRY

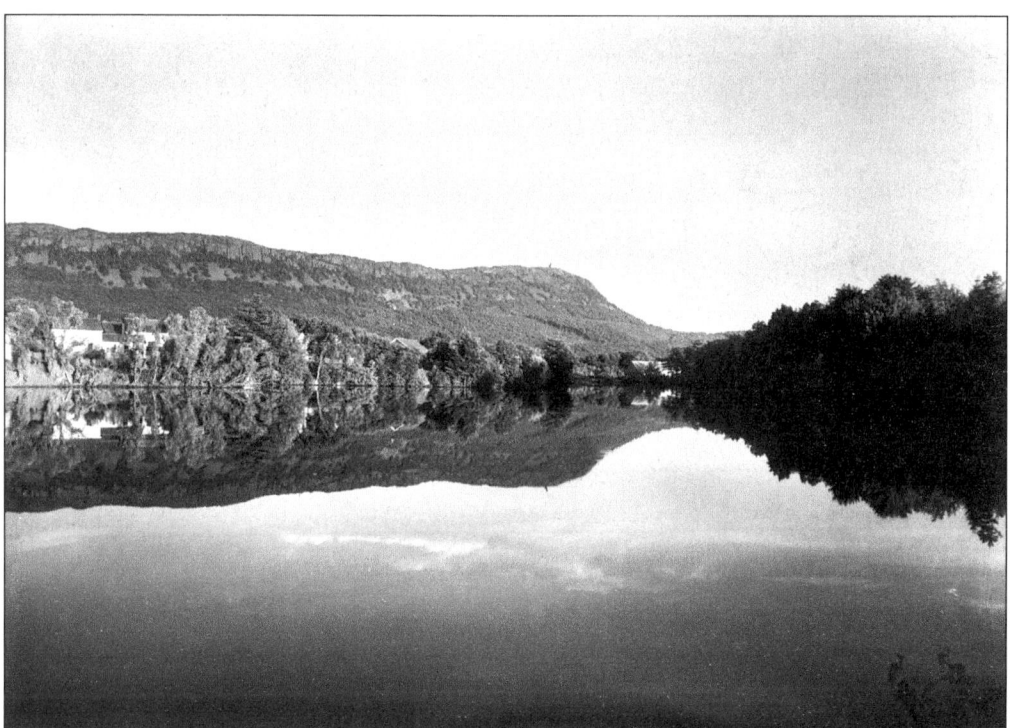

In 1847, Broad Brook was impounded with the construction of a dam, creating Nashawannuck Pond. The reflection of Mount Tom in the pond creates the appearance of a bottle. "The Bottle," as it is called, has become a symbol of Easthampton. The pond, a popular recreational site for townspeople, was named for the Nashawannuck Manufacturing Company.

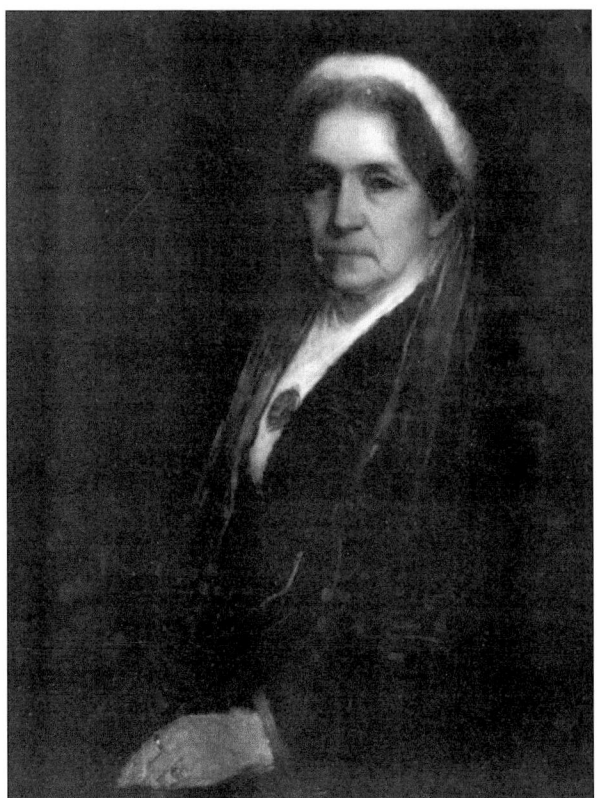

Emily Graves of Williamsburg married Samuel Williston in 1822, becoming his lifelong advisor. She hired many families for the covered button business and served as the company's first bookkeeper. As the wealth of the Willistons grew, the couple became benefactors of many colleges and charities.

Horatio Knight was born in Easthampton in 1819. Educated in the local schools, Knight became an employee, a protégé, and later a business partner of Williston. From 1875 to 1878, Knight served as the lieutenant governor of Massachusetts.

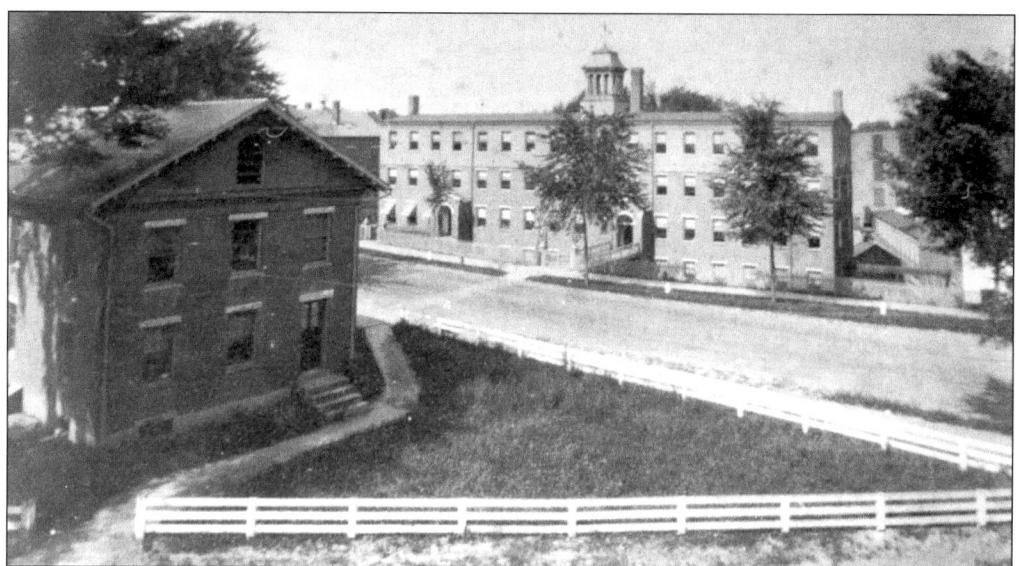

The Williston-Knight Button Company shop was opened in 1847, originally owned by Samuel Williston and Horatio Knight. The company made covered buttons, a popular fashion accessory of the late 19th century. The company went bankrupt in 1883, when Horatio Knight's son embezzled company funds. Although Governor Knight faced personal bankruptcy problems, he restored the company's finances and his own to strong footing. Eventually, the fashion trend of covered buttons went by, and the successor company closed in 1922. This building was later a warehouse and is now a furniture store.

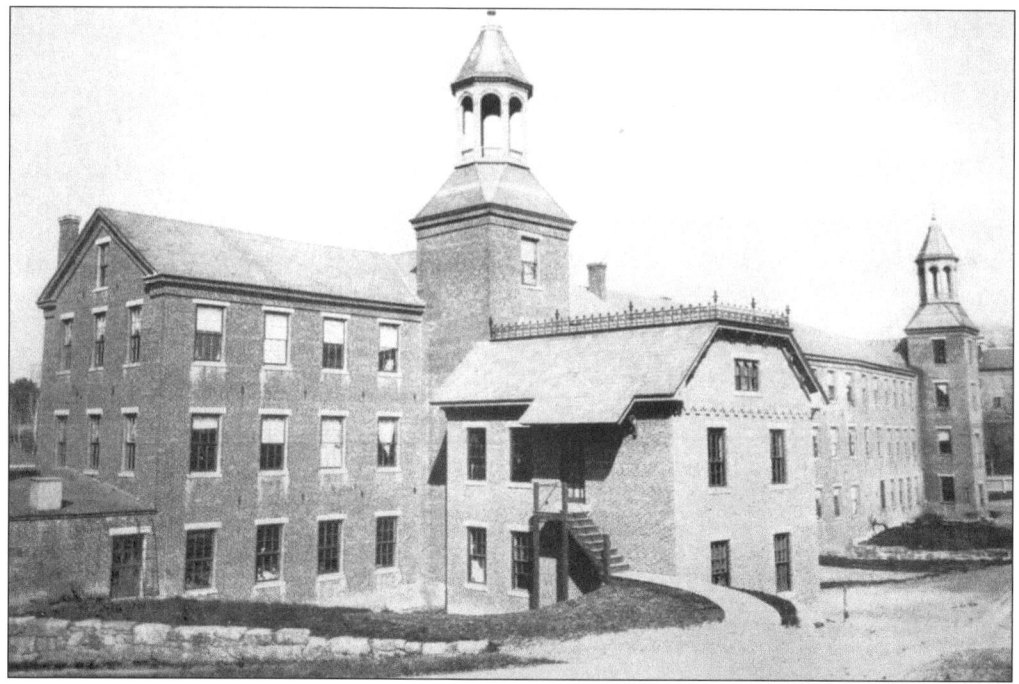

In 1848, the Nashawannuck Manufacturing Company was established to manufacture elastic for men's suspenders. The company was founded by Samuel Williston. It remained active until 1912, when it was sold to the Glendale Elastic Manufacturing Company.

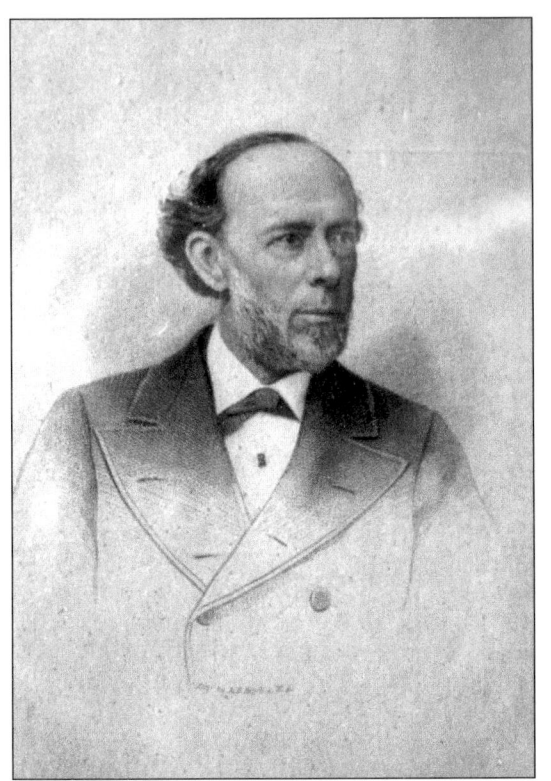

Edmund Sawyer was another protégé of Samuel Williston. Born in 1812 in Vermont, Sawyer was employed there by Nathan Williston, a brother of Samuel Williston. Impressed with the work he did, Williston hired him. Following his apprenticeship as a clerk, Sawyer became a member of the board of directors of the Nashawannuck Manufacturing Company, heading both local manufacturing and the New York sales offices. Sawyer also served as treasurer of the Williston Mills and helped return it to solid financial footing. He also served as executor of Samuel Williston estate. He died at age 58 on November 12, 1879.

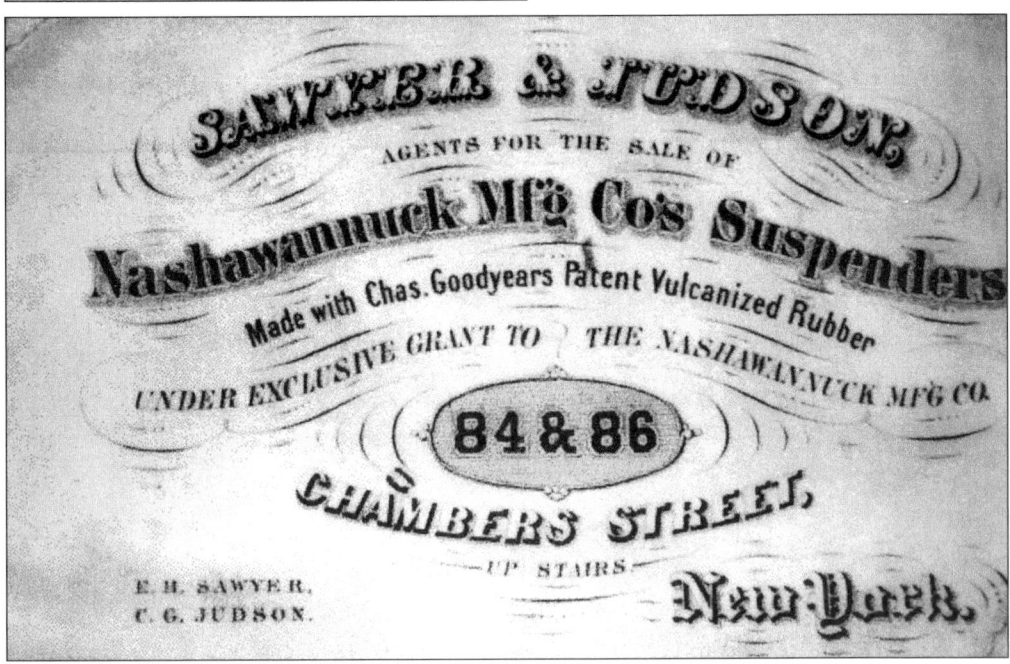

Shown is the business card for the New York sales offices of the Nashawannuck Manufacturing Company. The company was eventually sued over copyright infringements. The U.S. Supreme Court eventually heard the case in 1890, deciding in favor of the Nashawannuck Manufacturing Company.

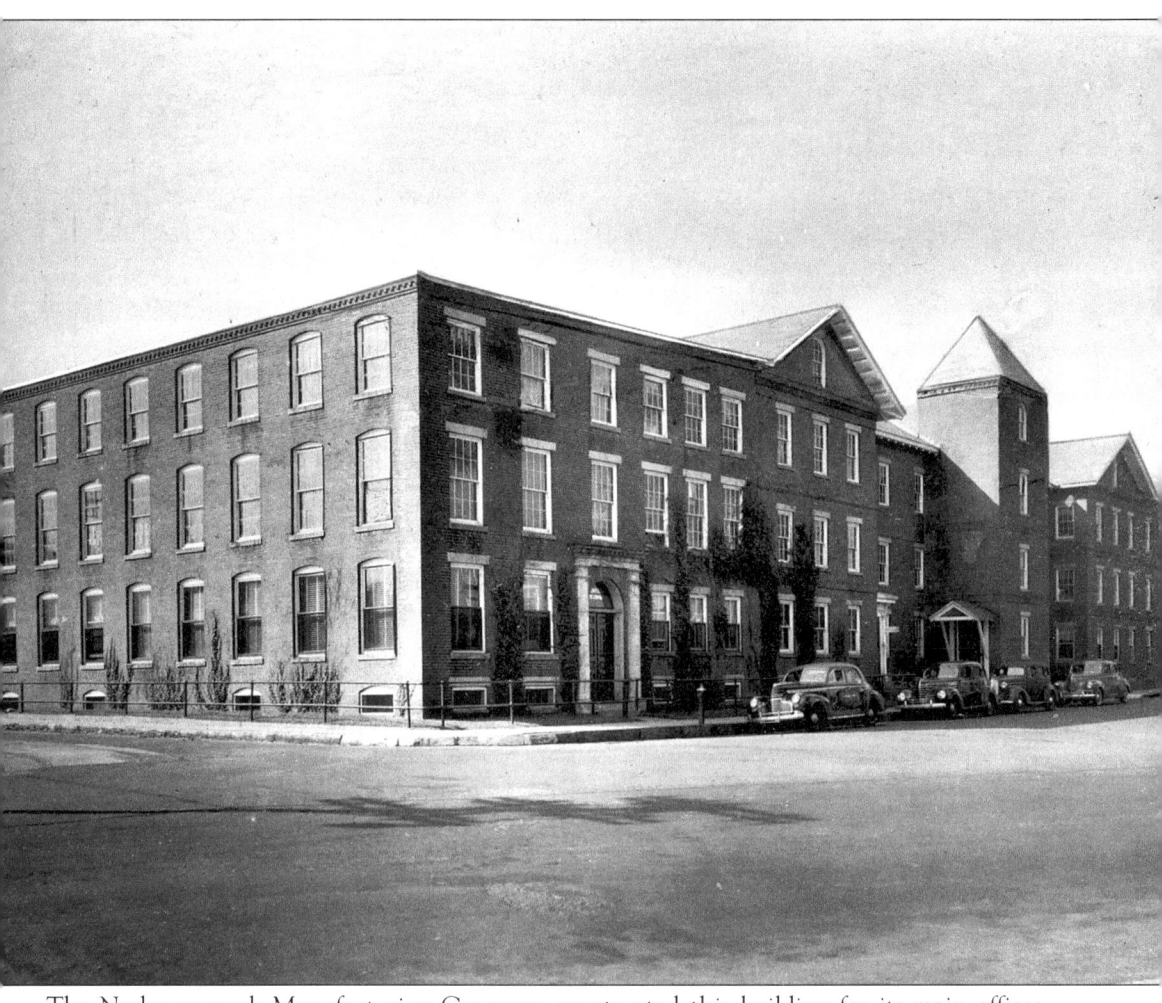

The Nashawannuck Manufacturing Company constructed this building for its main offices. When the company was sold to the Glendale Company in 1912, it served as the main offices for that company. From 1927, it served as the main office for the United Elastic Corporation. It was taken down in 1962 and replaced with a modern office.

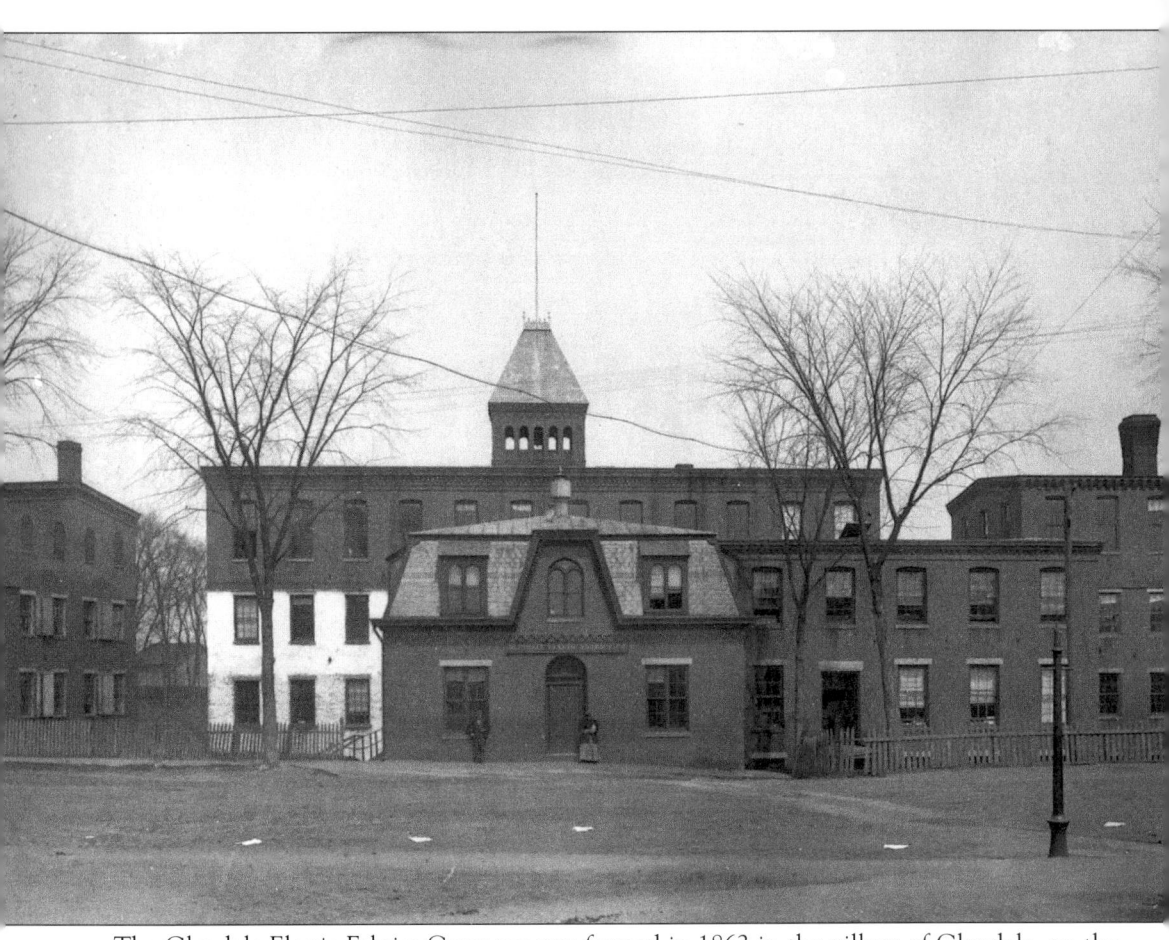

The Glendale Elastic Fabrics Company was formed in 1862 in the village of Glendale, on the Easthampton and Southampton line, where they manufactured elastics for shoes. In 1864, the company moved to Easthampton, where it constructed these mills next to the Nashawannuck Manufacturing Company. These mills were known as the Glendale division of the United Elastic Corporation.

Following the deaths of Williston, Knight, and Sawyer, new investors purchased stock in the Glendale Company. Joseph Green became company treasurer, serving until his death in 1905. Green's stepson, Clifford Richmond, later owned the Colton Elastic Mills plant and served as the president of the United Elastic Corporation.

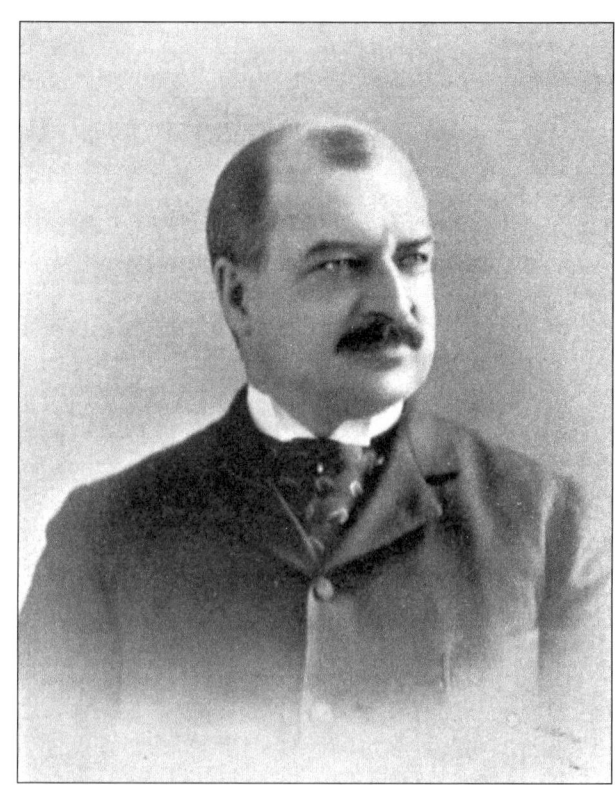

Glendale Elastic Fabrics Co.

EASTHAMPTON, JAN. 1ST, 1885.

It is expected that after this date every person in the employ of this Co. will observe habits of perfect cleanliness in the mills, both as to keeping their looms perfectly clean and their *hands* and *mouths*, for a person has no more right to scatter tobacco juice over the work, his loom, or the *floor*, than he has to come into your best room at home and spoil your floor. To those who think they can continue to work for this Co. and come in at times half intoxicated and who are obliged to "stay out" occasionally under the false plea of being "very sick", we have only to say if they continue in this course they will be discharged however good workmen they may be when sober—for, although we do not claim any control over our workpeople in their private affairs, yet no person can work for this company unless he keeps himself in proper *condition* so to do—Reading, conversation and visiting each other is not allowed and every one should be so busy while his loom is running, as not to have *time* for any sociability. The management have confidence that every person employed will see "the point" of all this and govern themselves accordingly. Overseers have full authority to discharge help at their discretion for a non-observance of these rules.

The quality of the work must be so much improved that goods can be delivered in continuous lengths without being cut on account of careless weaving.

JOSEPH W. GREEN, JR., TREASURER.

Many employees may have said, "And a happy New Year to you, too" when they saw this notice dated January 1, 1885. The notice warns workers to keep "habits of perfect cleanliness," saying that "a person has no more right to scatter tobacco juice over the work, his loom, or the *floor*, than he has to come into your best room at home and spoil your floor." It also warns against "reading, conversation and visiting each other" while on duty. There was little the employees could do but accept company's mandates.

George Colton was a Vermont native who arrived in Easthampton to set up machinery at the Glendale Company. He purchased a plot of land on Union Street, where he constructed a competing elastic mill in 1886. The company manufactured cords, braids, and other elastic goods with an initial workforce of just 10 employees.

In 1916, the Colton Elastic Mills (by then employing 175 people) was purchased by the corporate clerk of the Glendale Company, Clifford Richmond. Richmond was the stepson of Joseph Green, the late treasurer of the Glendale Company. Richmond ran the Colton Elastic Mills until its merger with the Glendale Company in 1927.

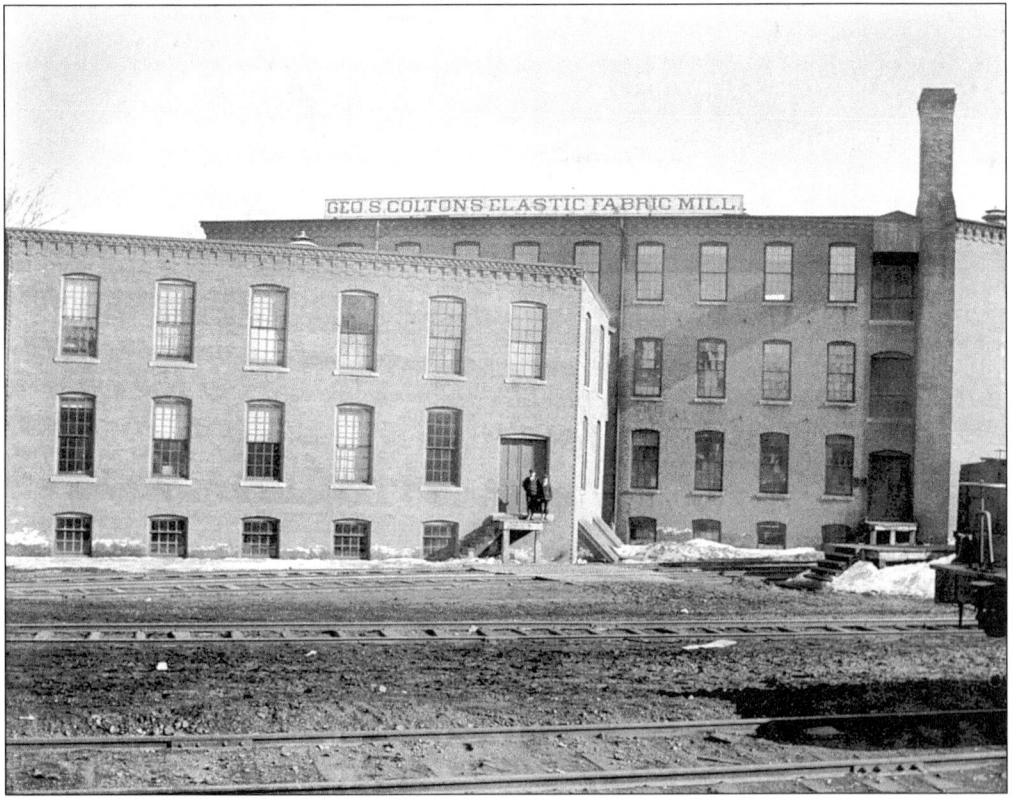

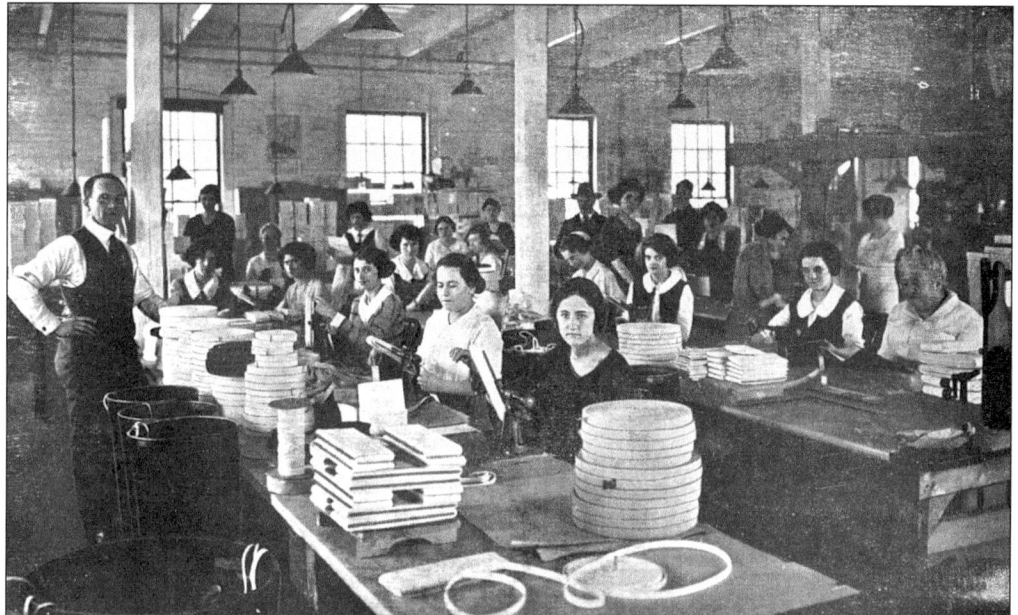

Following the 1927 merger, the Colton Elastic Mills concentrated production of elastics for sales in department stores and then sold them to consumers for the home sewing trade. Shown here are some of the employees of the finishing room.

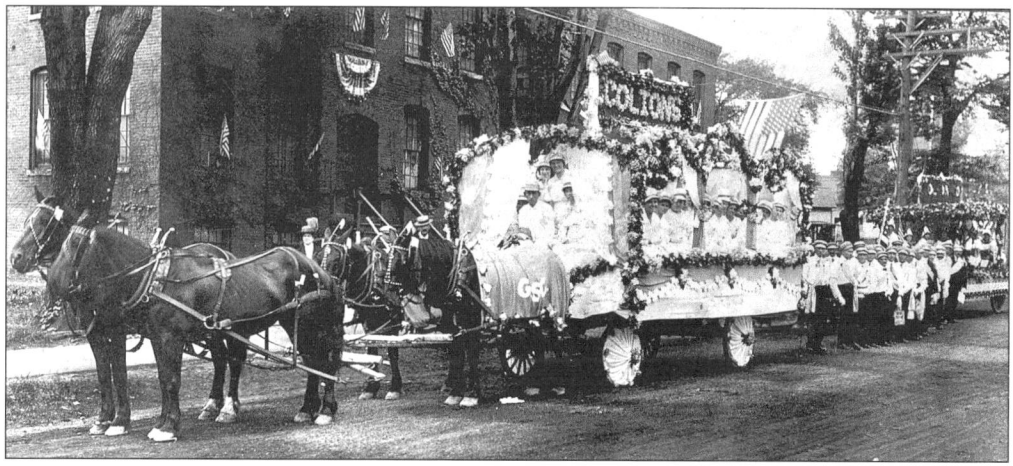

This Colton Elastic Mills float appeared in the 1910 parade. The float is on Union Street in front of the mill.

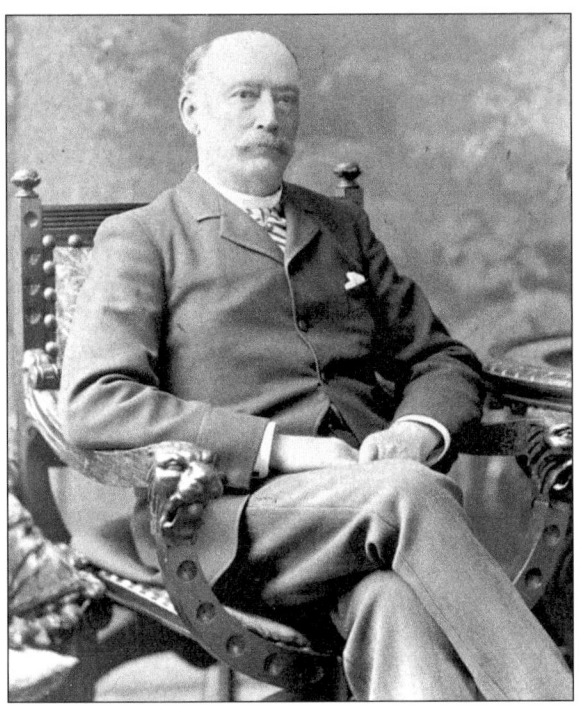

E. Thomas Sawyer was the brother of Edmund Sawyer and the engineer for the mills. Born in 1829, E. Thomas Sawyer was a rail and ship engineer before coming to Easthampton in 1859 to work for his brother. In 1873, he became the general manager of the Easthampton Rubber Thread Company, a position he held until his death in 1897.

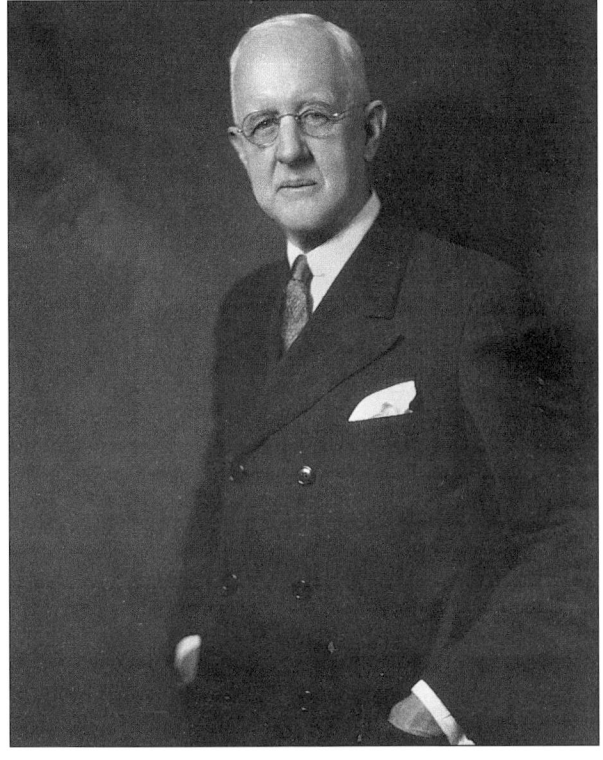

Born January 12, 1869, Robert Williston was a grandnephew of Samuel Williston. In 1904, Robert became a member of the board of the Easthampton Rubber Thread Company, becoming its president in 1923. He also served as treasurer of Williston Academy for over 30 years. He died January 11, 1934. His death marked the end of his family's ties to the local mills.

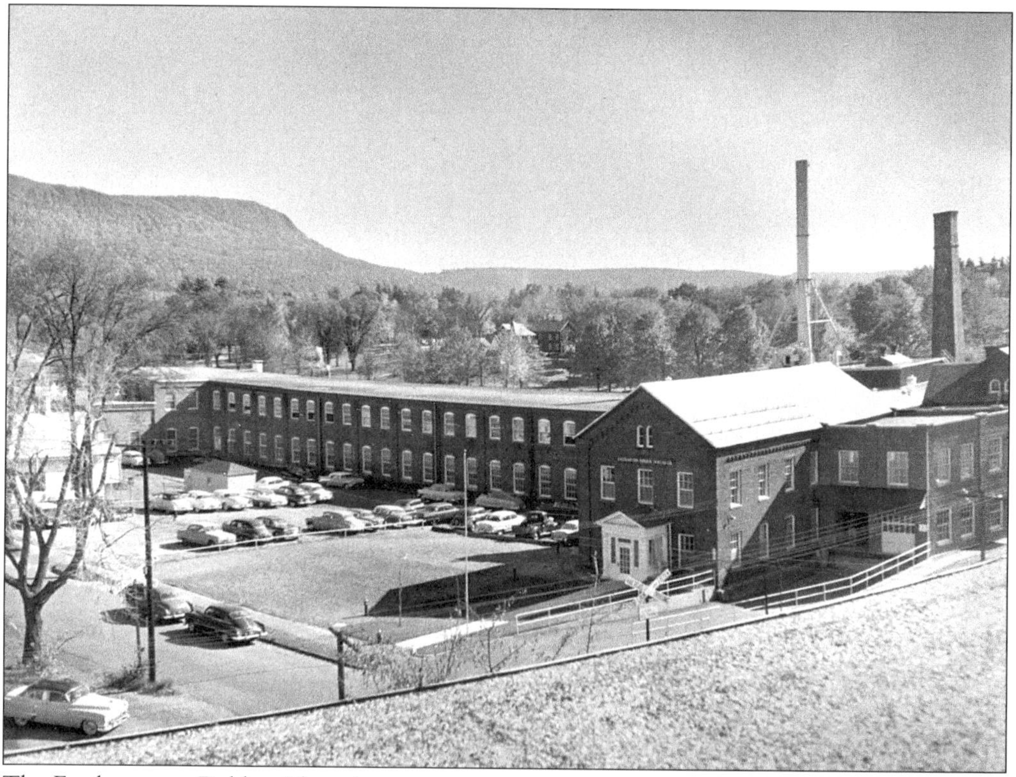

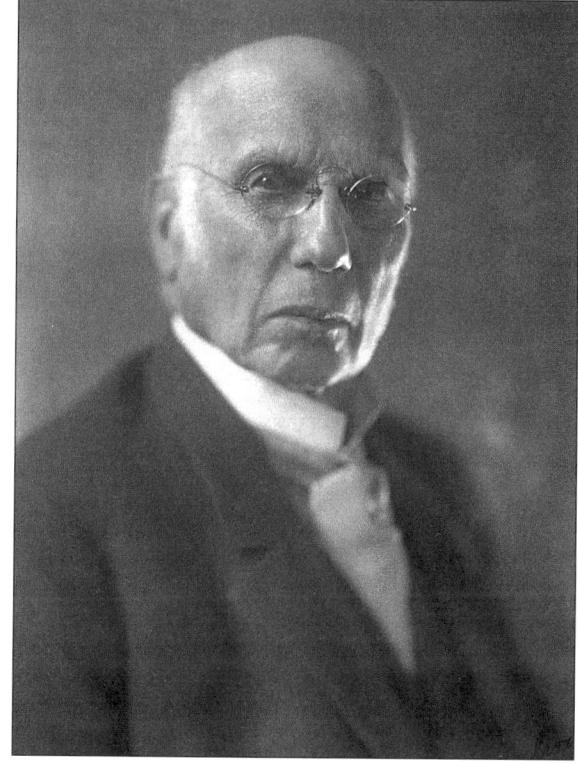

The Easthampton Rubber Thread Company was incorporated in 1863 to manufacture rubber strips for the Nashawannuck Manufacturing Company. Later, the company would also serve the Glendale Company and the Colton Elastic Mills. The mills shown in this 1957 photograph were constructed on Payson Avenue and were active until 1987. The site of the mills was cleared and replaced with the public safety complex.

Franklin Pitcher originally came to Easthampton to run the Williston Mills in 1885. He returned in 1891 to manage the Easthampton Rubber Thread Company. He became treasurer of the company, running it until his death in 1923. Both his son and grandson were also executives for the company. He also served as president of the Easthampton Savings Bank and on many local boards.

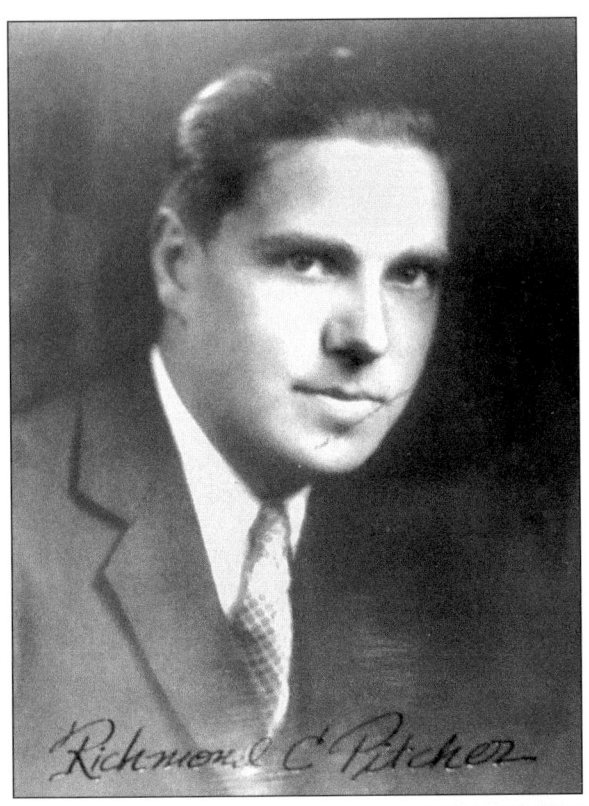

Richmond C. Pitcher

Richmond Pitcher, William Pitcher's son, was being groomed to become treasurer of the Easthampton Rubber Thread Company. In 1927, an accident involving a vulcanizing machine at the company took the lives of three workers. Following the incident, Richmond Pitcher took over operation of the machine. A defective valve, which had caused the first accident, again malfunctioned and badly burned Pitcher. He died December 26, 1927 at age 23.

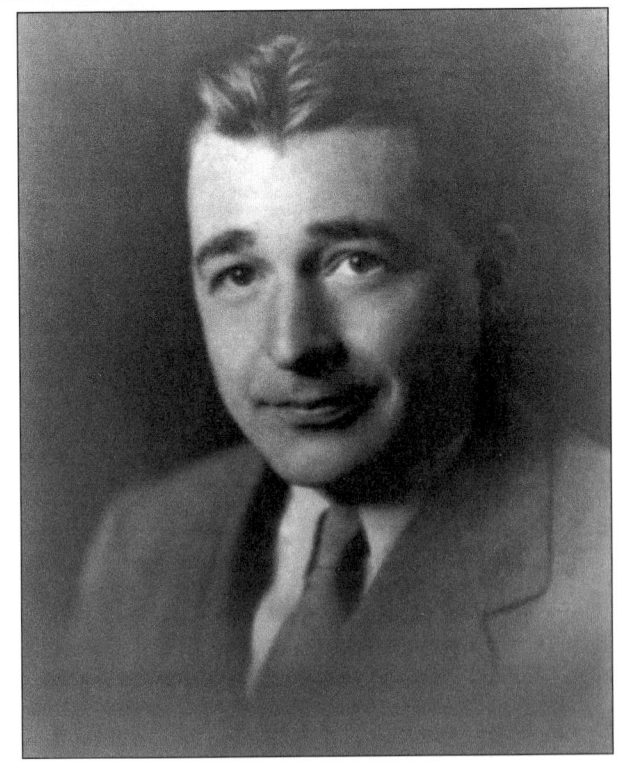

Ken Shaw was born on June 18, 1906. He graduated from Williston Seminary in 1924 and the Massachusetts Institute of Technology in 1928. He became an apprentice of William Pitcher and earned several promotions. By 1936, he had become a member of the company's board of directors, becoming the clerk of the corporation the next year. By 1943, he had also become assistant treasurer of the company. He began a plant modernization plan in preparation to fulfill WWII contracts. He passed away suddenly on July 27, 1943, at the age of 37.

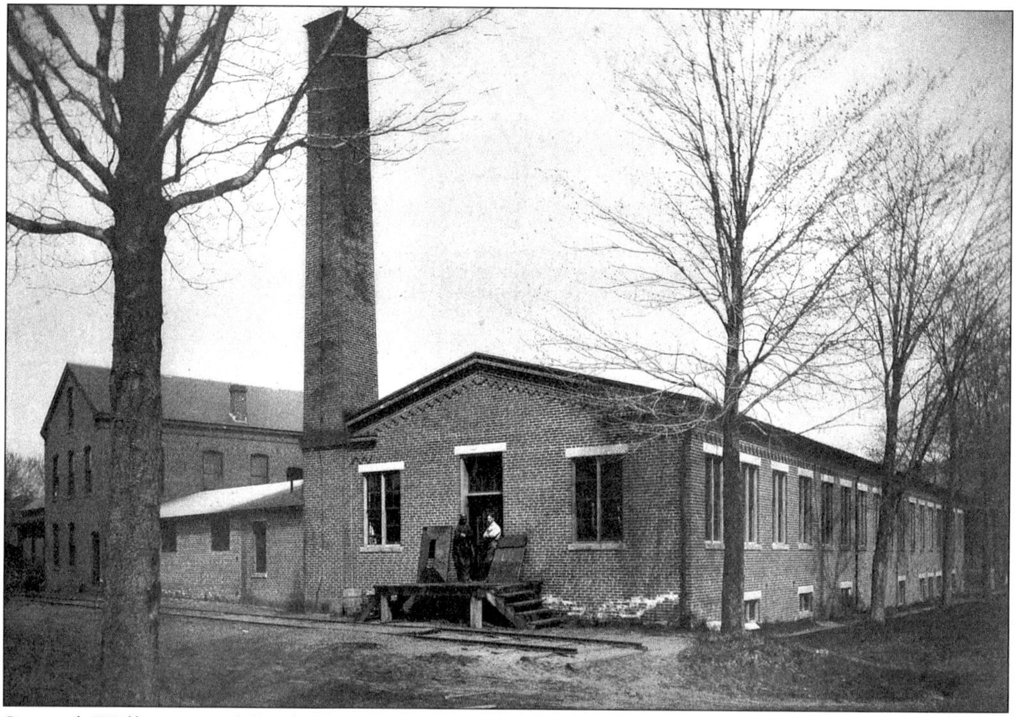

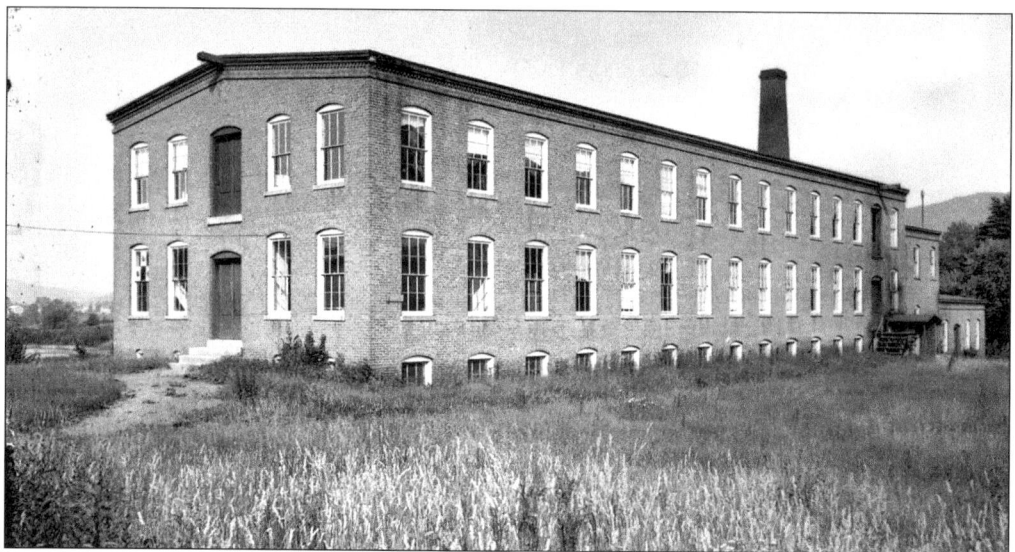

Samuel Williston and his business associates formed the Valley Pump Company in 1868 to manufacture pumps for the local mills. The company was sold to outside business interests who closed the factory. Later, this Payson Avenue plant was used as the printing plant for the *Easthampton News*, a weekly newspaper. It is now a mixed-use building.

The King Silk mill (not associated with the United Elastic Corporation mills) was built for a silk business. Mulberry trees were planted and silk worms were introduced to foster this industry. In 1905, the National Felt Company purchased this mill. Still located in this Mechanic Street mill, the company now known as National NonWovens also owns several Pleasant Street mills.

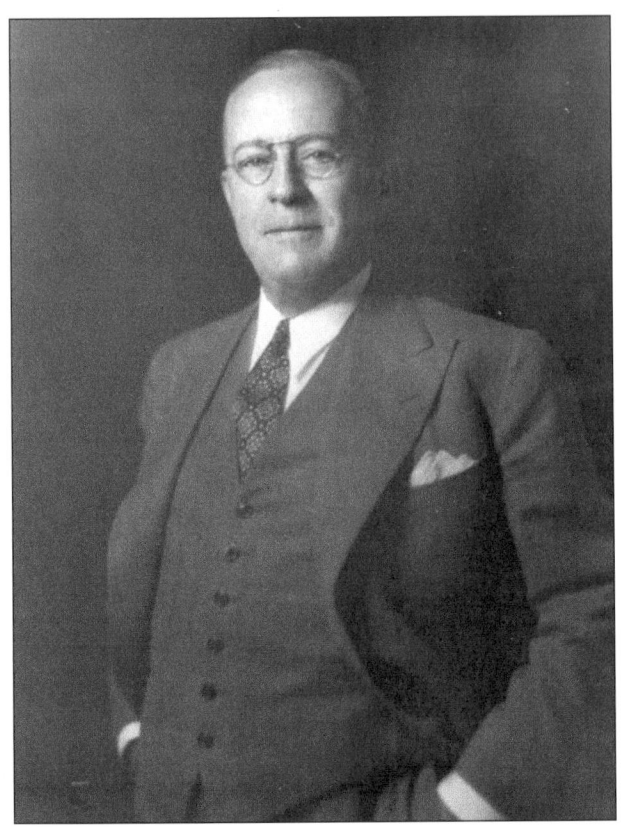

Edward Shaw became the first president of the United Elastic Corporation in 1927. He was born August 12, 1875, and graduated from Williston Seminary. He read law at a Northampton firm alongside Calvin Coolidge, the future president. An attorney in private practice until 1919, Shaw was appointed by Coolidge to the Massachusetts bench. He left the judiciary in 1922, becoming an attorney for many corporations, including the Glendale Company. He became president of the United Elastic Corporation, serving until his death in 1943.

Some Glendale Company employees pose in the finishing room. William Chipman was a foreman, appearing at the far left. The company produced many types of elastics for suspenders. The company concentrated on piece goods after the creation of the United Elastic Corporation.

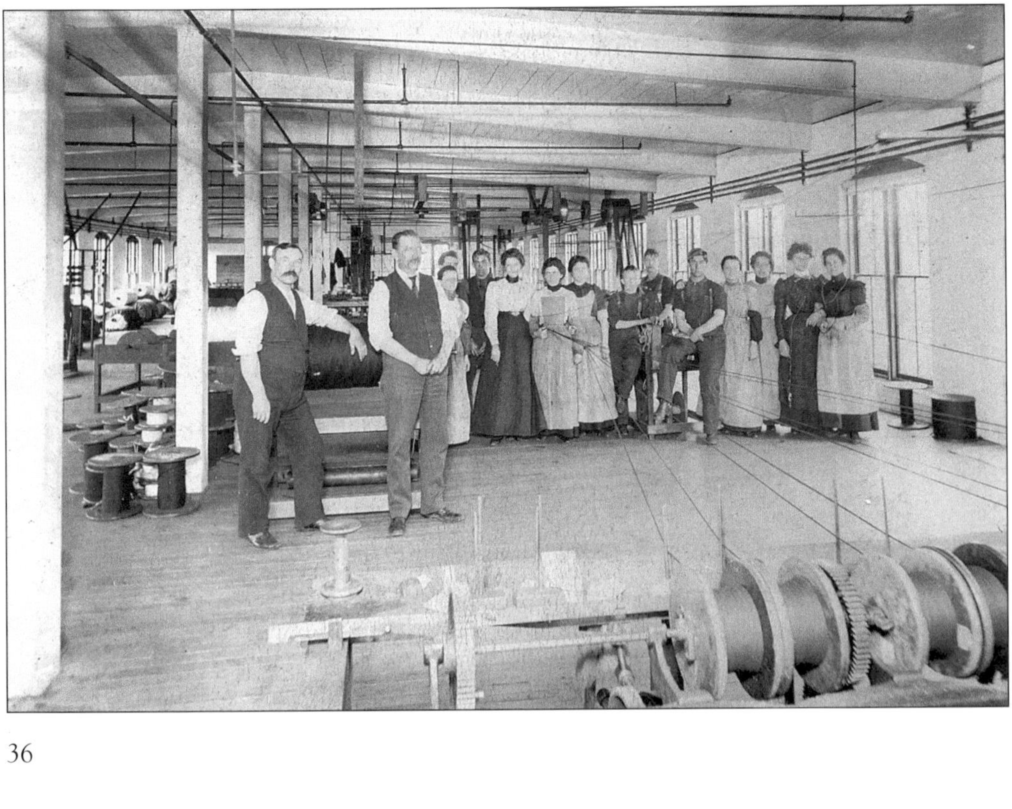

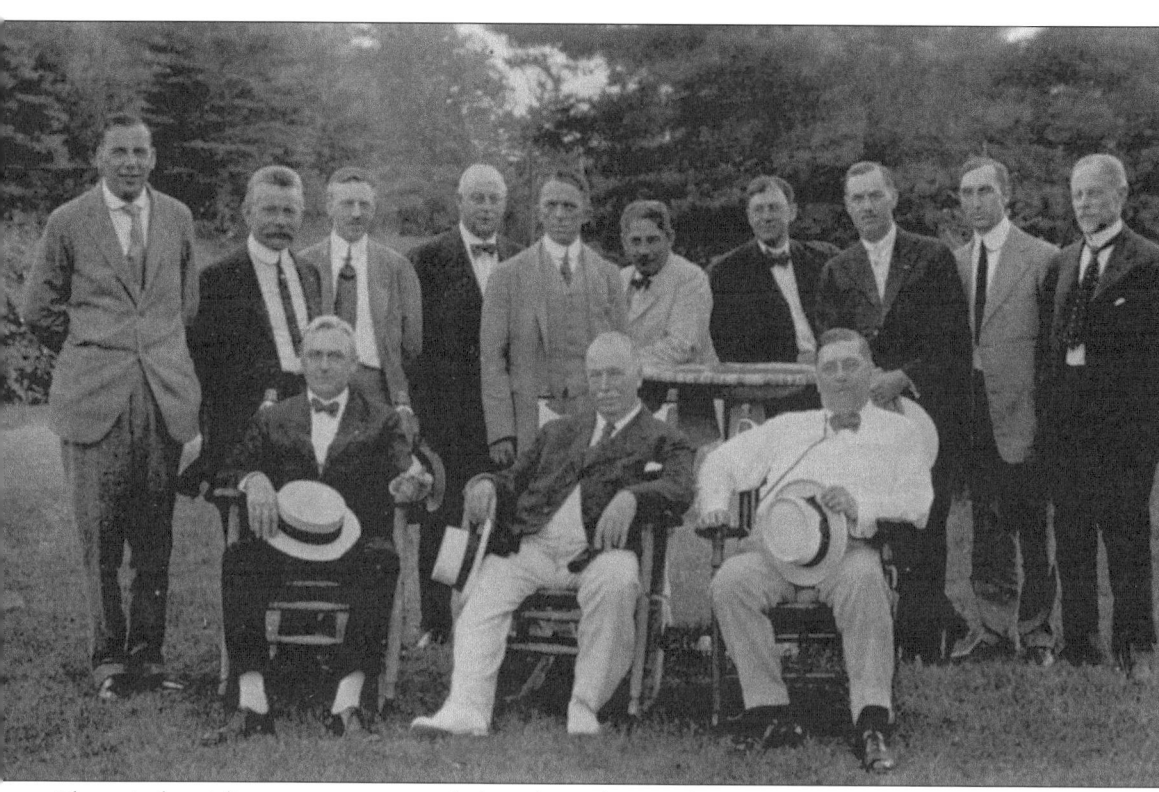

These industrialists are at rest, including (seated center) George Astill of the Glendale Company, (standing far left) William Pitcher, and (second from right) Clifford Richmond. The rest of the men are from out of town. William Pitcher, the son of Franklin and father of Richmond, was born in 1871. Following his graduation from Williston Seminary, he became a protégé of Thomas Sawyer. Pitcher served as the treasurer of the United Elastic Corporation in 1927. He served as the president of the corporation in 1943, managing the Easthampton Rubber Thread Company until 1954, when he died at age 82. Astill ran the Glendale Company from 1905 until the creation of the United Elastic Corporation.

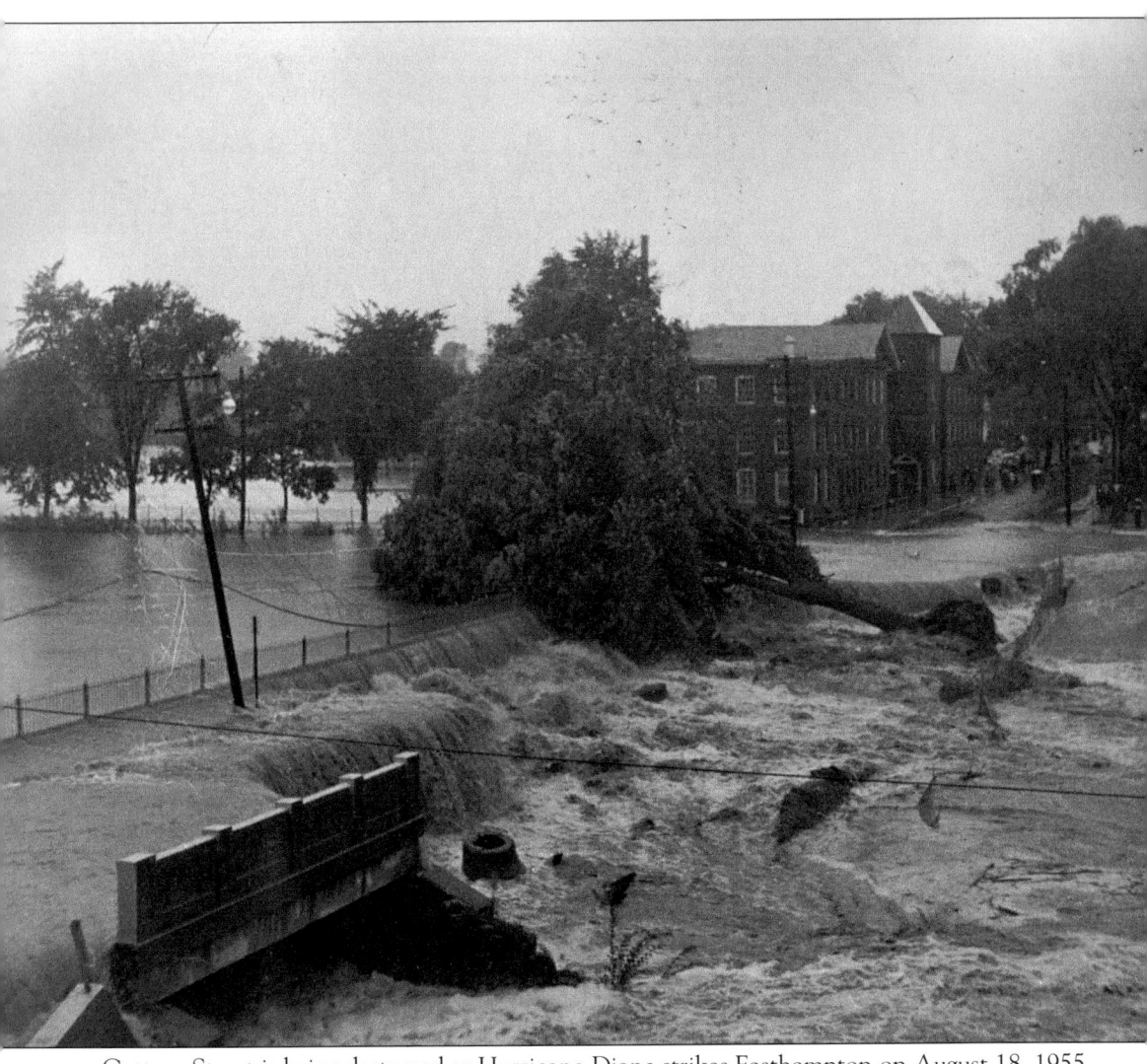

Cottage Street is being destroyed as Hurricane Diane strikes Easthampton on August 18, 1955. For several days before, ponds and rivers had swollen from heavy rain. The United Elastic Corporation main office is in the center, with the Glendale division in the foreground. Both the Glendale and the Hampton divisions were heavily damaged.

The United Elastic Corporation mills were modernized during WWII and the 1950s. Here, a warehouse is being constructed. In the rear is the power plant, which provided heat and power for the Easthampton Rubber Thread Company and the Glendale division, as well as for parts of Williston Academy.

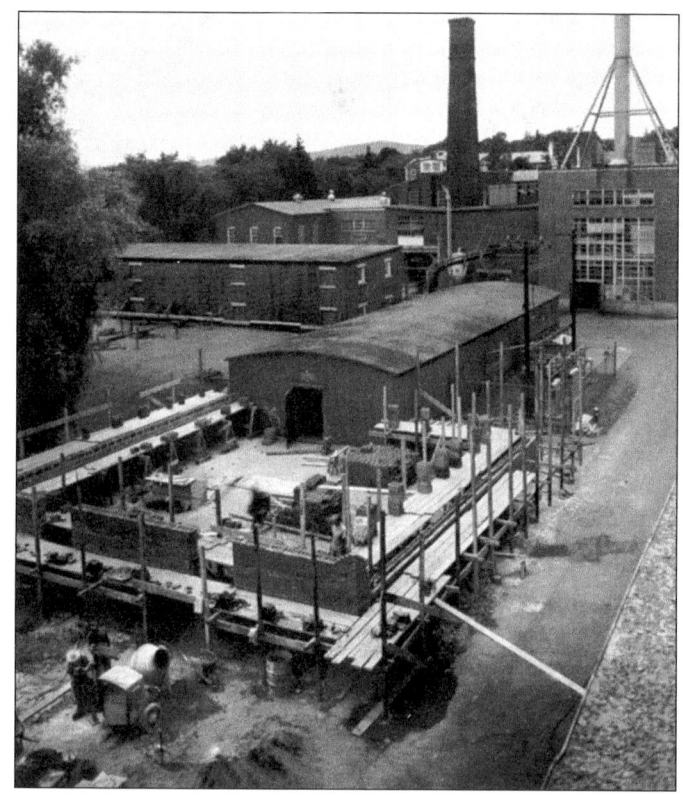

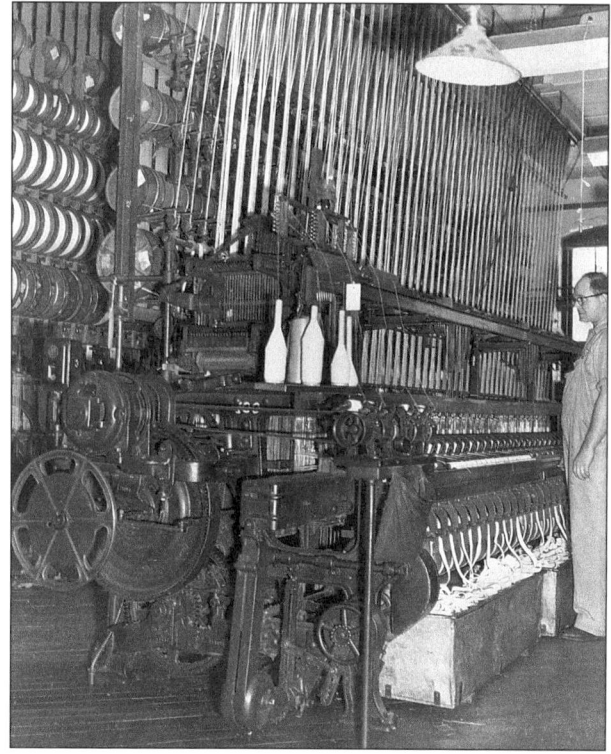

Shown in this 1950s photograph is a row of looms in the Glendale plant. Produced here were cotton yarns, elastics for home sewers, ribbon rubber thread, and golf ball thread. The plant also produced braided, wide, woven, and knitted elastics.

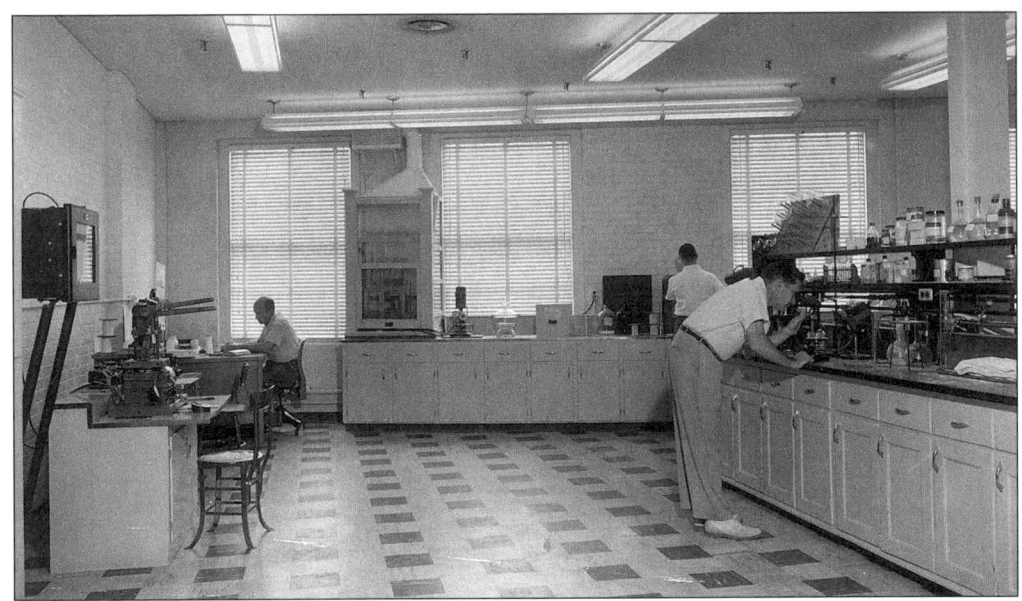

Many of the perfections made to rubber thread were done in this lab. Here, they either invented or perfected such materials as spandex, narrow elastics, and narrow rubber thread.

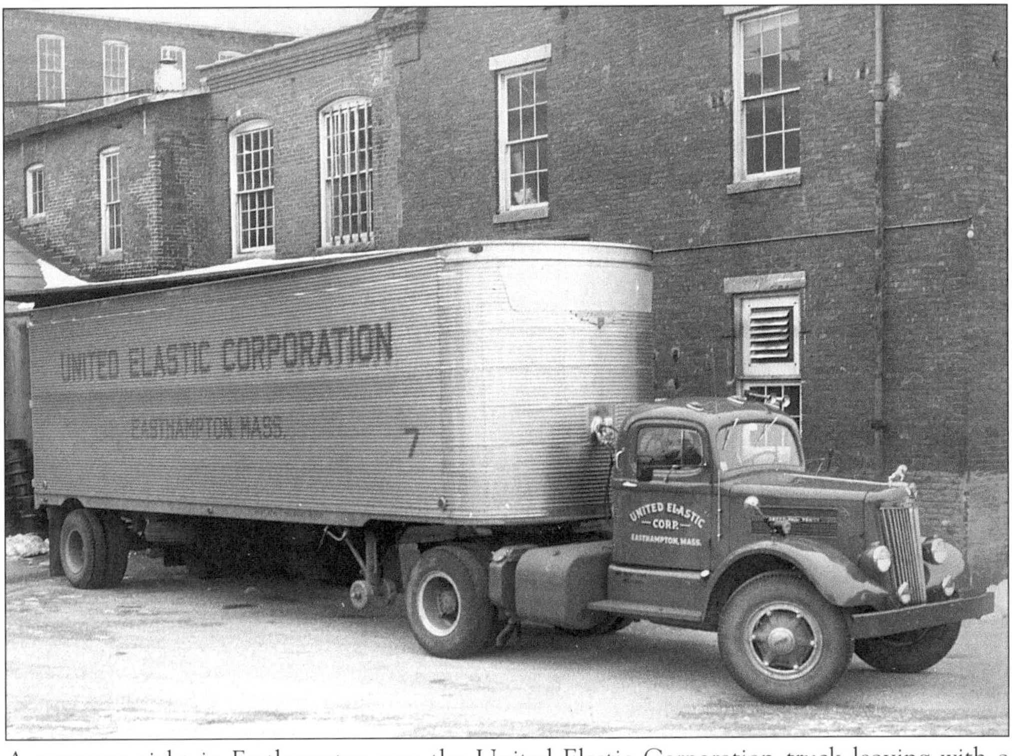

A common sight in Easthampton was the United Elastic Corporation truck leaving with a load of finished goods. In addition to the plants at Easthampton, Littleton, and Lowell, the company eventually had branches in the following locations: West Haven, Connecticut; Stuart, Virginia; West Boylston, Alabama; Woolwine, Virginia; Westfield, North Carolina; and Nova Scotia.

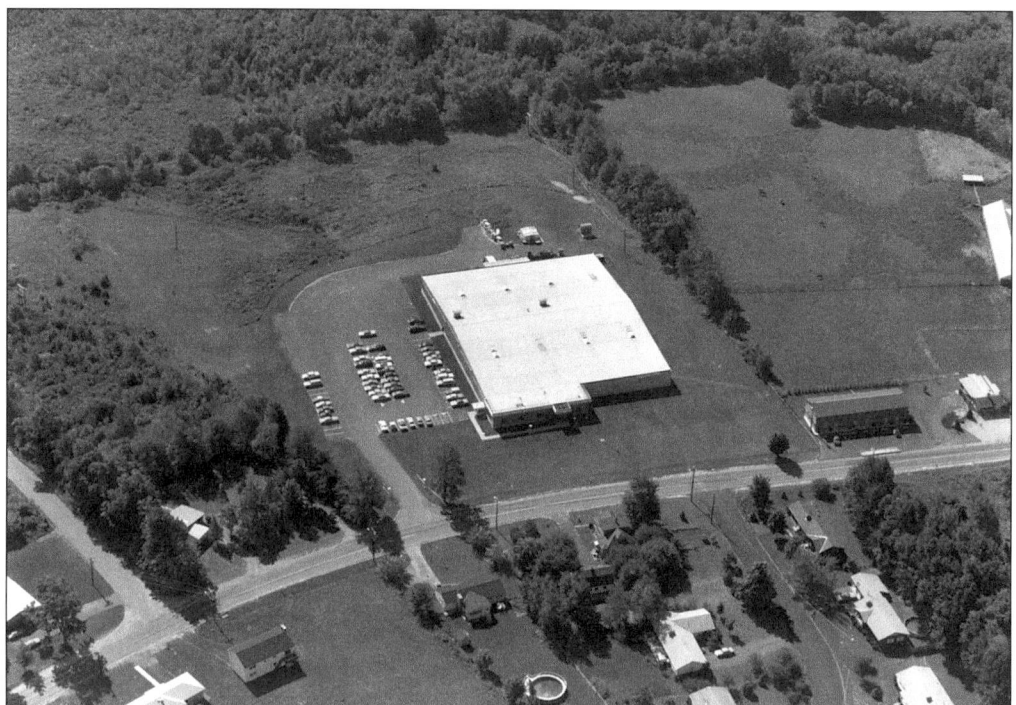

In 1963, the Molded Products division of the Easthampton Rubber Thread Company was opened in this mill. The building was constructed by the United Elastic Corporation on Southampton Road in Easthampton. Originally, the mill constructed laboratory stoppers, pharmaceutical closures, golf ball cores, and polyurethane products. Similar products are still manufactured here.

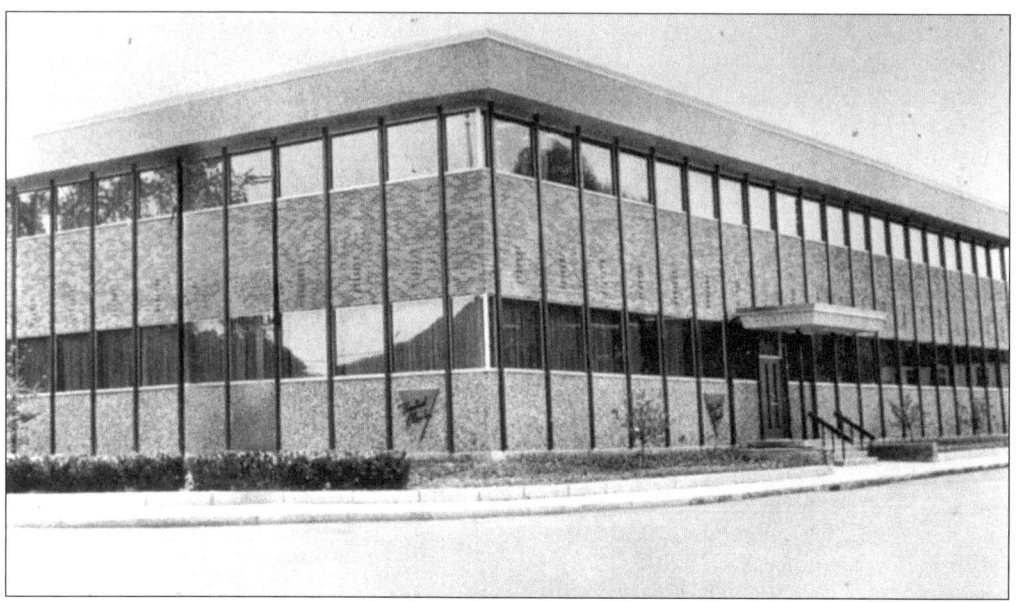

A new general office was opened in 1965, replacing the former Nashawannuck Manufacturing Company office. This building was used as the main office of the United Elastic Corporation until it closed. Since then, it has had several tenants.

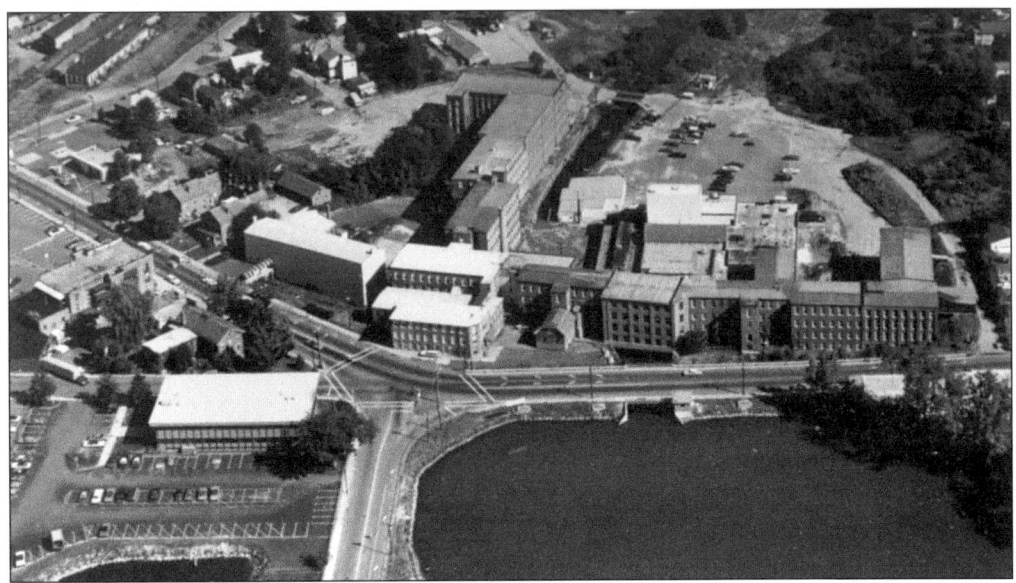

This 1968 aerial photograph shows the Glendale division of the United Elastic Corporation. A longtime executive for the company at the West Haven division, S. Clark Lilley became president and chairman of the board of the United Elastic Corporation. In 1968, he helped engineer the merger between the United Elastic Corporation and the J. P. Stevens Corporation. He was given a seat on the combined board of directors, but was removed the following year when the J. P. Stevens Corporation assumed control of all the United Elastic divisions.

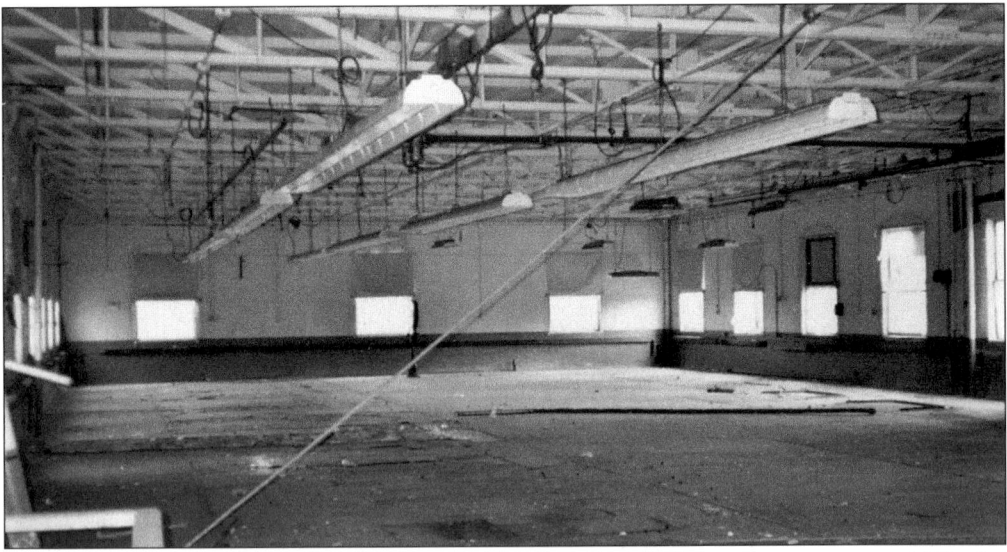

Following the closure of the Glendale division of the United Elastic Corporation in 1970, the J. P. Stevens Corporation operated the former Easthampton Rubber Thread Company as the Williston plant and the Payson plant. Both were closed in 1987. The former Glendale mills are now owned by Riverside Industries, which rents to several companies. After being vacant for several years, the former Easthampton Rubber Thread Company plant was torn down. This photograph shows the interior of the mill. The former site is now home to the public safety complex.

Three

LOWER MILL POND
INDUSTRY

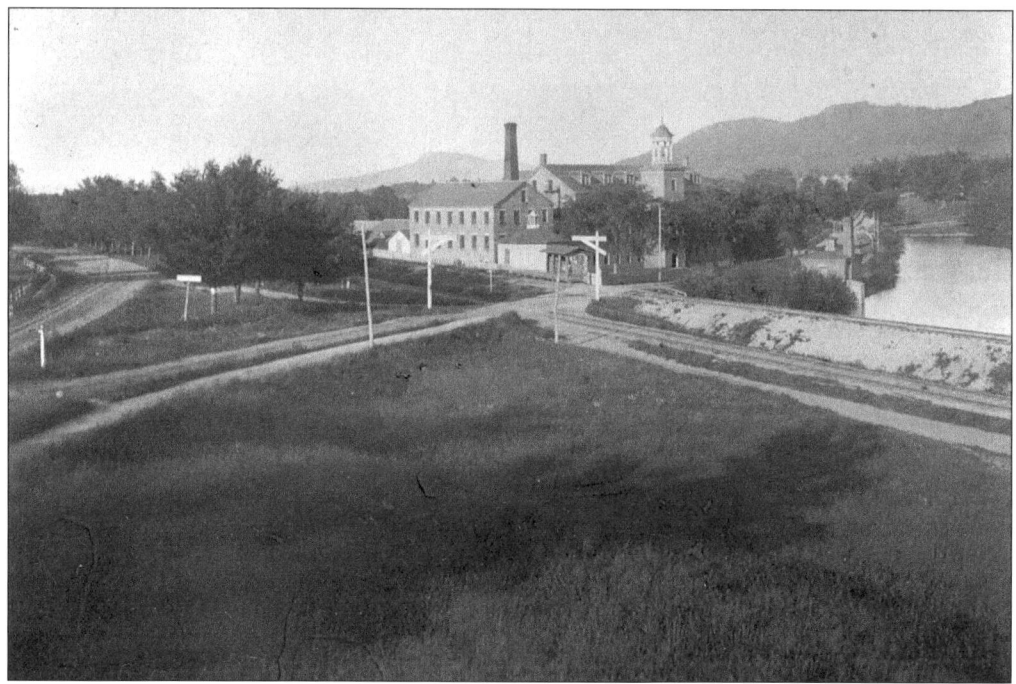

The Lower Mill Pond is less than a mile from Nashawannuck Pond and is connected by a canal. In 1859, Samuel Williston purchased the water rights of Broad Brook, where a sawmill operated during the 18th and early 19th century. Here, Williston constructed Williston Mill No. 1, a spinning mill. This picture was taken in 1899 after the purchase of the mill by the Hampton Company.

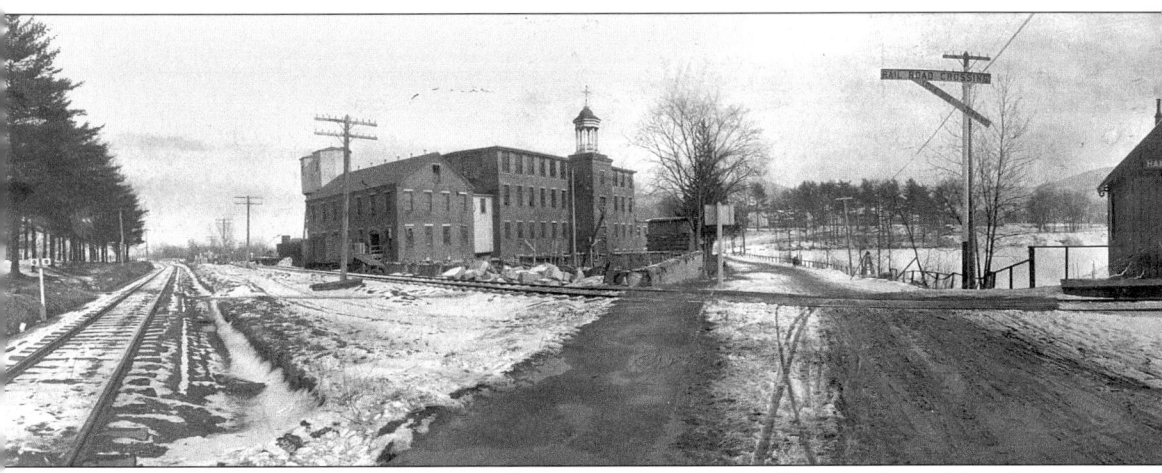

The Hampton Company was originally associated with the West Boylston Manufacturing Company. Cloth finished at the West Boylston plant was brought to the Hampton plant to be dyed or bleached. Later, the company dyed, bleached, or mercerized piece goods for other companies. The Hampton Company also had a division that dyed yarns and another division that made rayon.

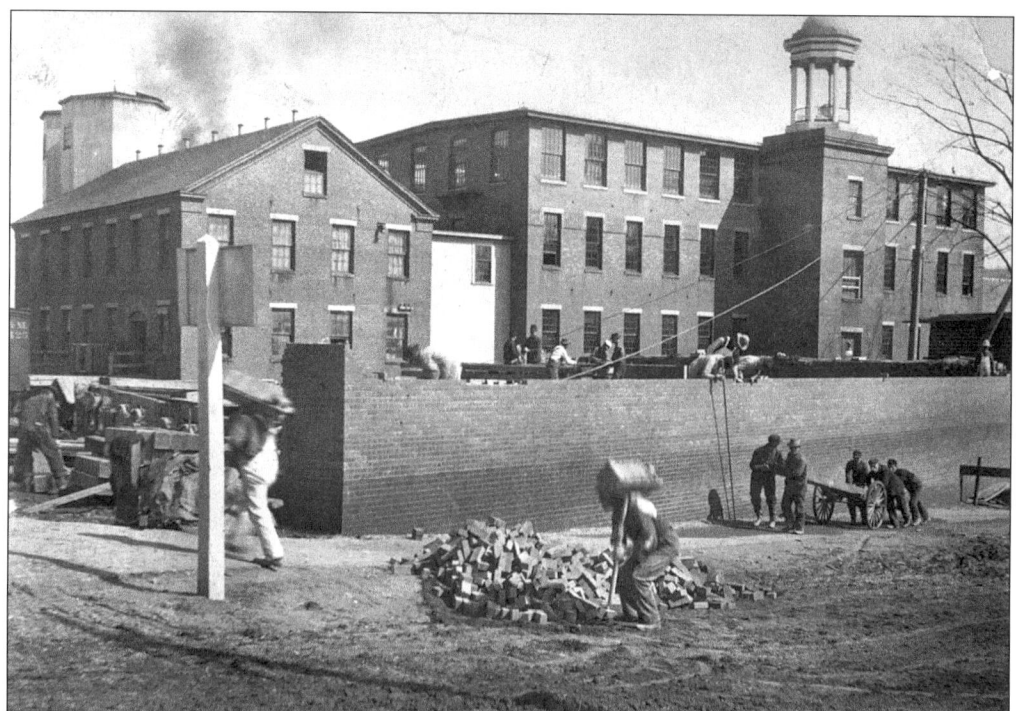

This c. 1900 photograph shows the construction of the Hampton Company's office. The Hampton Company eventually had over 30 buildings for manufacturing operations. Even more important for the company was the abundance of water from artesian wells, many of which were located in the well field behind the mills. The same source of water is used today by Easthampton for public drinking water.

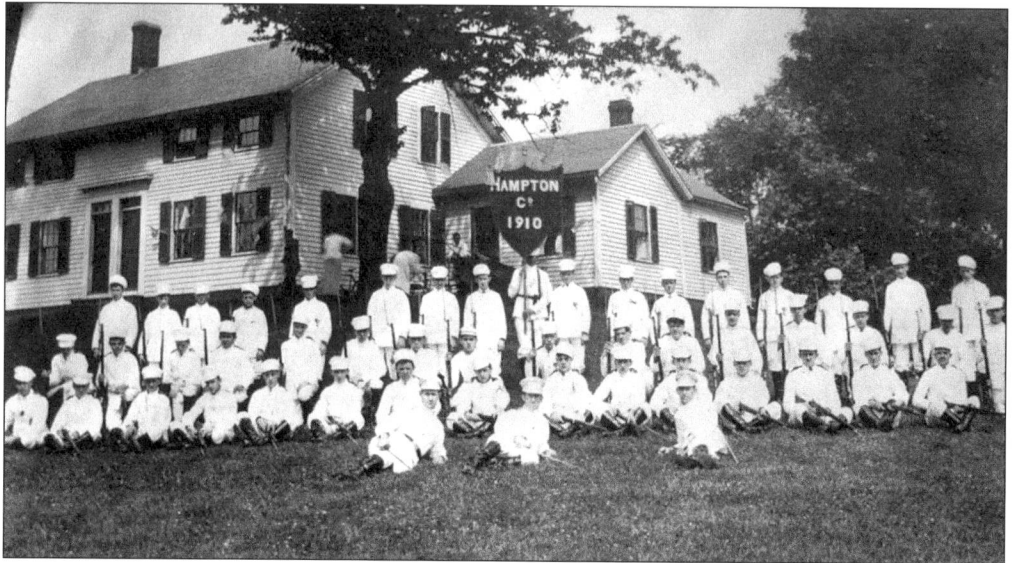

Employees of the Hampton Company pose at 197–199 Pleasant Street in 1910. The Hampton Company's need for workers was helped by immigrants from Canada and Poland who sought employment at the Hampton Company.

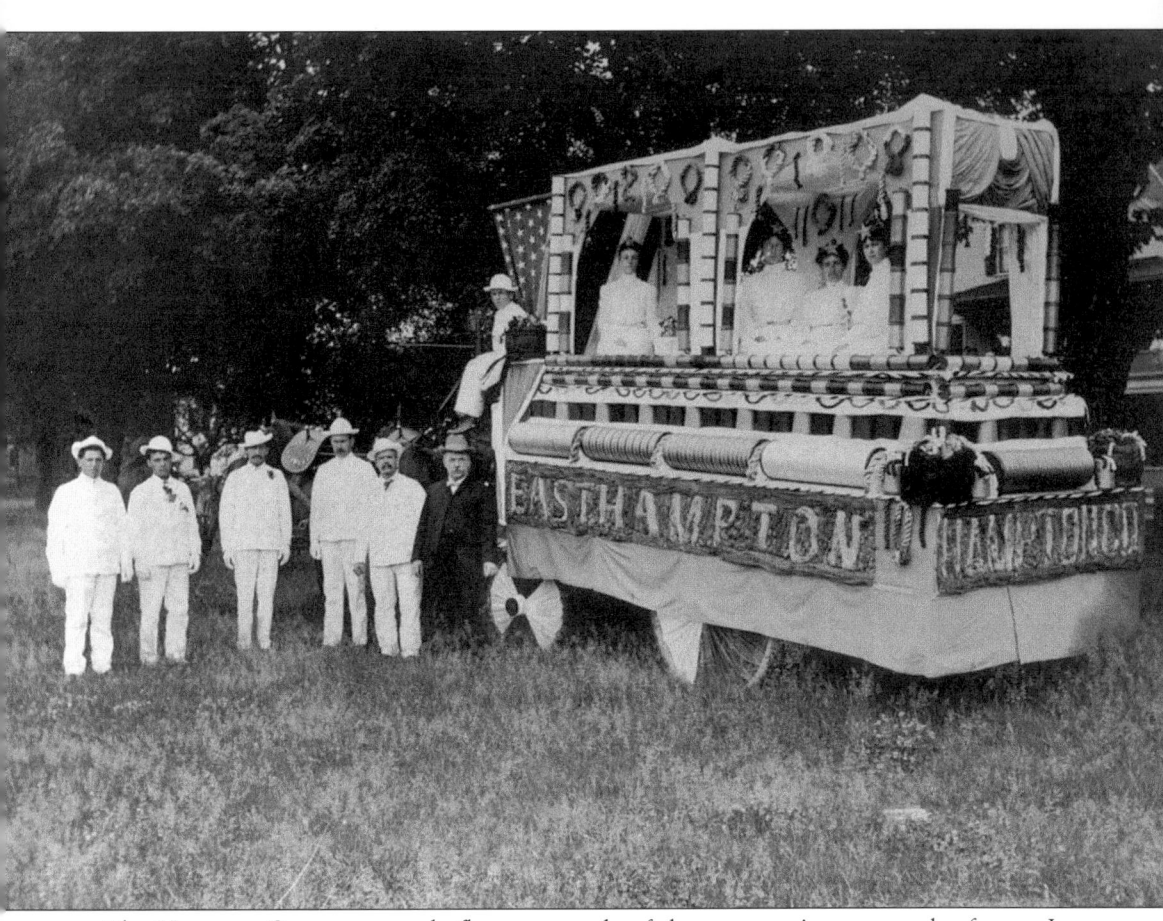

The Hampton Company parade float was made of the company's own spools of yarn. James McCallum (in the dark suit) was superintendent of the yarn division. This division, having always been operated as a separate division, was sold to American Thread in 1946. They closed it in 1949.

George Barton was born on January 30, 1862 in England, where he learned the textile business. He came to the United States in 1903 to set up mills, including one for the Hampton Company. In 1905, Barton returned to Easthampton to head production of the piece goods division. He died on December 17, 1935.

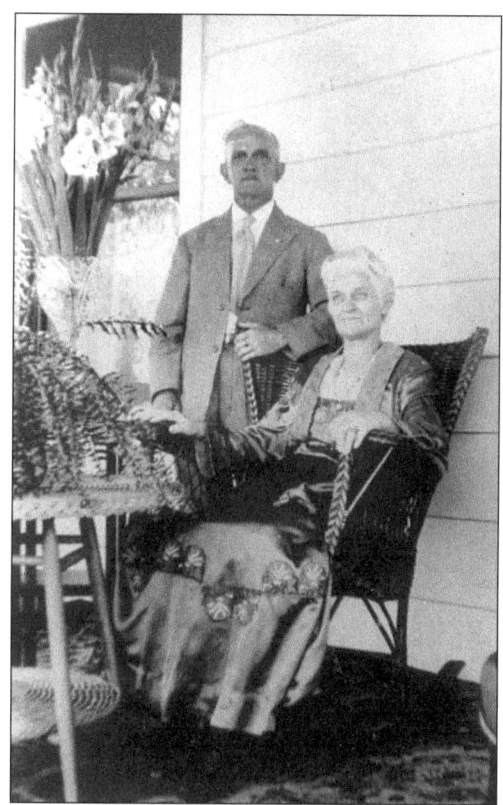

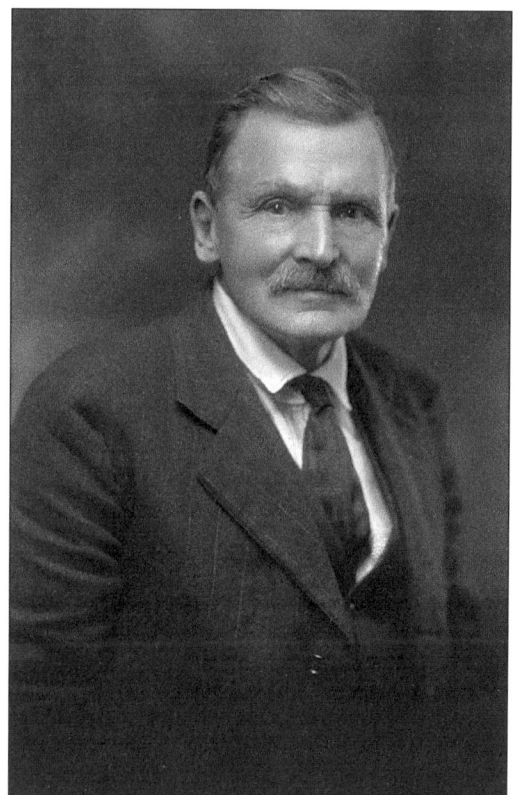

Charles Scott served as a master mechanic at the Hampton Company. His job was to set up machinery for other employees to operate and to fix the machinery that broke. He was regarded as a valued employee for his knowledge of the machinery and his skills in repairing it.

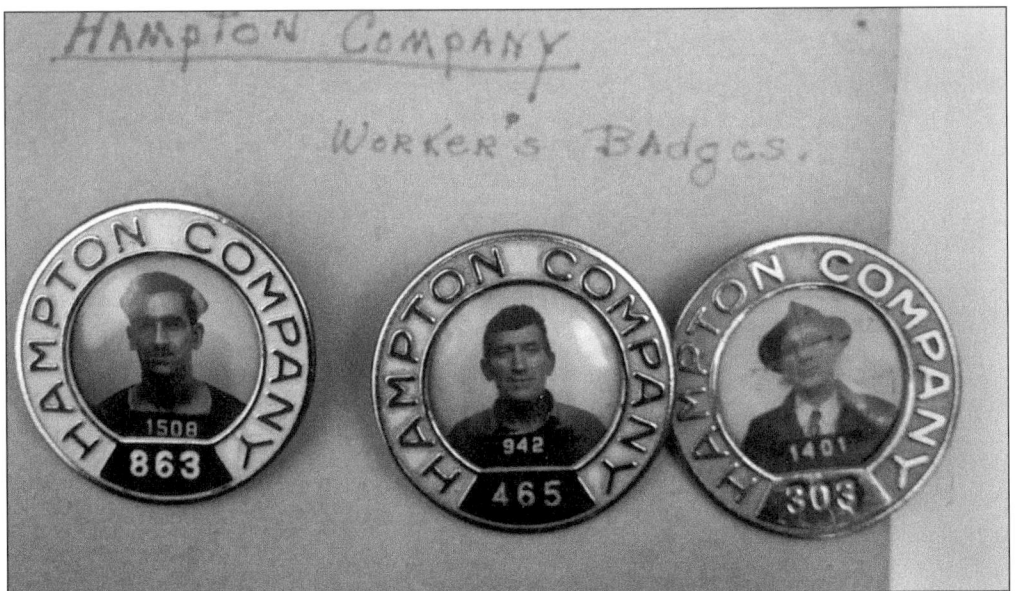

These employee badges for the Hampton Company symbolized its fear of industrial sabotage. Security became a concern for the company because of its need for large numbers of employees, including people hired for only a few days. Union activity also prompted the increase in security, especially after the 1934 strike, which lasted several days and resulted in a call-up of the National Guard.

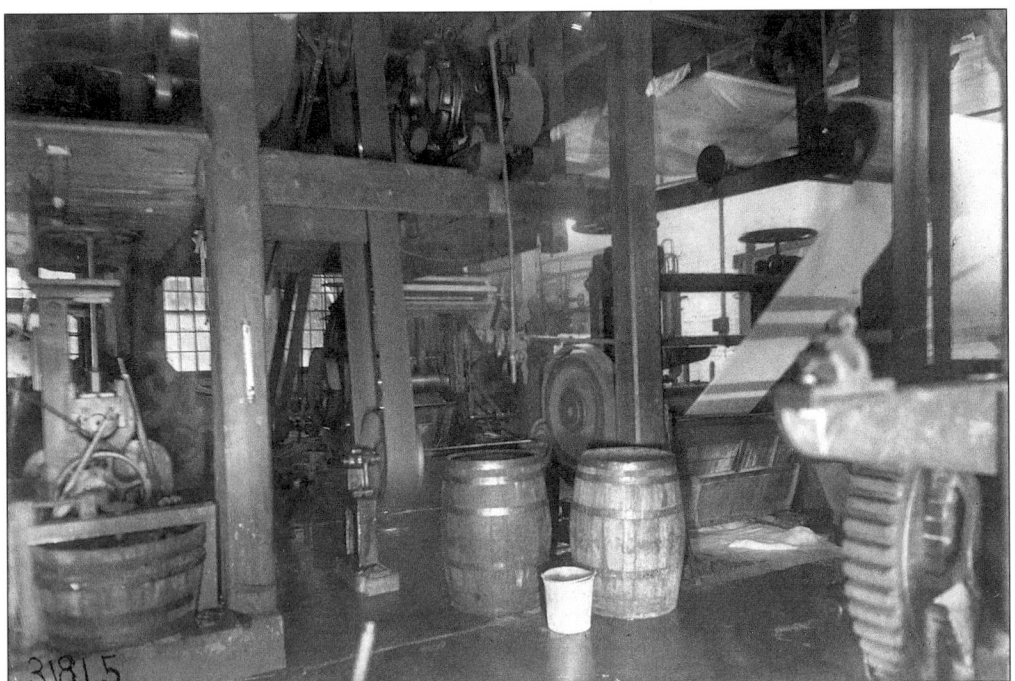

Machinery at the Hampton Company included this dying machine. The work was hazardous, as many types of caustic chemicals were handled during the manufacturing process. Today, the outdoor tanks in which processed waters were stored remain standing behind the mills.

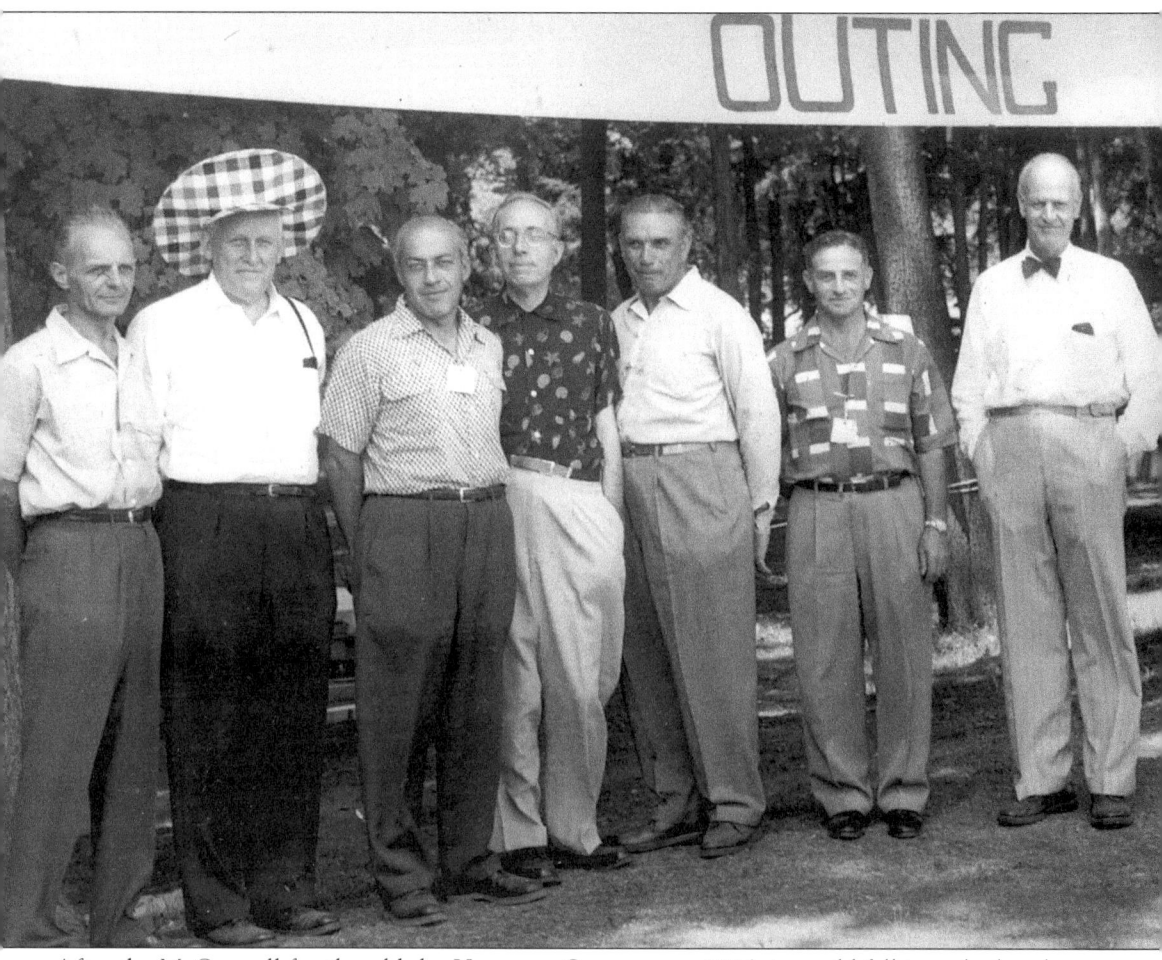

After the McConnell family sold the Hampton Company in 1946, it would fall into the hands of several owners: Textron, American Thread, and Fuller Fabrics. Here, D. B. Fuller (in hat), poses with employees, including William Guinan (far right), who headed plant operations from 1946 until the company closed in 1962.

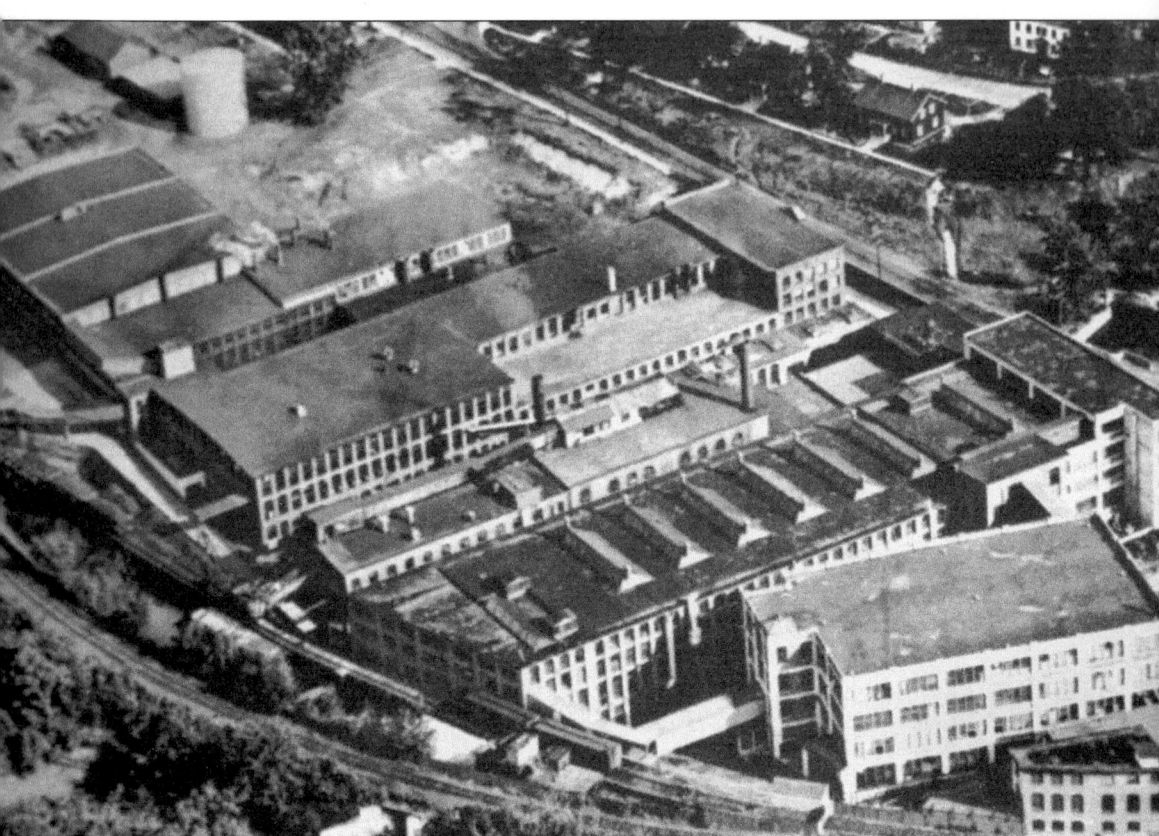

The J. P. Stevens Corporation bought the Hampton Company in 1955. Gradually, the company scaled back operations until it finally closed in 1962. The former Hampton Company mills are now used for a warehouse, with offices and space rented to light manufacturing. The October Company, a maker of wood products, uses the newer mills, located at the top left of picture.

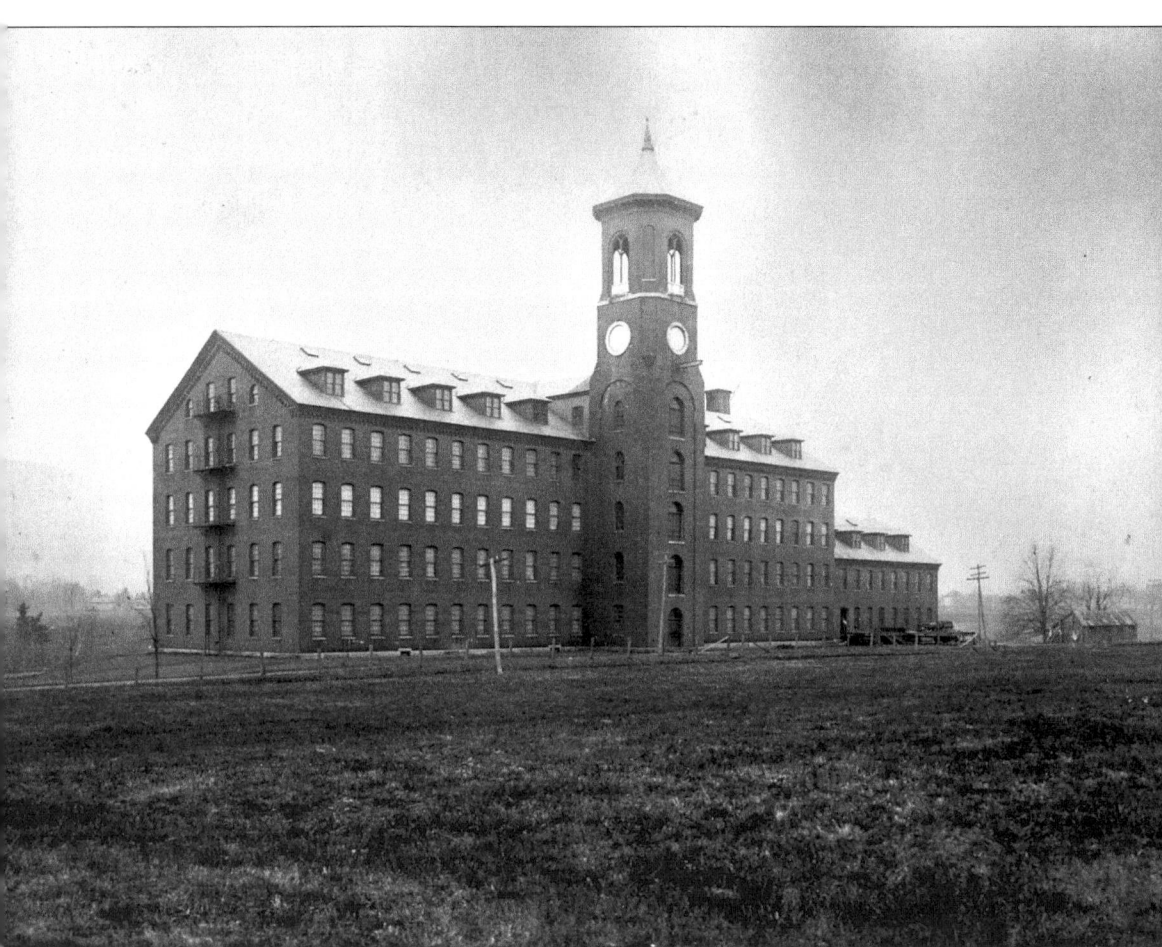

The Williston Mills, successful because of Civil War contracts, opened this second mill in 1865. The mills faced a post-war depression and had economic ups and downs through the balance of the 19th century. Both Edmund Sawyer and Franklin Pitcher had to be called in to help the company. The Easthampton Spinning Company succeeded the Williston Mills. The company went bankrupt in 1898, with Williston Seminary holding a mortgage. The next year, this building was sold to the West Boylston Manufacturing Company, which constructed five additional mills around this building. The mill was taken down in 1931. Today, the site is used as a parking lot, basketball court, and skateboard park.

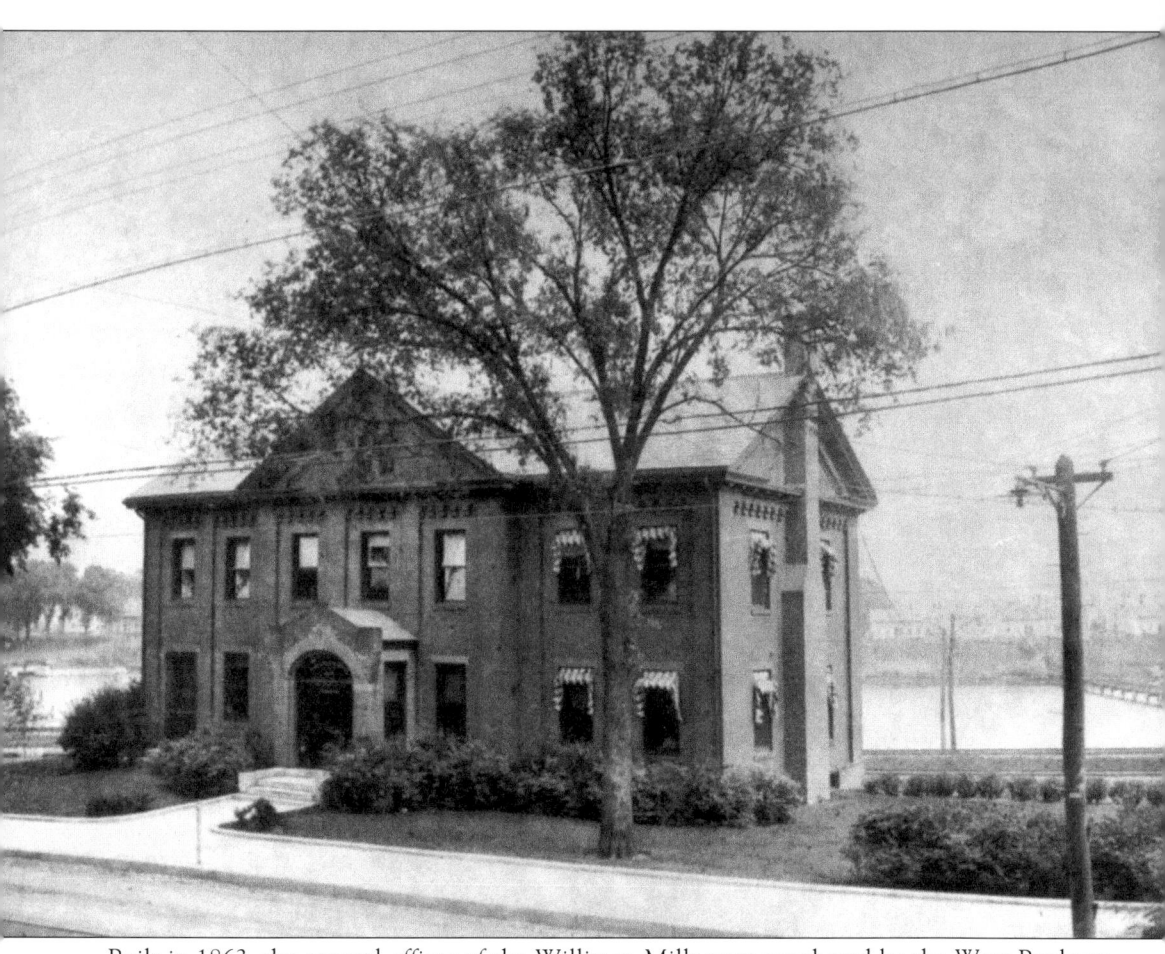

Built in 1863, the general offices of the Williston Mills were purchased by the West Boylston Manufacturing Company in 1899 for use as a main office. In 1814, the company was incorporated in the town of West Boylston, Massachusetts. This building was enlarged in 1917. After the closing of the company, this building remained unoccupied until 1942, when it became an office for Campagna Construction Company. Following this, the building was used by the MacMorin Metal Stamping Company as their manufacturing site. In 1949, Stanley Home Products bought the MacMorin Metal Stamping Company. Frank Stanley Beveridge then gave this building to the American Legion, the Dalton Lavallee Post No. 224, which converted the office to a club house, banquet hall, and bar.

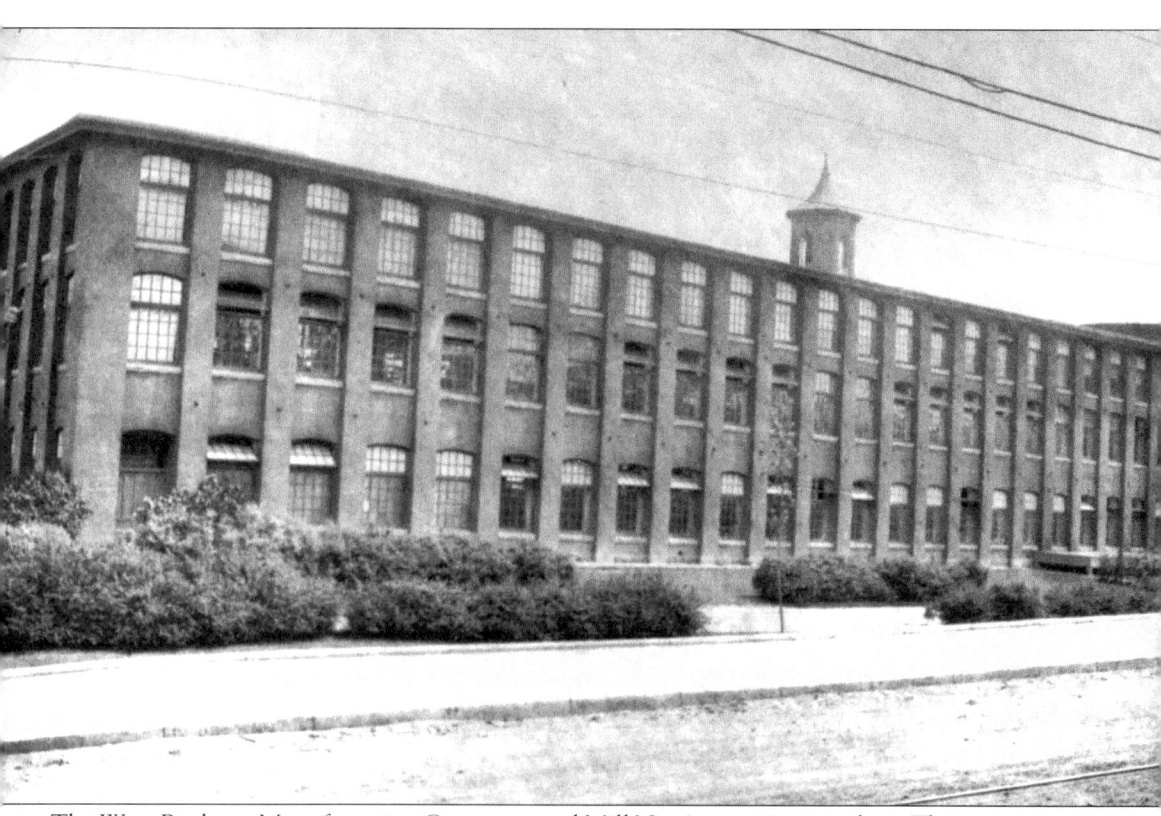

The West Boylston Manufacturing Company used Mill No. 1 as a spinning plant. The company constructed this mill from brick and timber salvaged from its mills in the town of West Boylston. The first tenant of Mill No. 1 after West Boylston ownership was the Advertising Corporation of America, which moved there from New York in 1932. This company, which produced printed materials, moved to Holyoke in 1958 and is now owned by the Blackfoot nation, located in North Dakota. Other tenants of Mill No. 1 included Interstate Slipper, American Maid Footwear, and Tubed Products. It has also been rented by the town. It now awaits a new tenant.

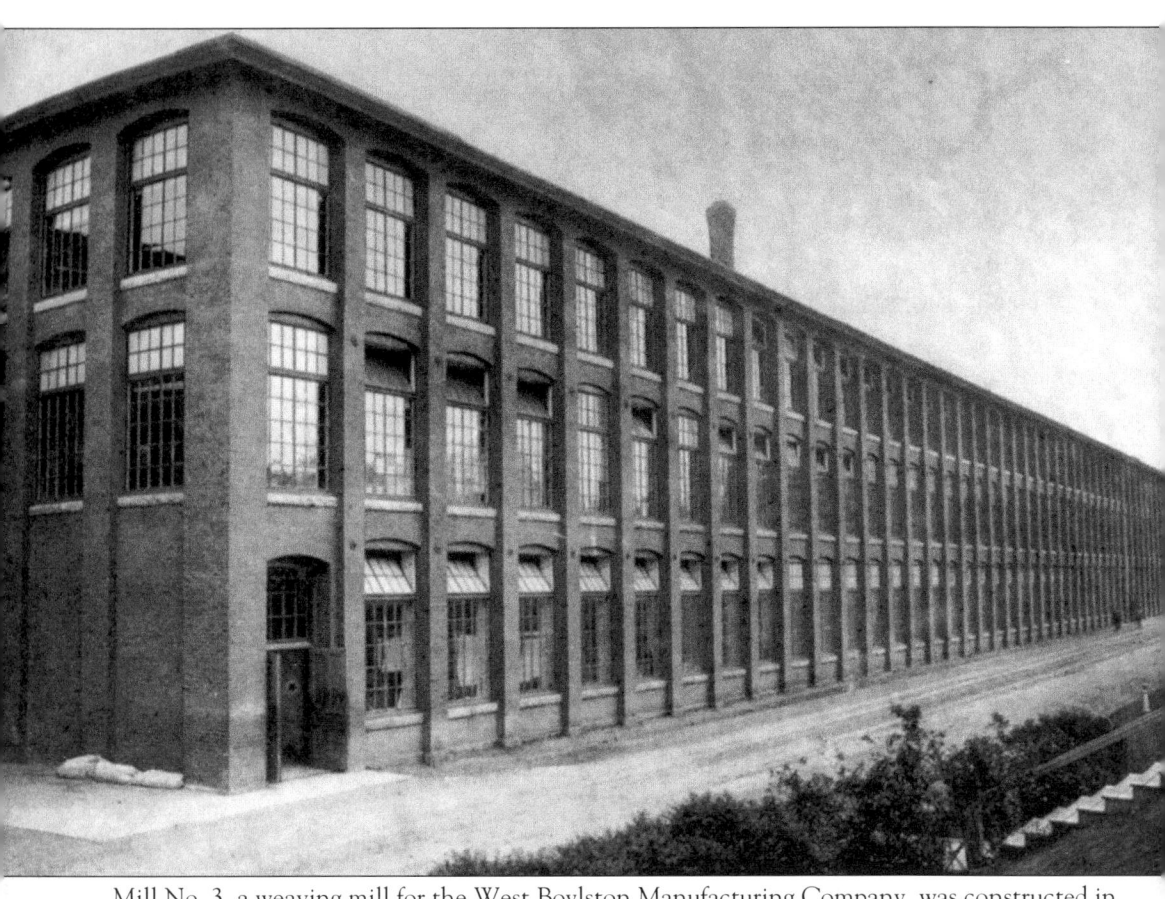

Mill No. 3, a weaving mill for the West Boylston Manufacturing Company, was constructed in 1900 and enlarged in 1907. In 1937, Paragon Rubber moved here from Brooklyn. This division and several subsidiaries of the company have been located in the mill, including American Character Doll, Noma Electric, Manhan Wallpaper, Spring Action, M&L Plastics, Rhodes Rubber, and Easthampton Weaving. Campagna Construction arrived in 1942, setting up in the other half of the mill to construct prefabricated housing for Europe after D-Day. Following the war, Nickle Cadmium Battery was located here from 1945 until 1963. National Felt took over this mill in 1963.

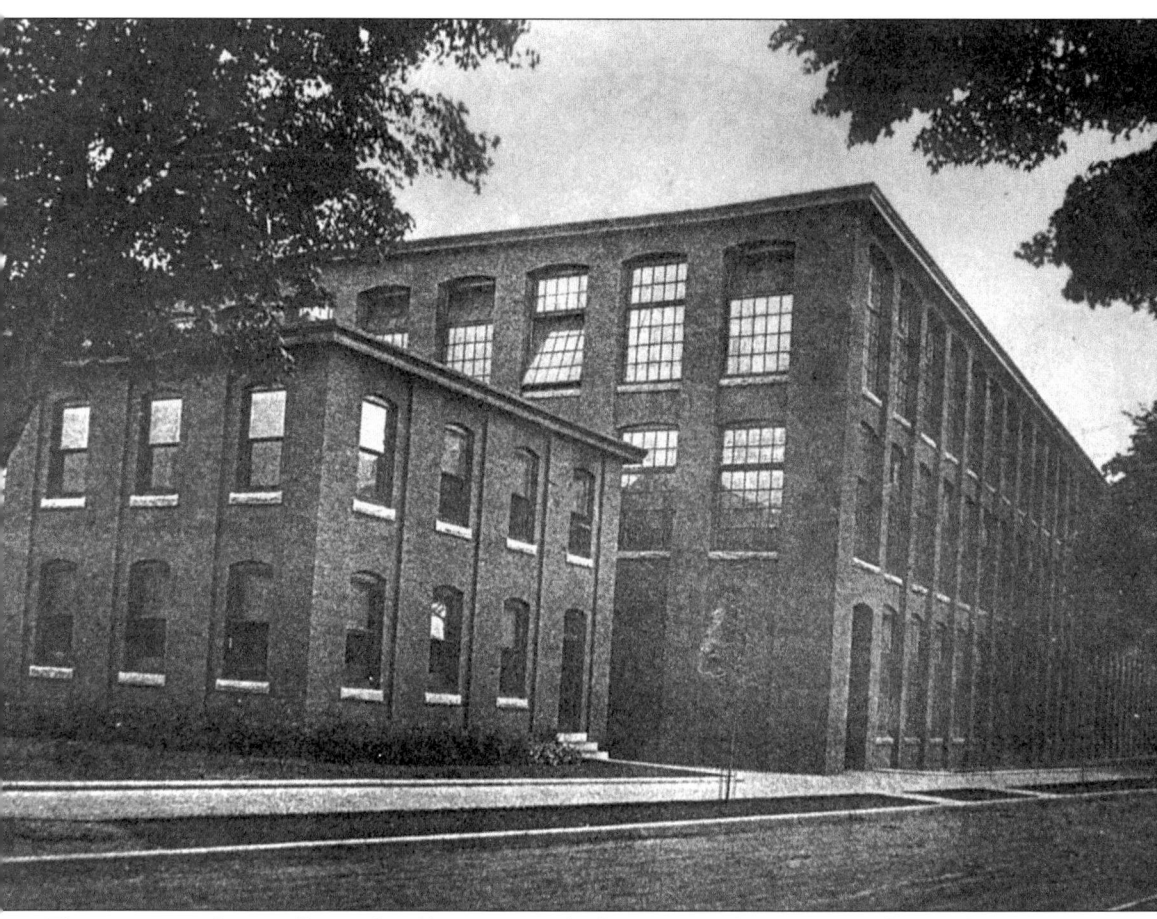

The superintendent's office and Mill No. 4 were built in 1907. The superintendent's office was expanded in 1917, doubling its size to accommodate a personnel and nurse's office. Mill No. 4 was later occupied by Standard Shirt, which moved from New Haven in 1938. The next year, the company became known as Lesnow Brothers and was sold to Textron. This company was here from 1943 to 1948. Lesnow Brothers was here again between 1948 and 1985. Hampton Specialty and American Maid Footwear also rented space here in the 1940s. In 1985, Kellogg Brush bought this mill, occupying it until 1996, when it moved to Ohio. The mill currently awaits a new tenant.

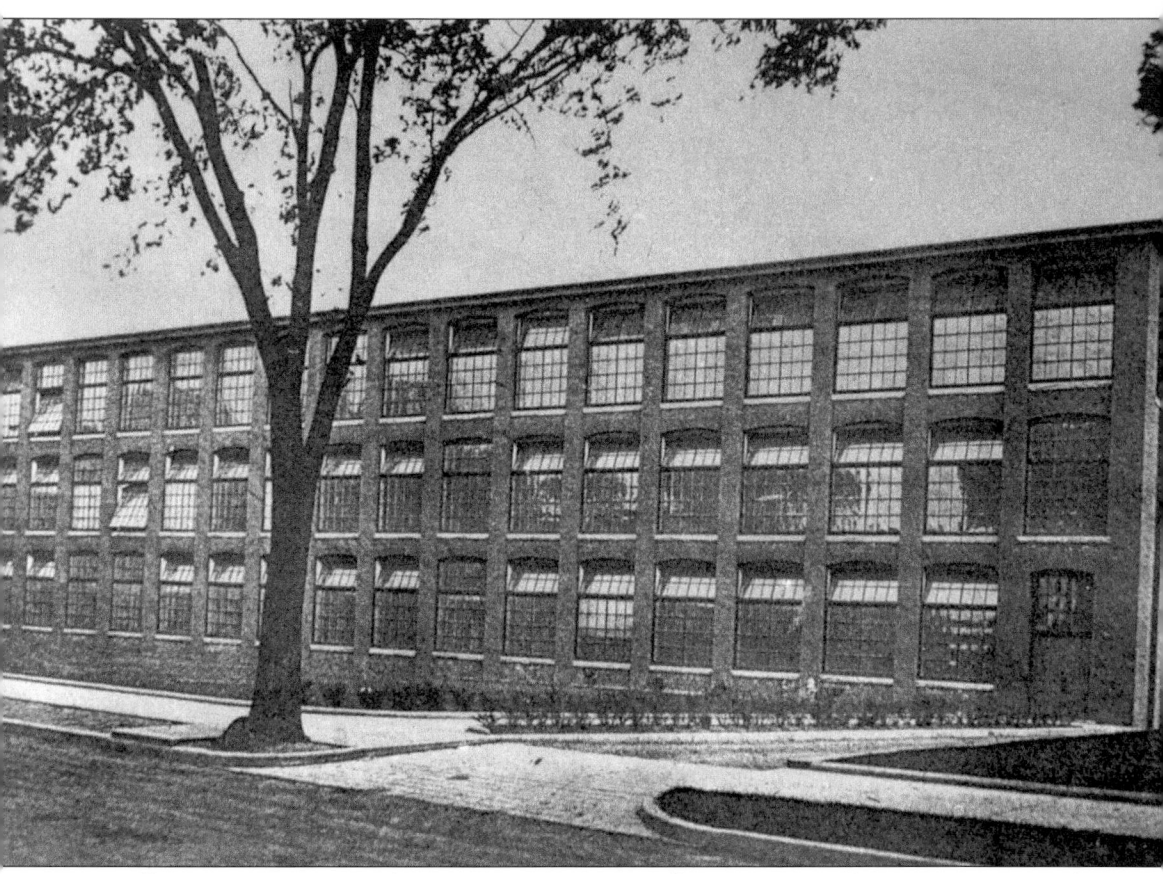

Mill No. 5 was constructed in 1912 as a spinning mill. It was vacant from 1931 to 1937, when Hampton Specialty moved here. This company manufactured metal chairs, outdoor furniture, and juvenile furniture. Its parent company went bankrupt and closed the plant in 1966. Kellogg Brush, a maker of brushes for domestic uses, moved here in 1967, staying until its move to Ohio in 1996. The mill is currently awaiting a new tenant.

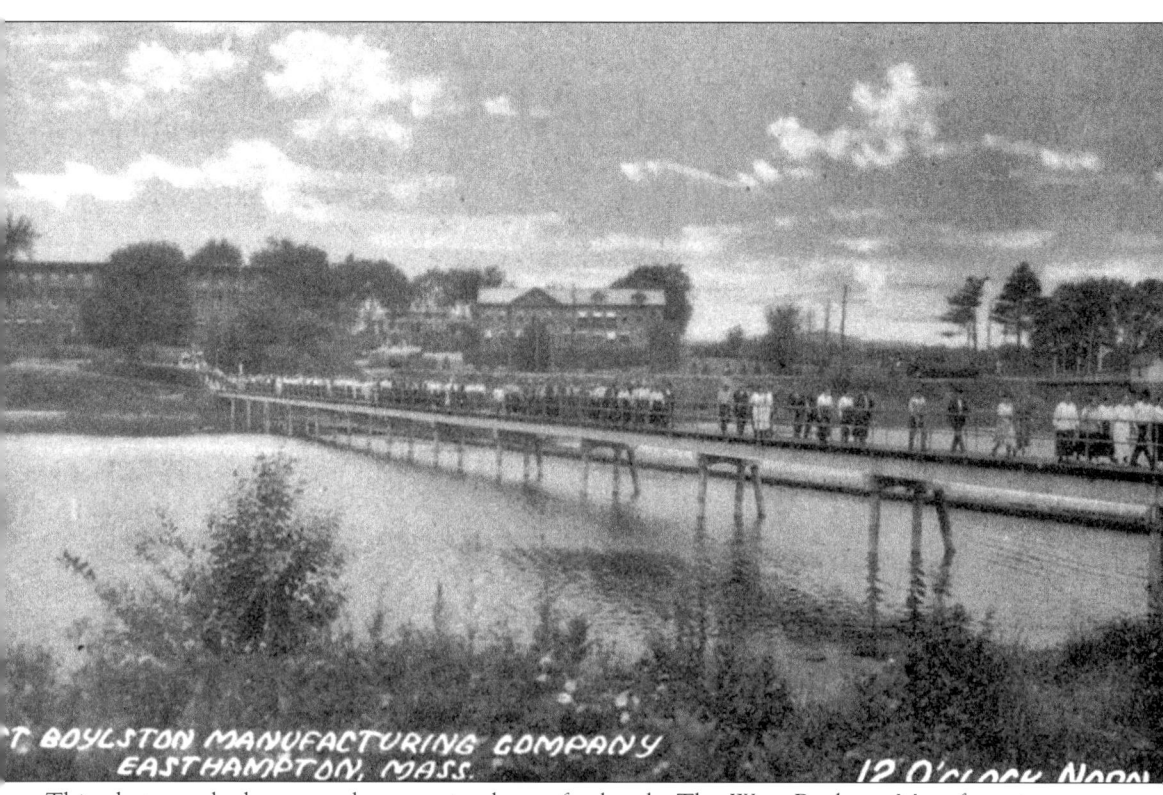

T BOYLSTON MANUFACTURING COMPANY
EASTHAMPTON, MASS.   12 O'CLOCK NOON

This photograph shows employees going home for lunch. The West Boylston Manufacturing Company hired employees of many nationalities for operatives, including people of Irish, French-Canadian, and Polish origin. The company initially had a 60-hour workweek, but reduced it a 48-hour workweek in 1920.

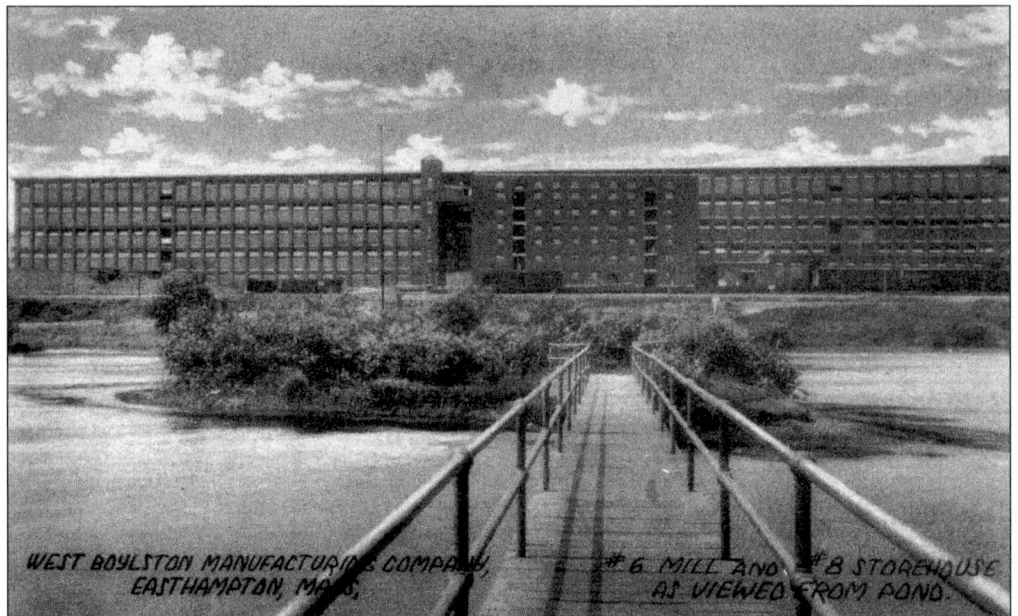

Mill No. 6 was constructed as a three-story building in 1915. Two additional stories were added in 1919. Here, the West Boylston Manufacturing Company made cloth tires and parachute materials for WWI contracts. The building was empty from 1931 to 1942. This photograph was taken from the West Boylston Everett Street village.

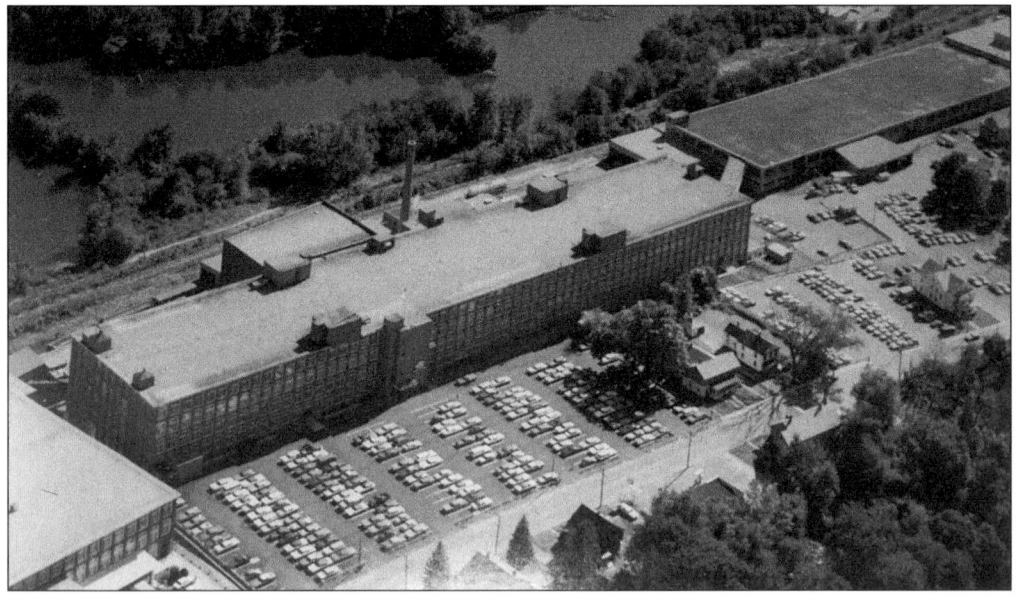

WWII revived the economy of Easthampton. In 1942 and 1943, the Cardanic Corporation set up a plant here as a back up manufacturing site for the Norden bomb site. For the next two years, General Electric had a vacuum tube plant here. Stanley Home Products moved its manufacturing plant here in 1947. The company, which closed in 1990, also constructed another building as a shipping and receiving plant. Today, the mill is a mixed-use development called EastWorks. The former shipping plant is owned by National NonWovens.

Fellow Textile Workers!

A TREMENDOUS

Massmeeting

Will be held on the

Easthampton Common, Main St.

Saturday, OCT. 5, 2 P. M.

Come and hear about the Ludlow sell out of the American Federation of Labor and the brutal Police attack on Fellow Worker Nat. Richards.

We will expose the latest plans of the West Boylston Mfg. Co. who are deliberately starving and crushing the workers in order to put over general wage-cuts and speed up.

All textile workers of Easthampton must come to this monster demonstration and show their solidarity with the Ludlow Workers.

Organize into the National Textile Workers Union, the fighting leader of the textile workers.

GOOD POLISH AND ENGLISH SPEAKERS.

Issued by Easthampton Local No. 7 National Textile Workers Union.

Two strikes broke out at the West Boylston Manufacturing Company in 1918. The first, centering on wage disputes, began in April and continued into May, when the weavers went on strike. This first strike lasted until early June, when an arbiter, who was appointed by the federal government, awarded raises. Lingering disputes brought another walkout at the end of June, resulting in a second strike.

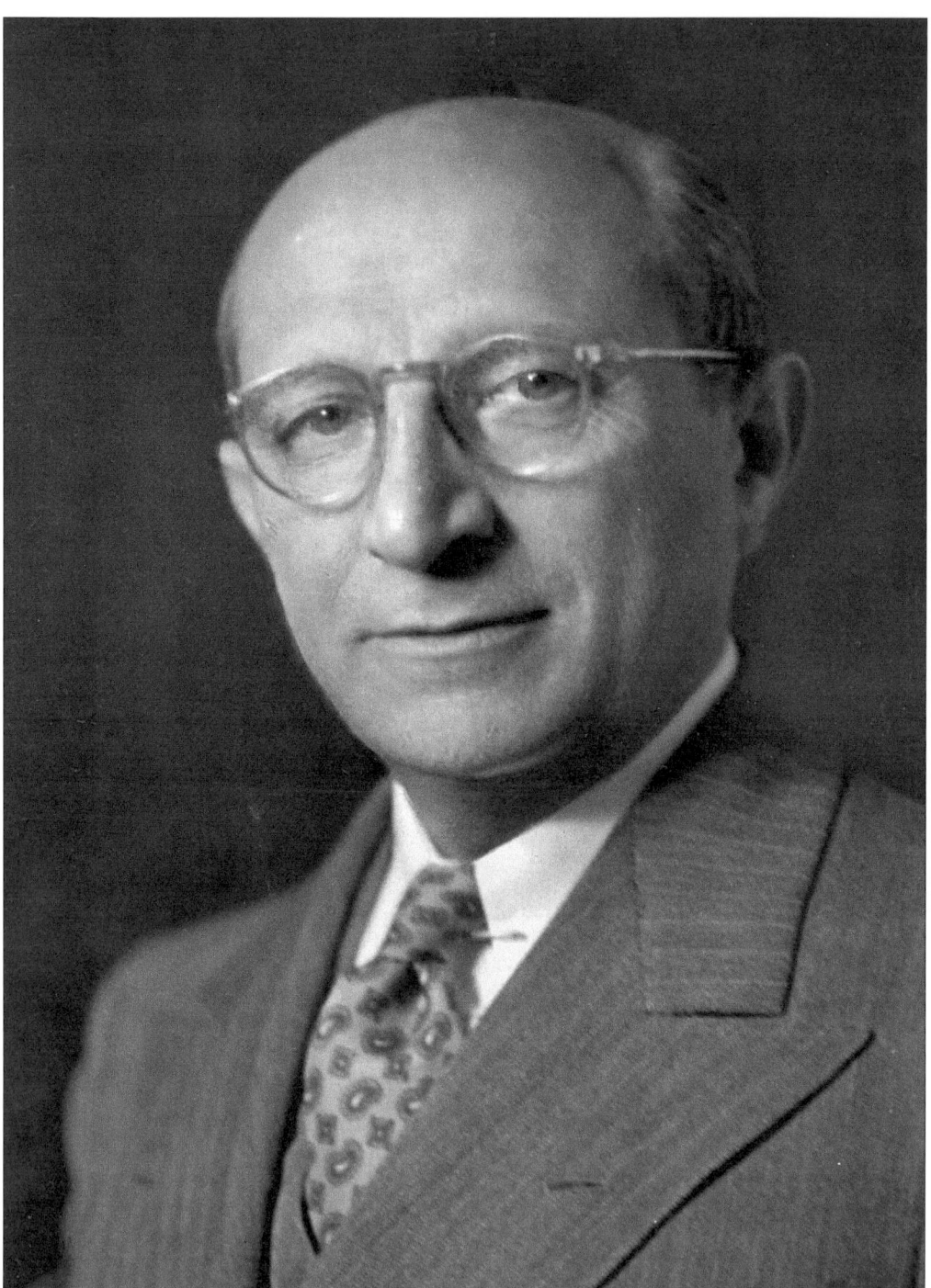

Stanley Lesnow helped the Easthampton economic recovery in the years following the West Boylston Manufacturing Company. In 1937, he moved his Standard Shirt Company here from New Haven. Although he sold the company to Textron in 1944, he re-acquired the company and Mill No. 4 in 1949, making men's shirts and raincoats. His son, George Lesnow, ran the company until 1985, when he found he could no longer compete with foreign imports.

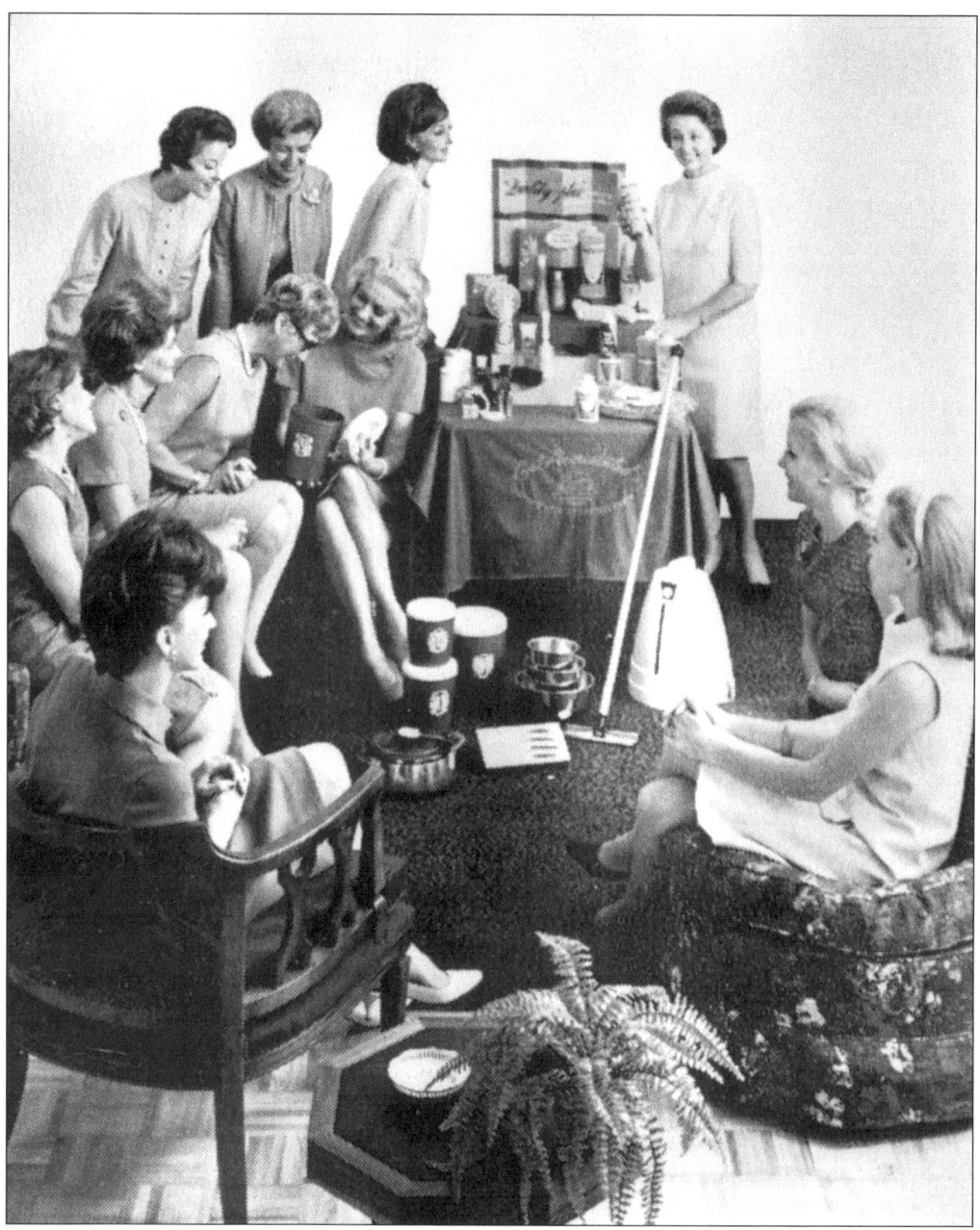

Stanley Home Products offered goods through direct sales at parties held in homes. In this photograph, we see one of these "Stanley Home Parties." The company sold products at a discount to its dealers, who in turn sold them for retail prices at parties. Stanley Home Products sold many lines of household goods during its stay in Easthampton.

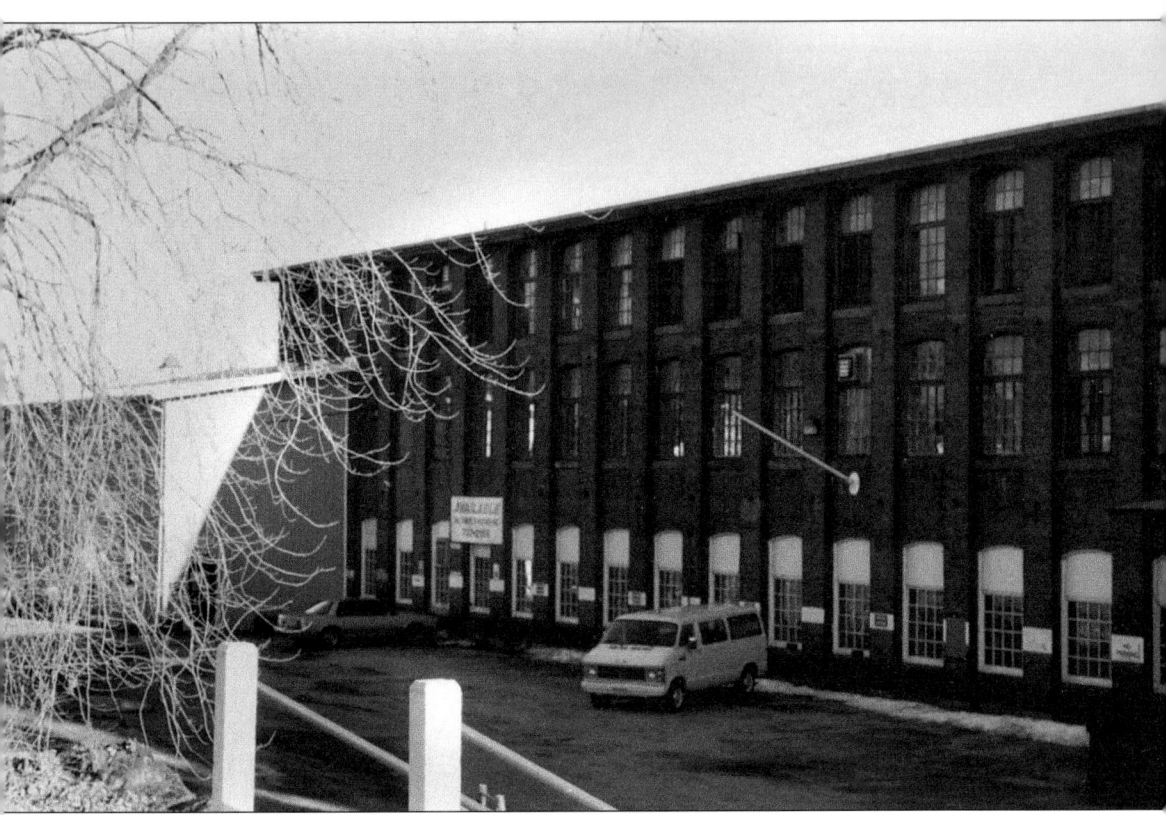

O'Neil Street was designed to foster a new industrial park. The project was initiated by the town board of public works and named for Michael O'Neill, the longtime town engineer. It was originally hoped that the Hampton Company would locate here. In 1962, the first three tracts were sold. The industrial park on O'Neill Street included six mills. One occupant was Tubed Products, which had left its previous location at Mill No. 1. This photograph shows Mill No. 1 awaiting a new tenant.

Four
RECREATION

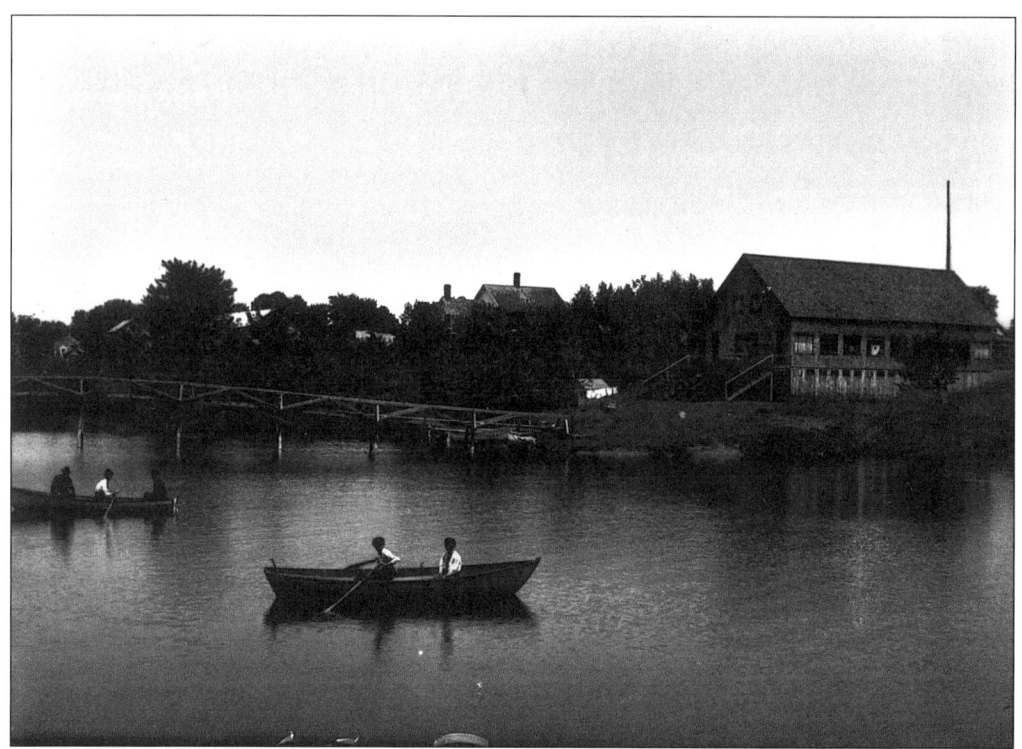

Nashawannuck Pond has long been a recreational site for the town. The boat club was active for many years. The pond has also been used for skating, swimming, and fishing. The town maintained a beach off Water Street until the community pool opened at Nonotuck Park.

BULLETIN

RECREATION ASSOCIATION :: WEST BOYLSTON MFG. CO.

EASTHAMPTON, MASS.

WEEK OF AUGUST 8

SUNDAY, AUGUST 8

Building open from 9.00 A. M. until 10.30 P. M.

BASEBALL

Girls' Team vs Hampton Mills. West Boylston Field at 3.00 P. M.
Association Team vs Baush Machine Tool at Springfield.

MONDAY, AUGUST 9

BASEBALL.

Field open.

BILLIARD TOURNAMENT

Mr. Witherell and Mr. Knox, 7.30 P. M.
Mr. McTurk and Mr. Witherell, 8.30 P. M.

FOUR TABLE BRIDGE CLUB

Meets in Quiet Room at 7.00 P. M. Miss Evelyn Judd and Miss Pearl Graves, hostesses.

BOWLING

Association Team (5 men) vs the Red Men 'of Northampton, 8.00 P. M. 10 strings.

TUESDAY, AUGUST 10

GIRLS' HEALTH LEAGUE

Meets at 3.00 P. M. in Women's Social Rooms.

BASEBALL

Field reserved for use of girls.

BILLIARD TOURNAMENT

Mr. Burns and Mr. McLear, 7.30 P. M.
Mr. McLean and Mr. Martin, 8.30 P. M.

BAGATELLE TOURNAMENT

All girls who have entered or who wish to enter the bagatelle tournament will meet in the Social Room at 7.30 P. M.

BOWLING

Ladies' Night in bowling alley. Men accompanying ladies will be admitted to the alleys.

WEDNESDAY, AUGUST 11

WELL BABY CONFERENCE

Advice and demonstration on how to bathe and care for a well baby. Bring your baby and have it weighed. Women's Social Rooms.

NUTRITION CLASS, 3.30 P. M.

This class is for children between the ages of 6 and 14 years. Class meets in Women's Social Rooms.

BASEBALL

Field reserved for boys. (Junior teams may arrange with Recreation Manager for games on Wednesday nights).

MOVING PICTURES at 6.30 and 8.30 P. M.

PROGRAM

"Jiggs in Society"—"Bringing Up Father."
Pathe News.
HOBART BOSWORTH in "BEHIND THE DOOR."
(A Paramount-Artcraft Feature.)

The captain's day had come! The man who had stolen, outraged, slain his bride, was paying—there behind the door. And the maddened seamen watched two terrible, silent, moving shadows and saw the wreaking of a vengeance that almost froze their blood. This is a virile, thrilling, he-man tale of adventure, love, and the sea, presenting Hobart Bosworth in the greatest role of his career.

"YOU WOULDN'T BELIEVE IT."—Mack Sennett's New Comedy.

BOWLING

Match Game. Mr. Church and Mr. Gagnon versus Mr. Johnson and Mr. Sexton.

THURSDAY, AUGUST 12

BASEBALL

Association Team practices at 6.00 P. M.

BOWLING

Match Game at 7.30 P. M. Mr. Chas. Wood and Mr. Tommy Wood versus Mr. Johnson and Mr. Sexton.

BILLIARD TOURNAMENT

Mr. Witherell and Mr. Osgood, 7.30 P. M.

GUEST NIGHT for men in Women's Social Rooms. Girls may bring and entertain men from 7.00 until 10.30 P. M. Men not admitted unless accompanied by ladies.

FRIDAY, AUGUST 13

BASEBALL

Inspectors vs Section Hands. West Boylston Field, 6.00 P. M.

BILLIARD TOURNAMENT

Mr. Osgood and Mr. Lowe, 7.00 P. M.
Mr. Church and Mr. Witherell, 8.00 P. M.

BOWLING

Machine Shop vs Card Room. 6 men teams. 8.00 P. M.

SATURDAY, AUGUST 14

MOVING PICTURES at 6.30 and 8.30 P. M.

PROGRAM

"He Married His Wife." Christie Special.
"THE WHIRLWIND"
Episode 10—"The Human Bridge."
SHELDON LEWIS in "DR. JEKYLL AND MR. HYDE"
This is a brilliant version of Stevenson's great masterpiece, presenting Sheldon Lewis in the dual role of Dr. Jekyll and Mr. Hyde. Mr. Lewis will be remembered for his remarkable work in "The Iron Claw," one of the most popular serials ever released.

"Snub" Pollard in "Getting His Goat." Rolin Comedy. Music by Recreation String Orchestra. Admission 17c and 10c.

BASEBALL

Association Team vs Gilbert & Barker at Springfield. West Boylston Field open. Any team wishing to secure the field should see Mr. Lowe.

BOWLING NOTES

Mr. Church, Mr. Gagnon and Mr. Powers make bold to accept the presumptuous challenge of Messrs. Wood, Johnson and Sexton on the one condition that the chicken supper be fully and amply sufficient to wholly appease their appetites after they have won the match.

A match game for next week is being arranged with the Glendale Mills, each team consisting of five men and five women, and each bowler will roll three strings. All girls who wish to try for the team should see Mr. Wood in the bowling alley.

The ten string match on August 2nd between Mr. Gadreault and Mr. King ended in a victory for Mr. King by the narrow margin of seven pins.

The cool evenings are increasing the popularity of the bowling alleys. Requests for the reservation of alleys should be made one week in advance.

GENERAL NOTICE

An exciting series of nine games of pinochle was played July 30th wherein Mr. Emil Johnson and Mr. Fred Foster, persistent contenders for the championship title, were fortunate enough to win two games from Mr. Mathew J. Smith and Mr. Robert Kennell, according to the reports of the excited bystanders.

Mr. Church says that he might win a game now and then in the billiard tournament if he didn't get so many kisses. Never mind, Charlie, for it isn't every man who gets too many kisses!

One of the most exciting baseball games of the season was played at Holyoke, August 1st, when the Association Team beat the Germania Mills by a score of 3 to 2. Captain Brown distinguished himself by holding the opposing team to two hits, striking out 14, and rapping out 3 hits himself.

Employees wishing to use the Recreation Building before 6 o'clock in the afternoon must secure a written statement signed by their overseer, showing that they are excused from work during the day or are working nights.

Miss Edna Russell accepted the challenge of Miss Beatrice Lyman for a bagatelle match and won a three game match. Miss Russell now states that she is ready to accept the challenge of any girl in the mill.

Mr. Emil Johnson, erstwhile claimant for pinochle honors, while spending a four day vacation in Rhode Island, was kindly remembered by his local friends who sent him a box of apples and a pinochle deck with a complete edition of the rules of the game. Mr. Johnson says he did not mind paying the C. O. D. charges but that the apples were a little green and the deck was short one card.

Complete results of the billiard tournament will be given

This was the schedule for the West Boylston Manufacturing Company recreation hall for August 8, 1920. Billiards, bowling, and movies seem popular. Bridge and bagatelle, an offshoot of pool, were also played. The company maintained the hall for the benefit of its employees. In addition to a baseball field, the company also owned an outdoor pool at the Parsons Street school.

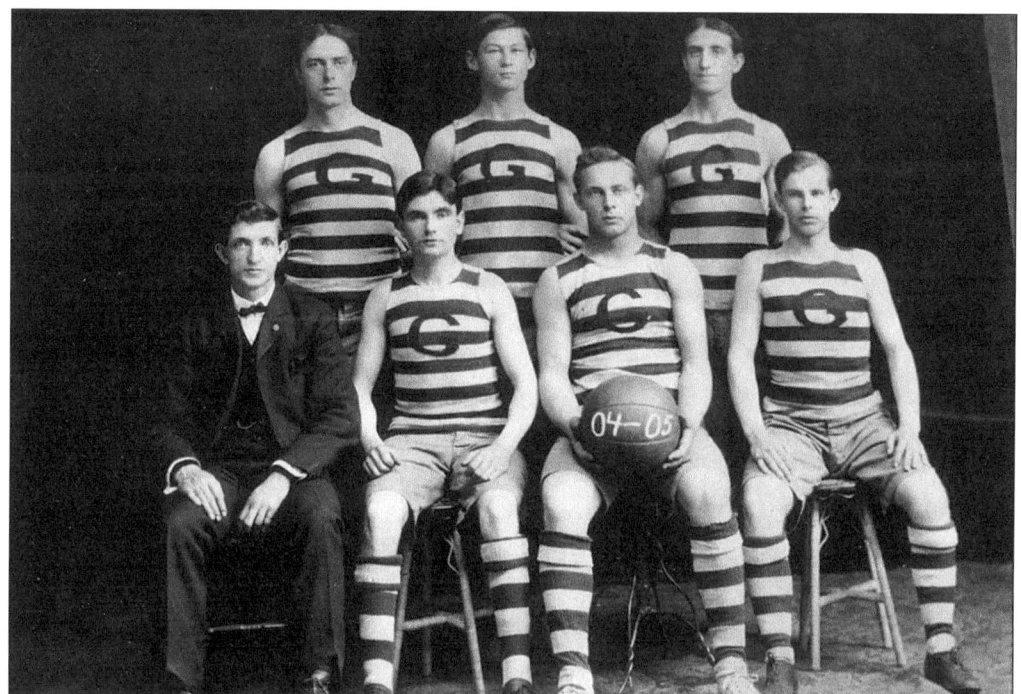

Industrial interests sponsored most recreational organizations, including the 1904–1905 Glendale basketball team seen here. Basketball had long been a popular recreational pastime. The team played in an industrial league, playing games at the Williston and Turn Verin Gyms.

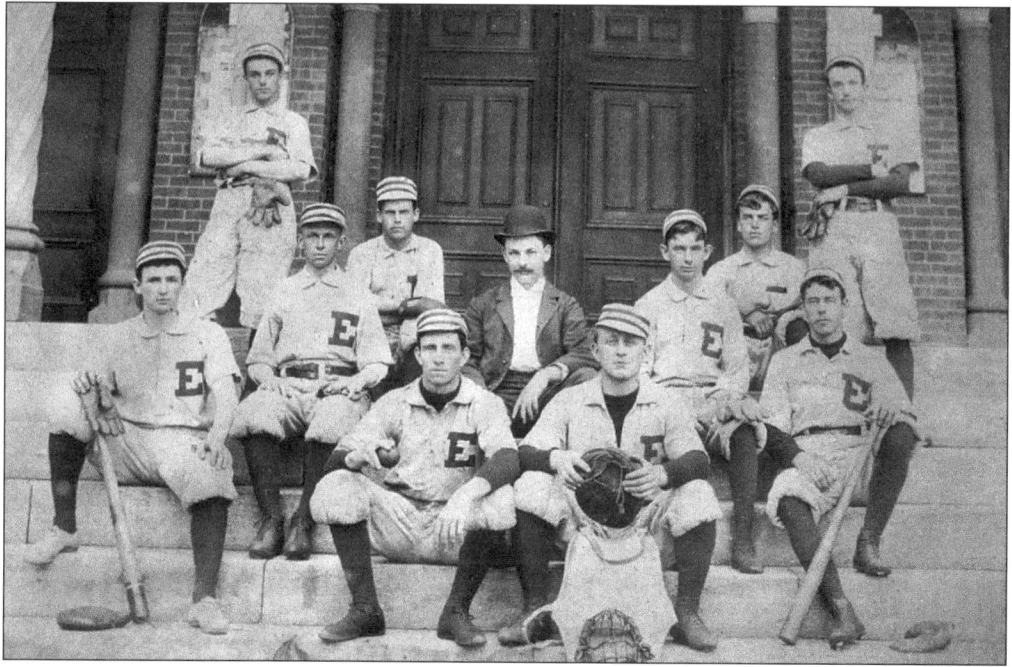

The Easthampton town baseball team poses on the front steps of the town hall. The team, which competed against other towns, would play its home games at Williston Academy.

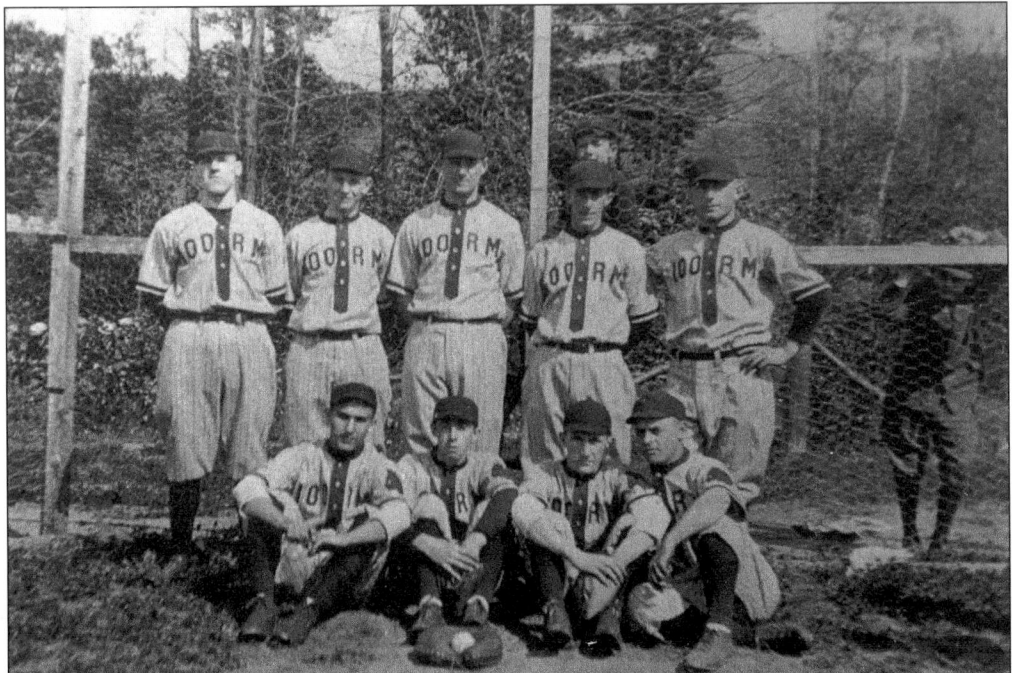

The Improved Order of Redmen baseball team poses near the backstop of the West Boylston athletic field. The field, located off Lovefield Street was the site of many baseball, football, and soccer games. The field, later owned by the Hampton Company as the "Hampton Bowl," fell into disuse after the town opened Daley Field.

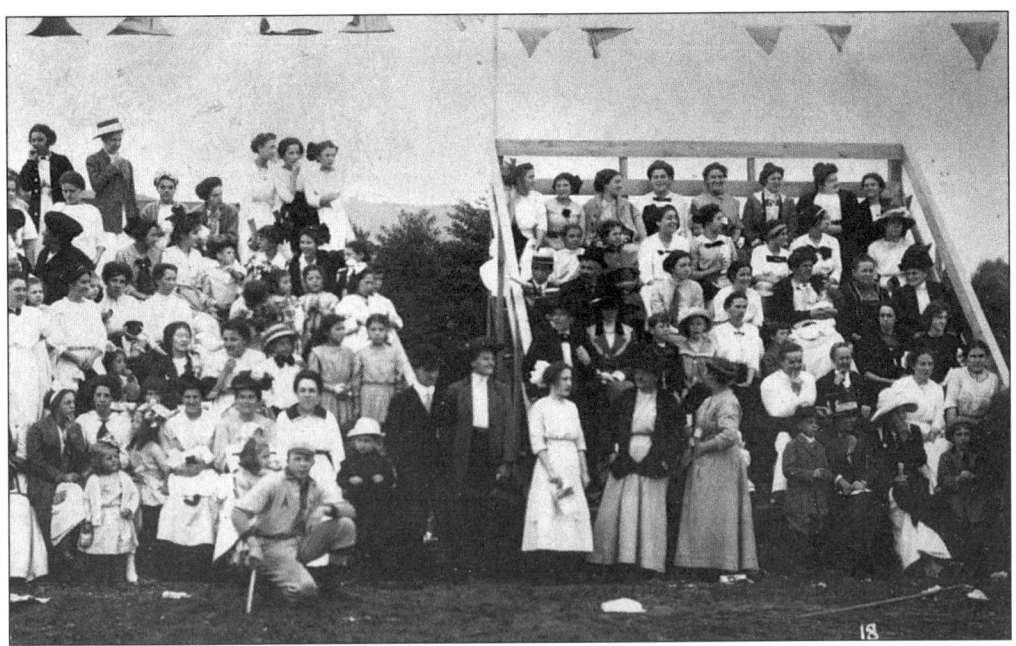

The Hampton Company offered its employees this baseball field on present-day O'Neill Street. Through the Hampton Athletic Association, the company offered baseball, cricket, soccer, and football.

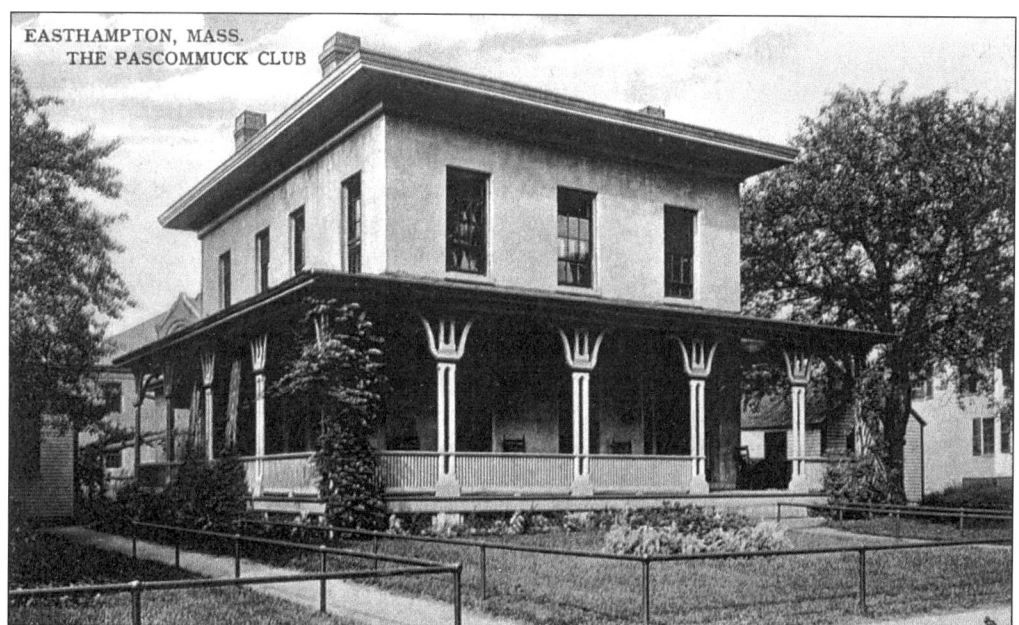

The Pascommuck Club was originally organized as a bicycle club in 1892. By 1898, it became a social club. In 1903, the club purchased the former Union Street home of Judge Alonso Fargo and converted it to clubhouse. It is still in use as a clubhouse.

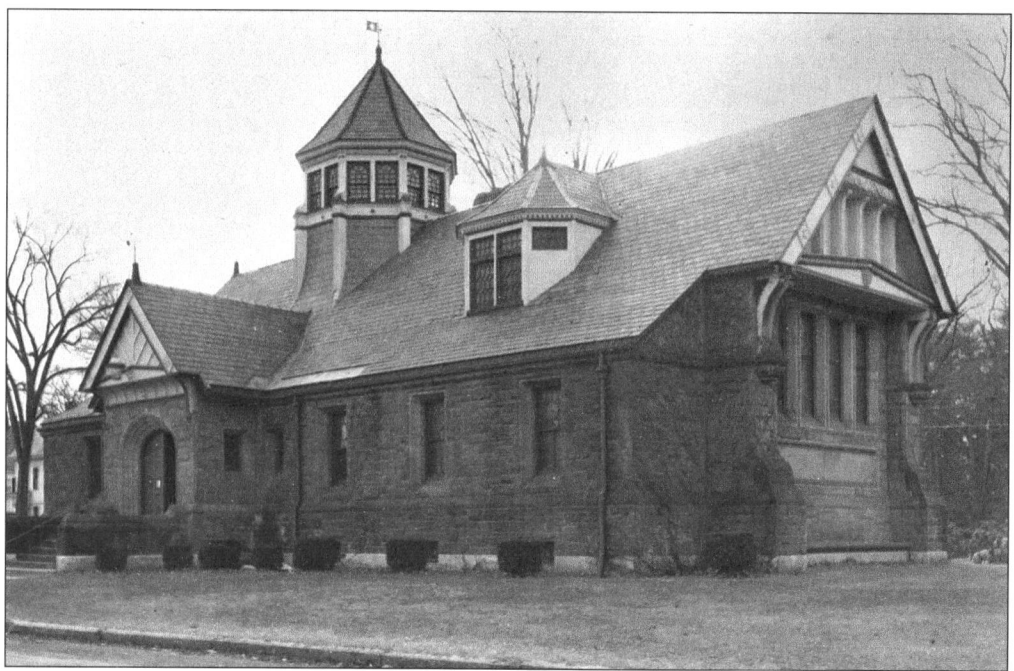

There has been a library as long as there has been a town. The Public Library Association was formed in 1869. While the library was housed in the town hall, Emily Williston purchased a small park owned by Lt. Gov. Horatio Knight and had this stone structure built. Payson Williston helped the library grow by contributing many books from his own collection. The library opened in 1881 and is still used as the library.

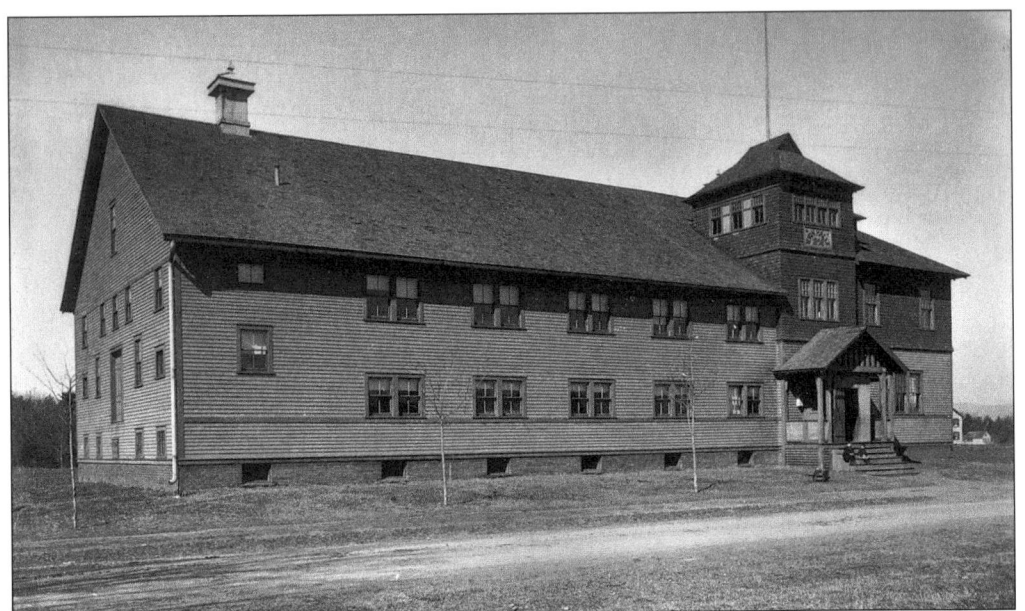

The Turn Verin Club opened to serve the German-born population of Easthampton. This gym was constructed in 1898, and was a gymnastic and shooting club. The gym was later used by a local entrepreneur as a hat factory. The gym was destroyed by arson in 1924.

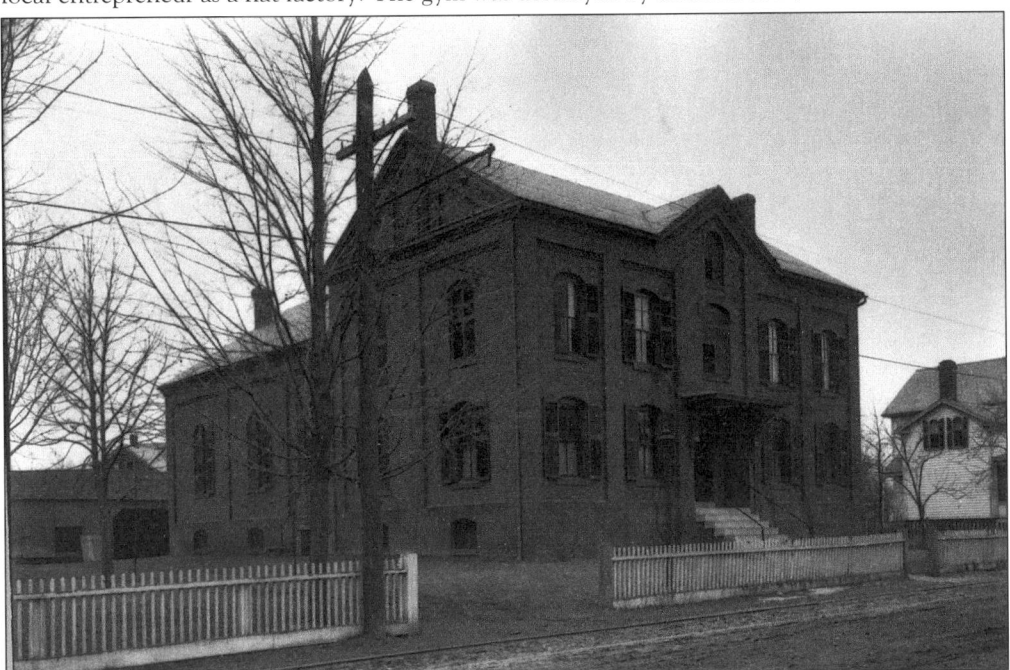

In 1881, the German Club was formed as a social club for German-born immigrants. The building was sold to the Improved Order of Redmen in 1924. The Nonotuck Tribe No. 91 was organized October 10, 1900 with 40 charter members. By 1952, the Improved Order of Redmen was losing members. The group sold this building to former actress Alice Kagan, who with her family operated the nightclub called the Manhattan Club. It is now the Easthampton Community Center.

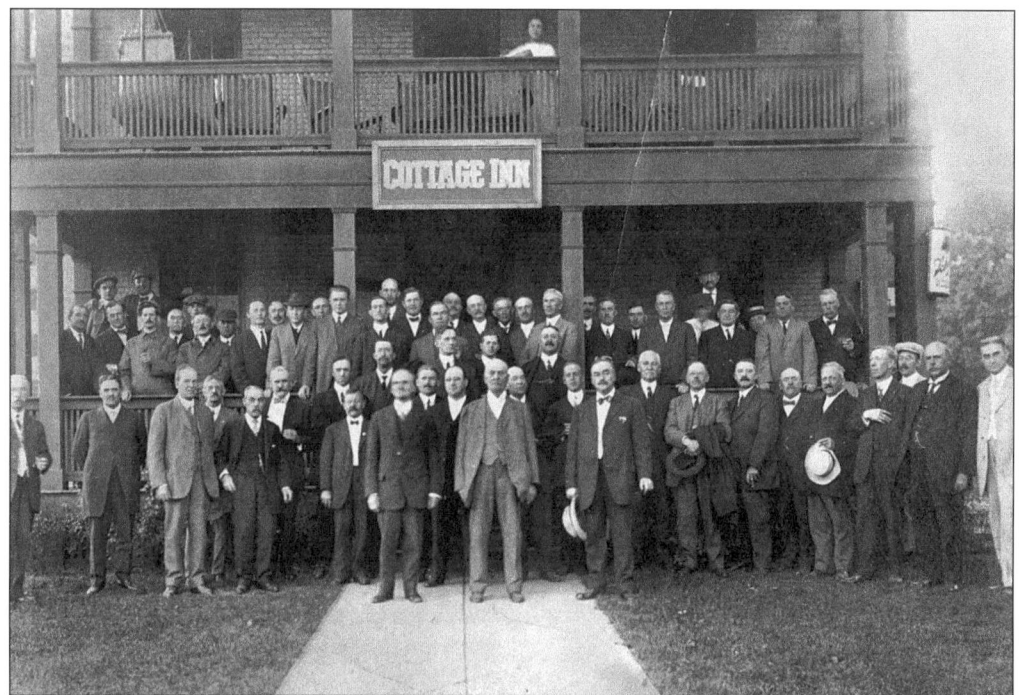

The Easthampton Businessmen Association stands on the front steps of the Cottage Inn. The group, a precursor of the chamber of commerce, met to organize strategies of attracting businesses to Easthampton. The Cottage Inn, a converted boardinghouse, was a small hotel. It was taken down in 1920 and is now the site of a service station.

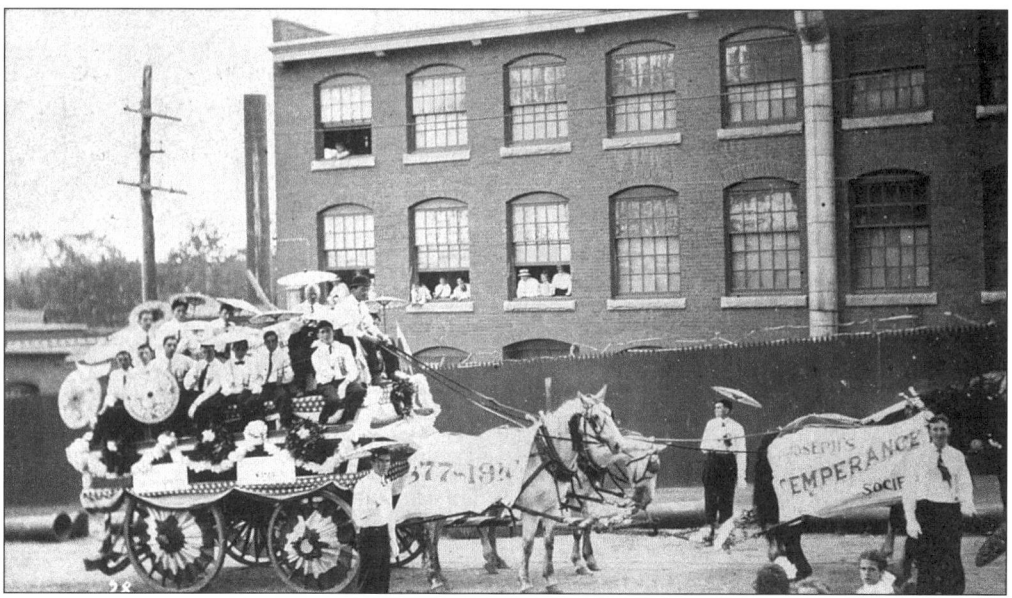

Easthampton boasted several temperance clubs, including the Catholic Benevolent League, the Pioneer Lodge, the Women's Christian Temperance Union, and the St. Joseph's Catholic Total Abstinence and Beneficial Society. Most of these organizations ceased to exist following Prohibition, except for the Catholic Benevolent League, which was active until 1946.

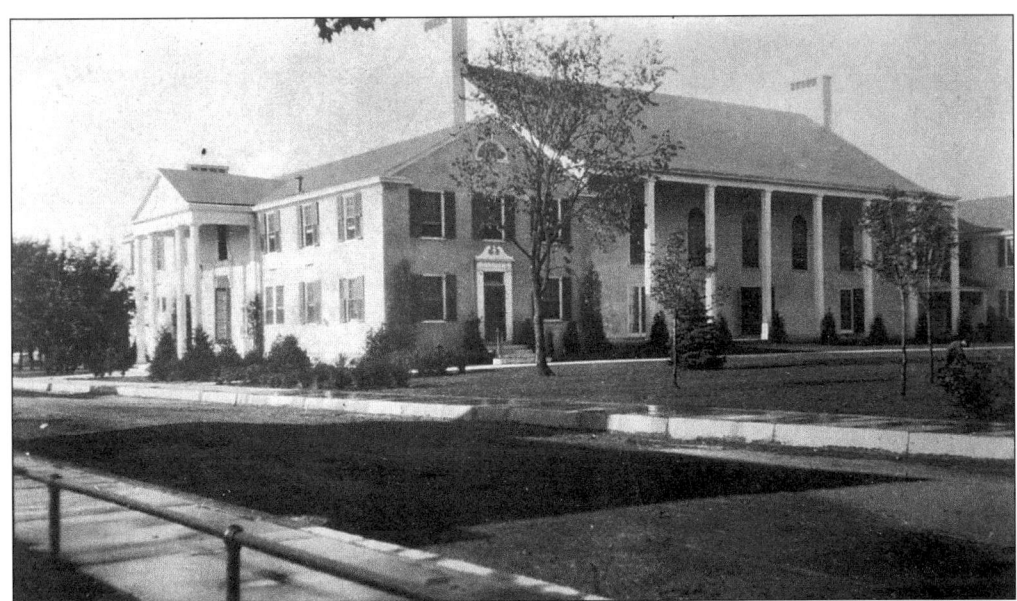

In 1919, recreation took a step forward when the West Boylston Manufacturing Company recreation hall opened on Pleasant Green. The hall offered social rooms, a luncheonette, a bowling alley, and a hall for basketball games or silent movies.

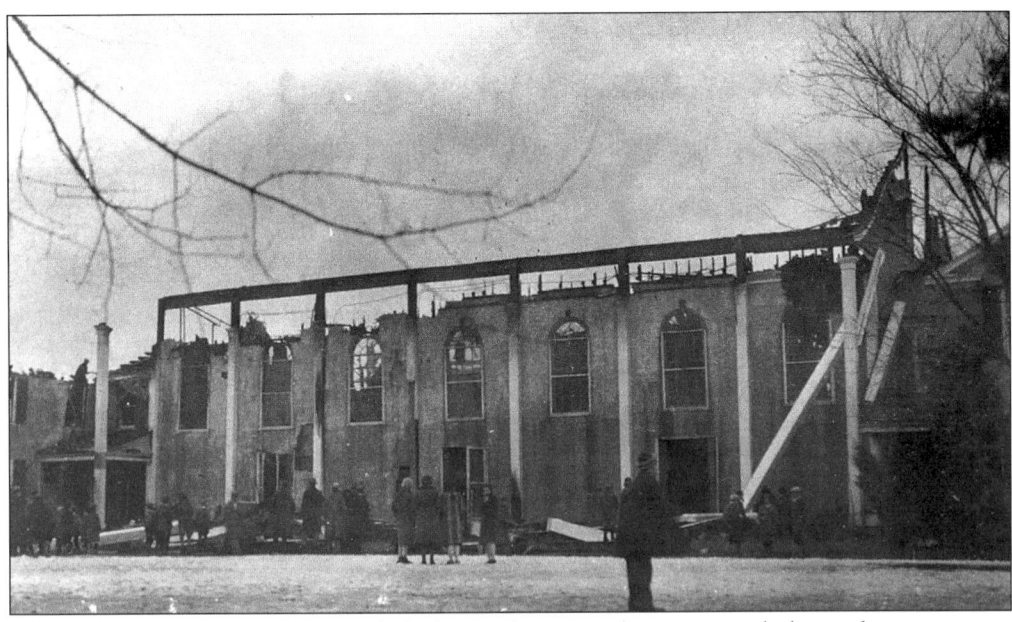

In 1931, the recreation hall—which had rented to several tenants, including a furniture store, and the local Rotary club—was destroyed by fire. The site was cleared and stood empty for two years until the town purchased the site. A Works Progress Administration (WPA) project converted the empty lot to Pleasant Green, a playground.

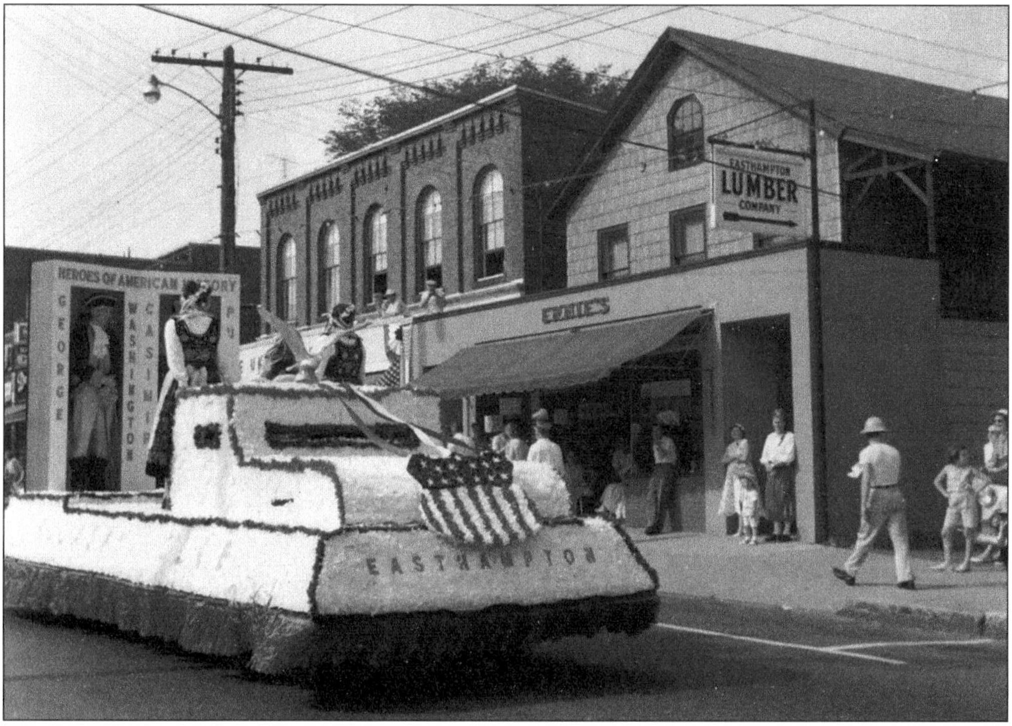

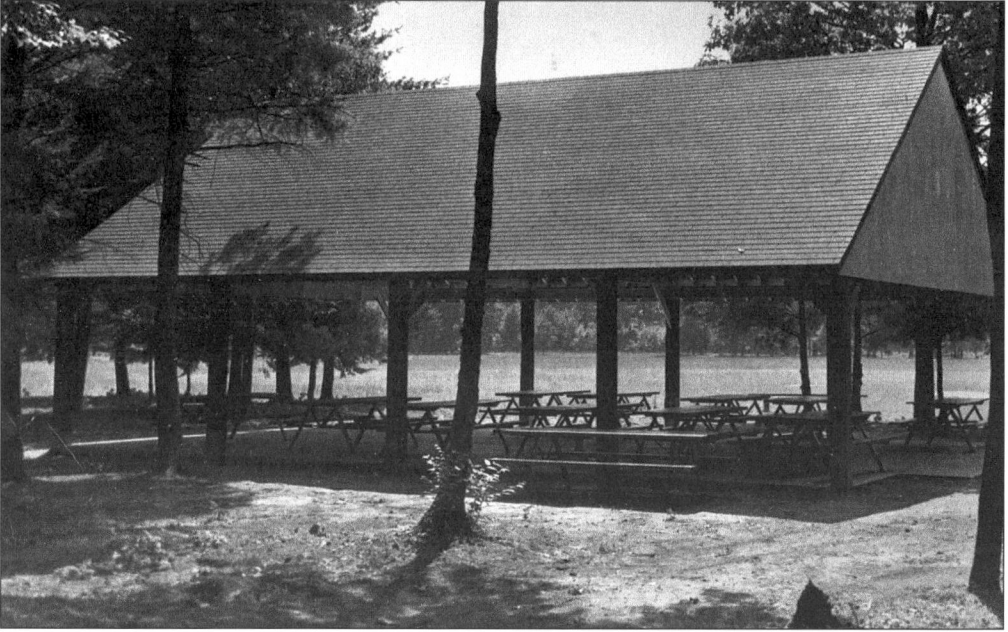

The Pulaski Club float, seen here, participated in the 175th anniversary parade in 1960. The club was formed in 1912 to promote the social and educational interests of people of Polish birth and descent. The club is still an active social organization.

On March 12, 1923, the town purchased the remaining acreage that makes up Nonotuck Park. The park is maintained by the town, and represents a break from industry-sponsored activities, which were the only available options in the late 19th and early 20th centuries.

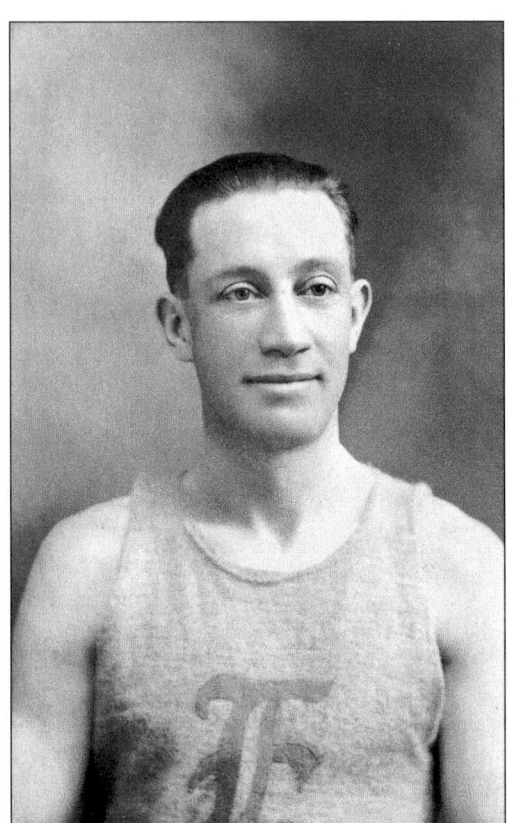

Marty Friedman played with the Easthampton entry of the Interstate League in 1920 and 1921. Friedman, a forward, came from New York and was considered one of the best players of the era. He later played and coached in Cleveland and was inducted into the Basketball Hall of Fame.

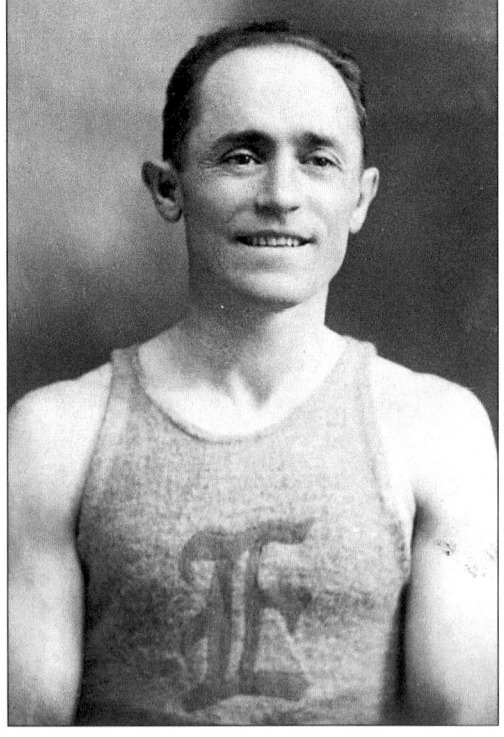

Barney Sedran (along with Friedman) made up the other half of the "Heavenly Twins." A guard, Sedran was regarded by Nat Holman (a longtime coach at City College of New York) as one of the greatest guards who ever played the game. He has been inducted in the Basketball Hall of Fame.

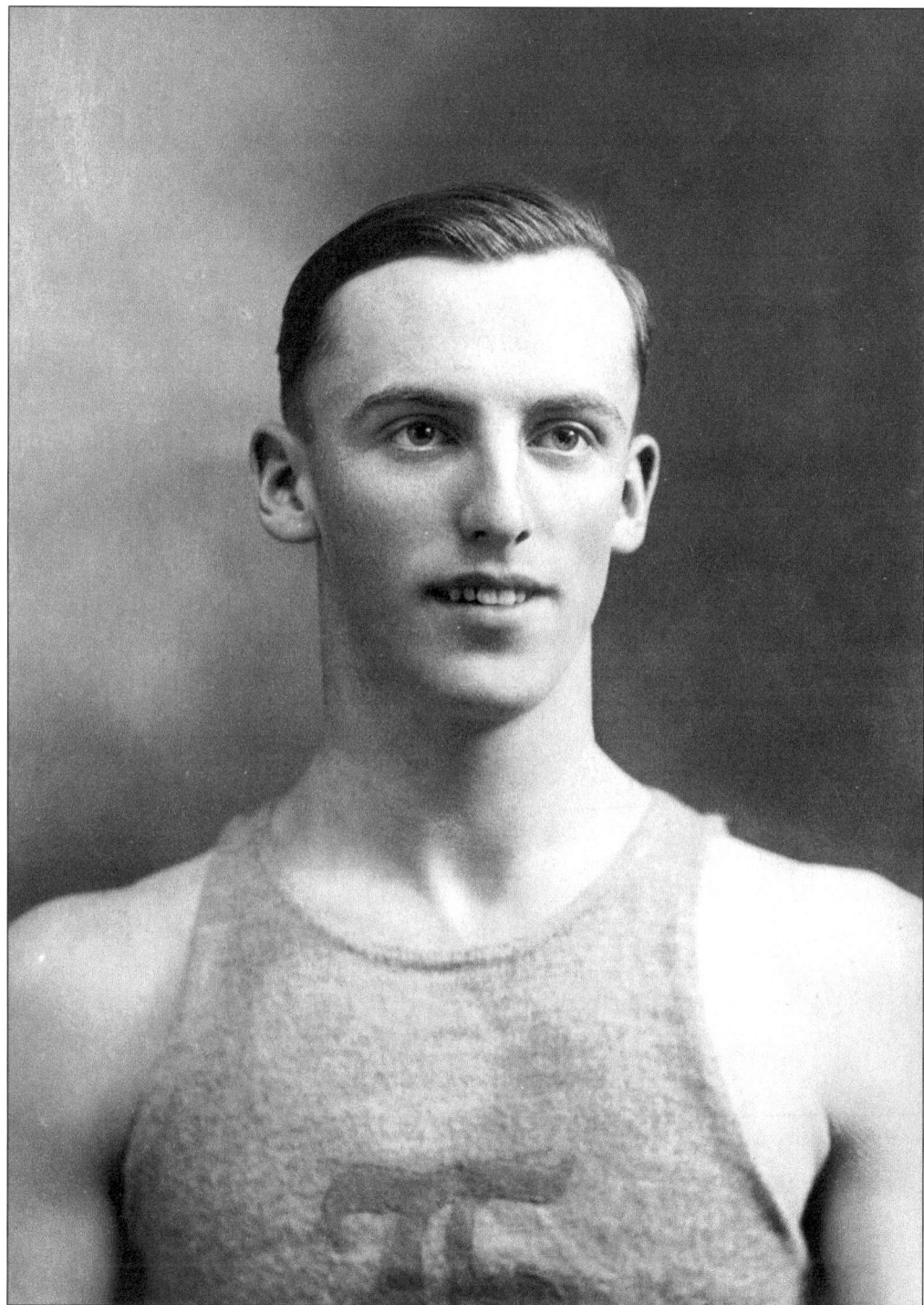

Although John "Honey" Russell was only 18 years old when he began to play for the Easthampton team, he had been a pro since his mid-teens. A defensive specialist throughout his career, Russell later served as coach for Seton Hall College. He was the first coach for the Boston Celtics and was inducted in the Basketball Hall of Fame.

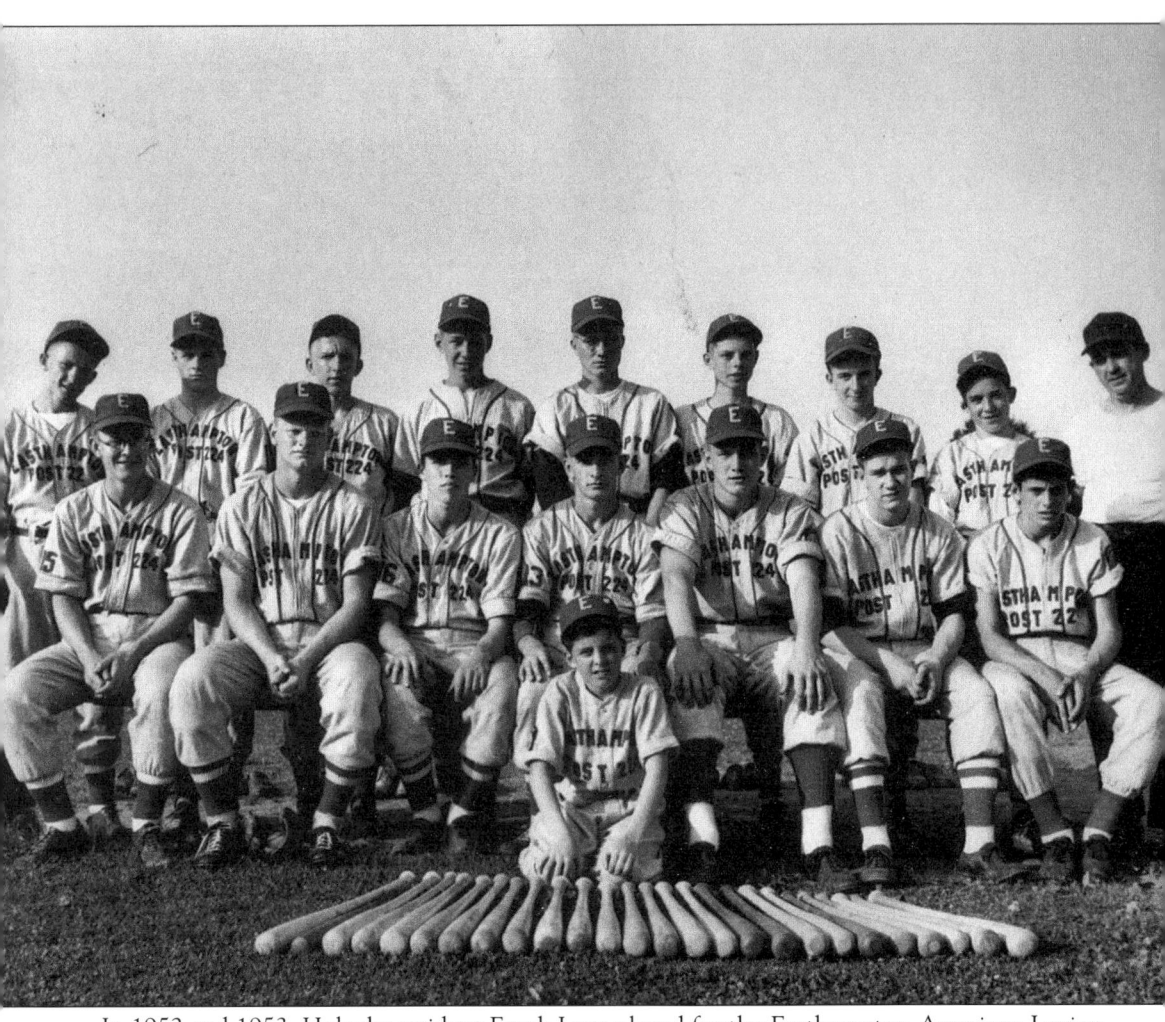

In 1952 and 1953, Holyoke resident Frank Lega played for the Easthampton American Legion team at Daley Field. Lega (seated third from right) was a sought-after prospect. He signed with the New York Yankees for a big bonus and was on the roster for the 1954 and 1955 seasons.

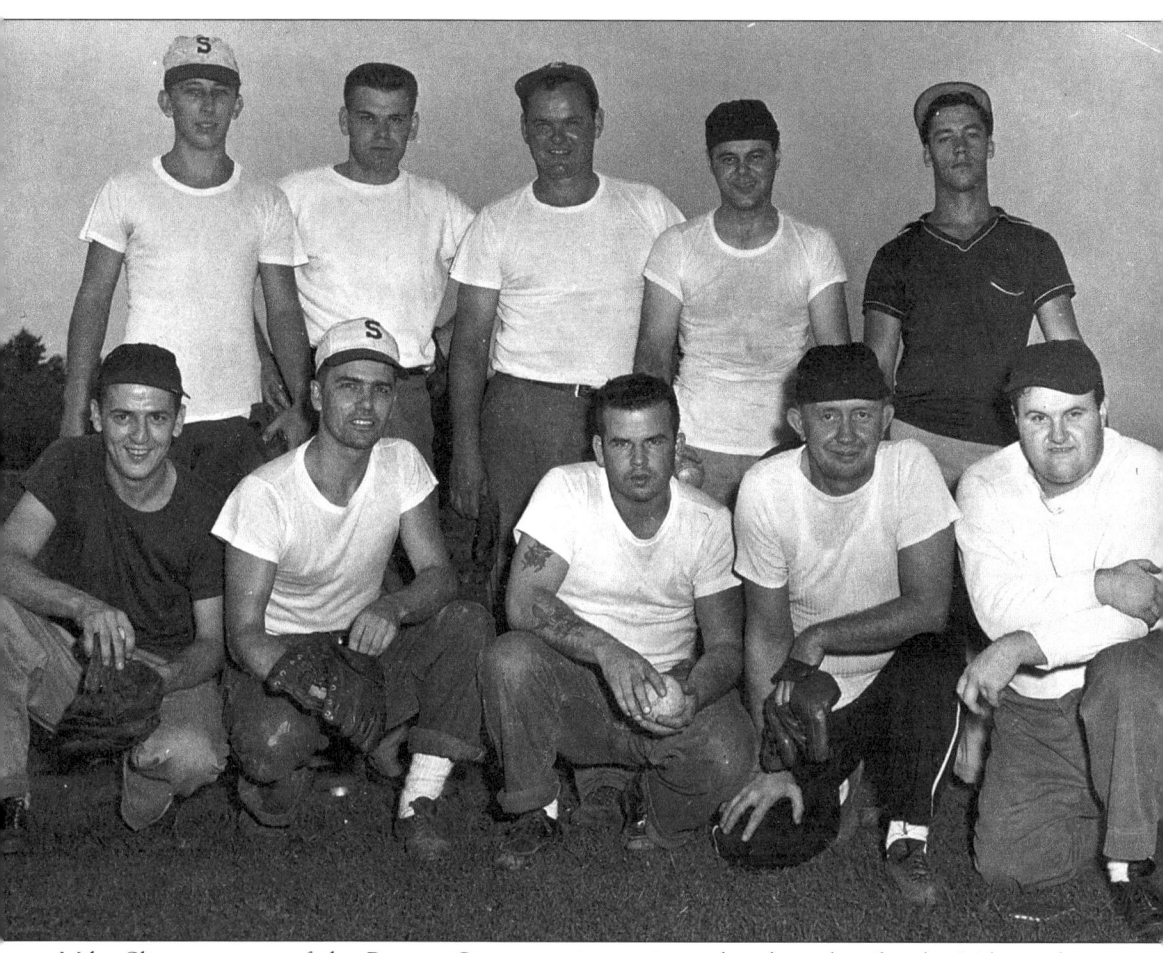

Mike Sliz, co-owner of the Parsons Street service station, played catcher for the Mike and Mollie softball team, seen above in 1952. He was a former semi-professional baseball player. In the late 1940s and 1950s, many teams played at Daley Field. The town purchased the field on March 12, 1923, comprising 13 acres.

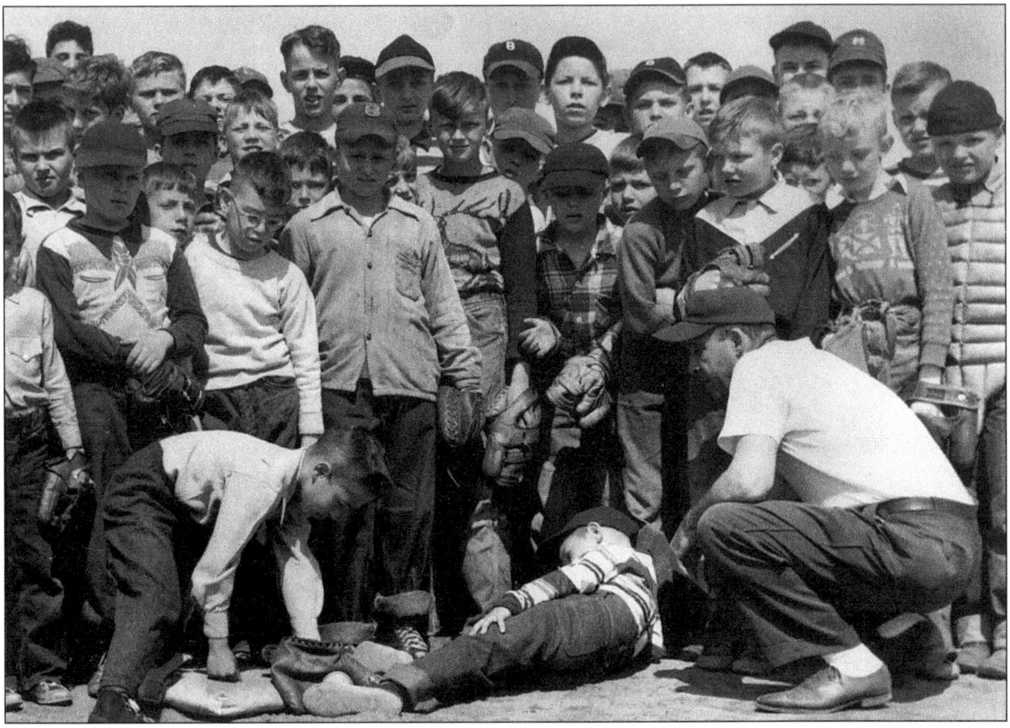

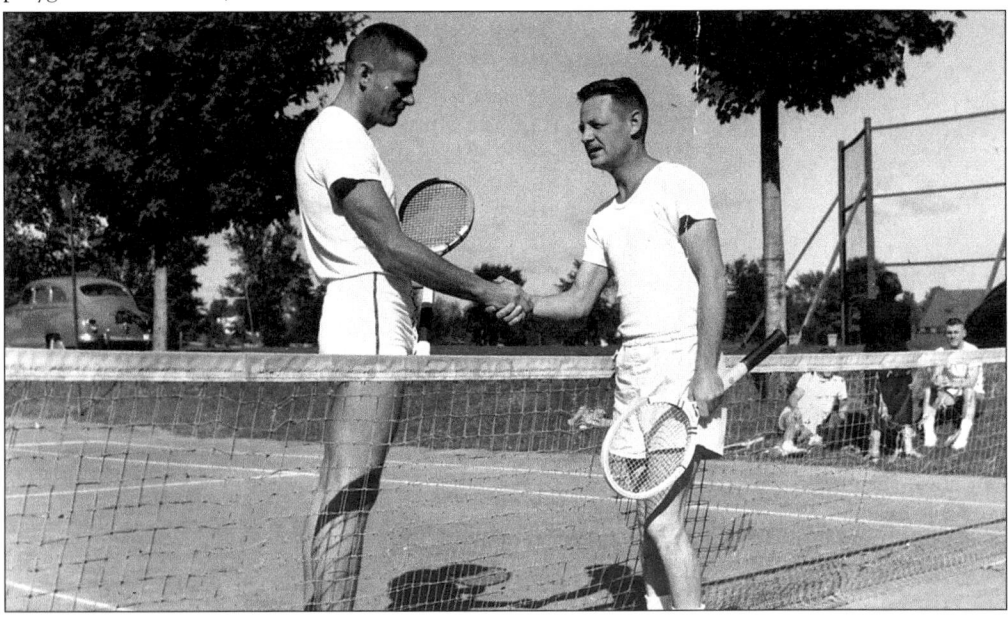

Howard Stone teaches base-running techniques. Stone was appointed in 1935 by the Works Progress Administration to run recreation programs at Pleasant Green. Three years later, he was promoted to recreation director for the WPA. From 1939 to 1945, he served as director of playgrounds. In 1945, he became director of recreation for the town. He died in 1954.

Later recreation improvements include the tennis courts at Daley Field. Here, Roland Reed, a longtime high school coach and teacher, just beat Hank Dombrowski (left) in a late 1950s tournament.

Five

HOUSES OF WORSHIP

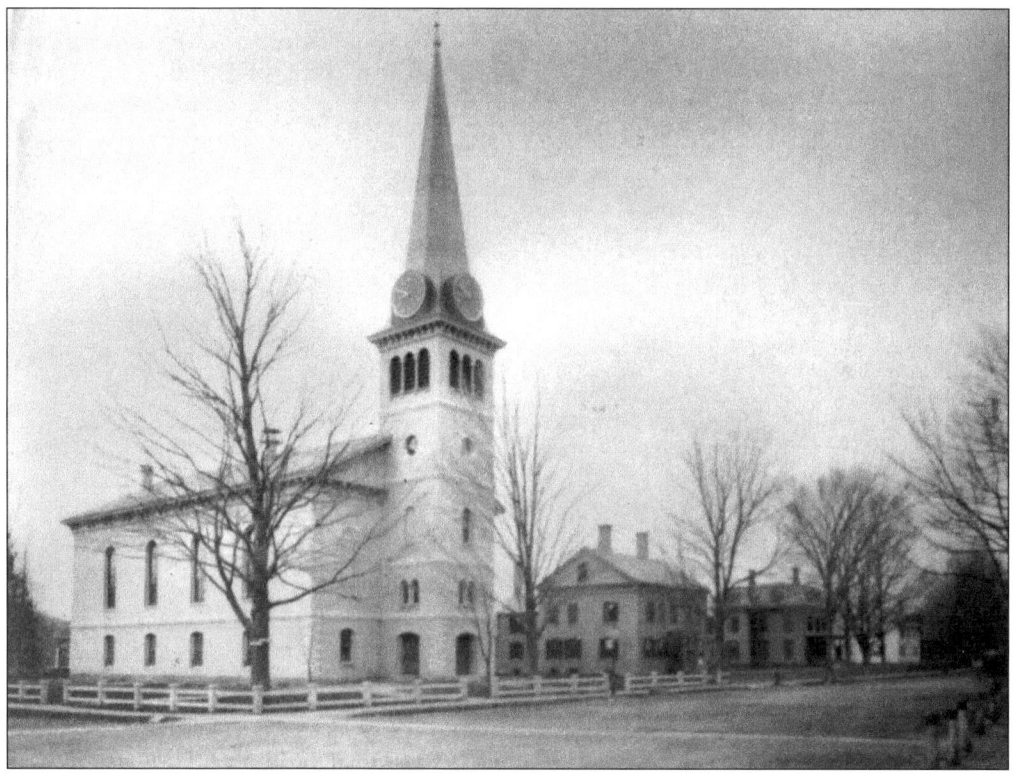

When the population increased as a result of the presence of the Williston-Knight Button Company and Williston Seminary, the need arose for a second Congregational church. In 1852, the Payson church was built. The Payson and First Churches eventually merged in 1918, taking the name the Easthampton Congregational Church, which is still active today. Note the Payson Church rectory, the brick house located next to the church. The clock on the steeple is owned by the town.

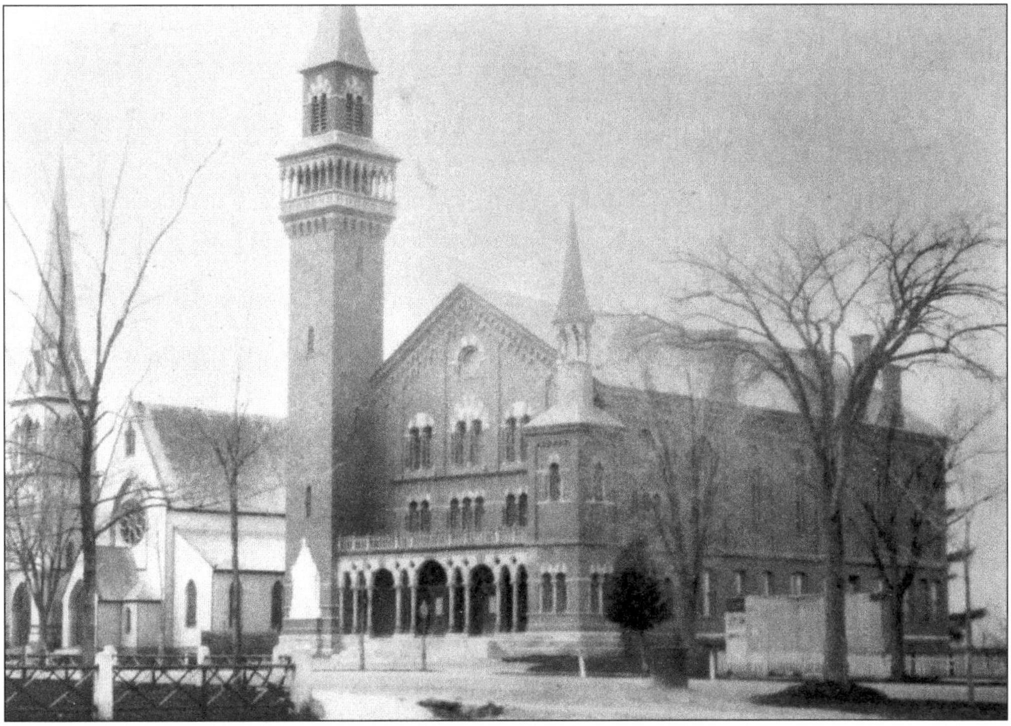

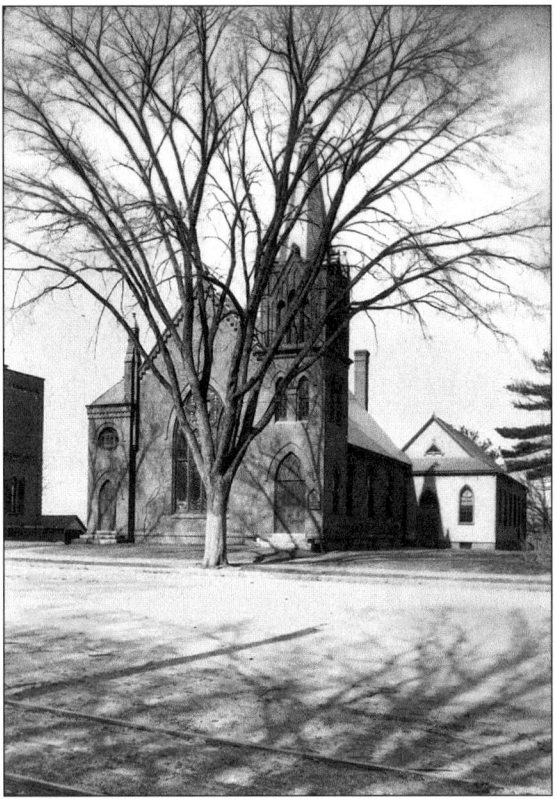

The town gave the former cemetery (located between the town hall and Shop Row) to the Providence Methodist Episcopal Church. The church, erected in 1860, represents the second religious denomination to establish a church in town. On January 10, 1892, it was destroyed by fire despite the efforts of some Williston Seminary students who ran across the street from their campus to help battle the fire and save valuables from the church.

The Methodist church was rebuilt following the 1892 fire. The church was merged with the Northampton Methodist Church to form the Christ United Methodist Church, located in Northampton. This building is now used as a day care center.

In 1871, the St. Philip's Episcopal Church began a mission, offering services in the lower town hall. This church, built in 1886, was located on the corner of Union Street and Chapman Street. It was replaced by the Rust Wilson department store.

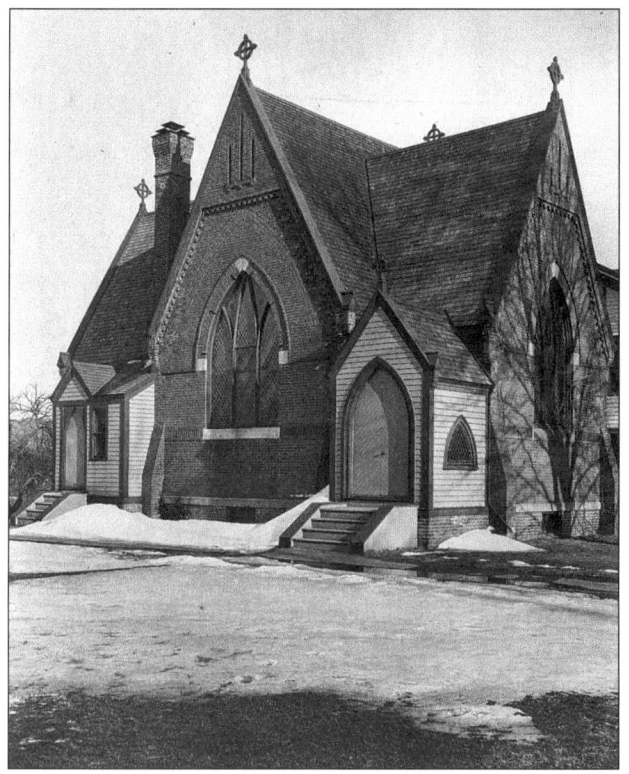

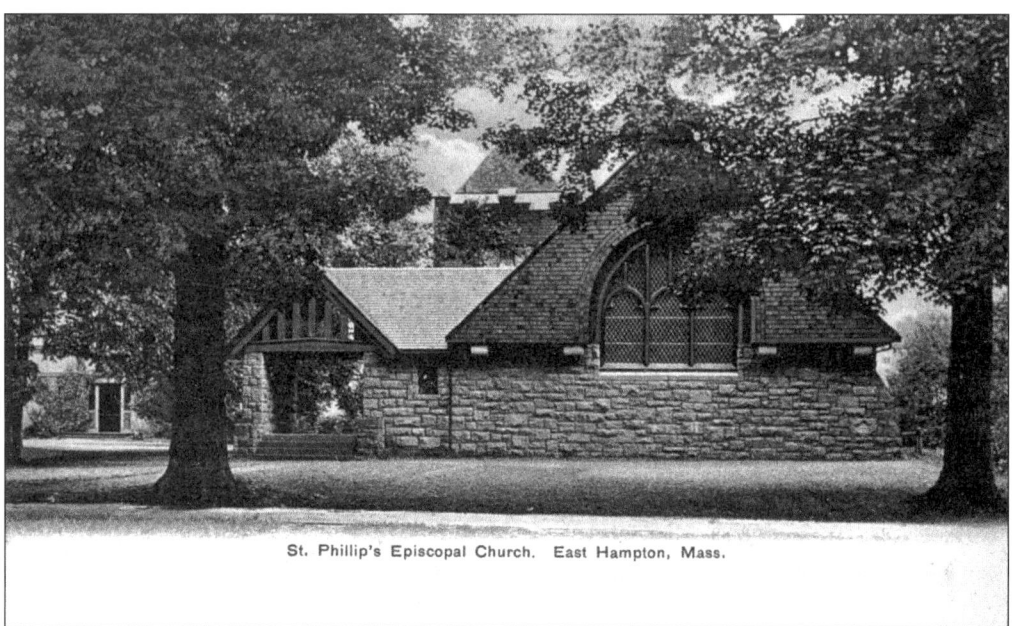

St. Phillip's Episcopal Church. East Hampton, Mass.

The St. Philip's Episcopal Church purchased the land around the mansion of industrialist E. Thomas Sawyer. The church was built on the lawn of Sawyer's former estate, which the church purchased. The former house was converted to a rectory, while barns were converted for use as a parish hall.

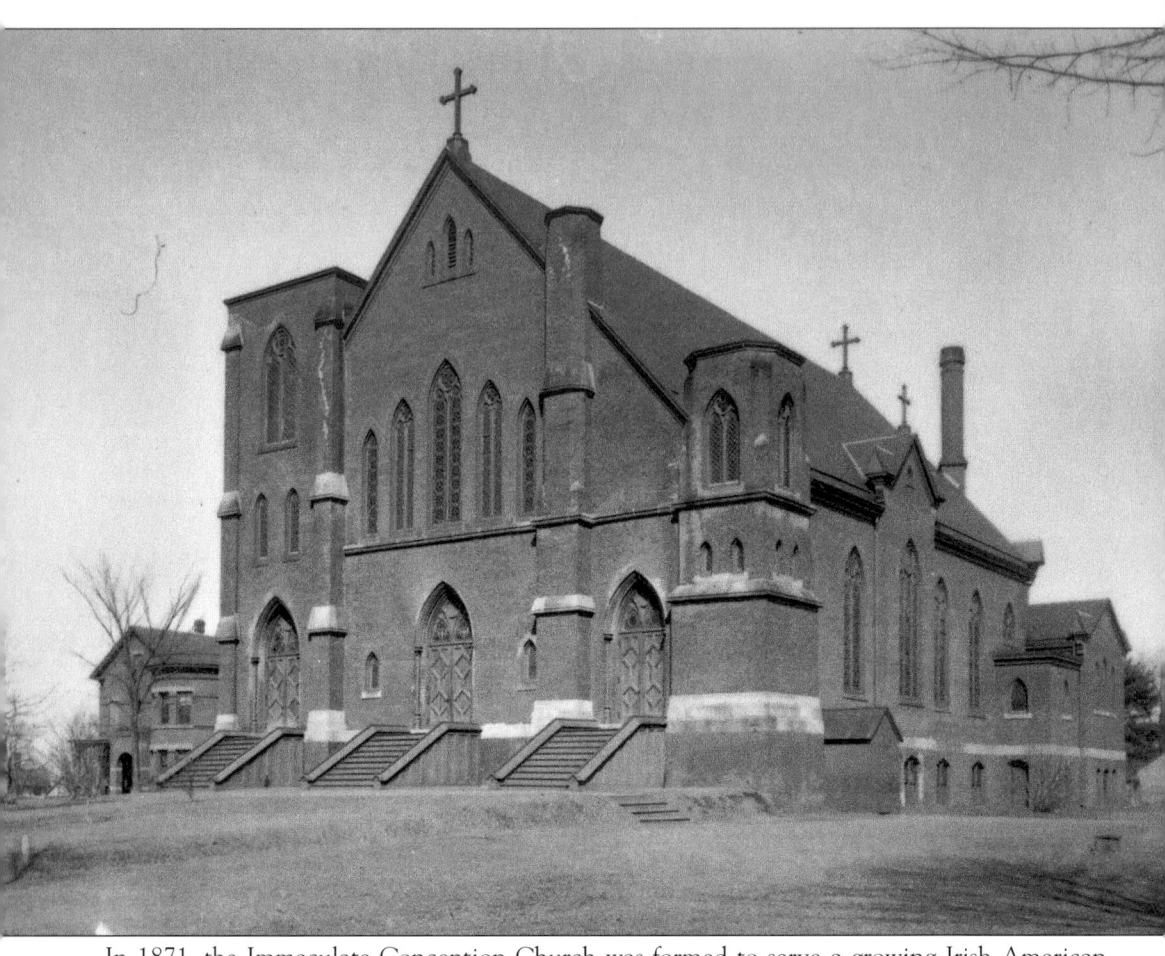

In 1871, the Immaculate Conception Church was formed to serve a growing Irish-American community. It was the first Roman Catholic Church in Easthampton. Despite initial local opposition, church buildings were constructed in 1871 and 1874. Both were destroyed by fire, and this third church was built on Adams Street. After this photograph was taken, the steeples in the front of the church were completed.

The first offshoot of the Immaculate Conception Parish was the Notre Dame Church, as French-speaking parishioners came to the area seeking employment. At first, Mass was held in the lower town hall. A former Union Street farm was purchased and its barn was converted into a house of worship. The farmhouse became a rectory. Both the farmhouse and barn were used as a parochial school until they were taken down in 1949, as a new Notre Dame school opened.

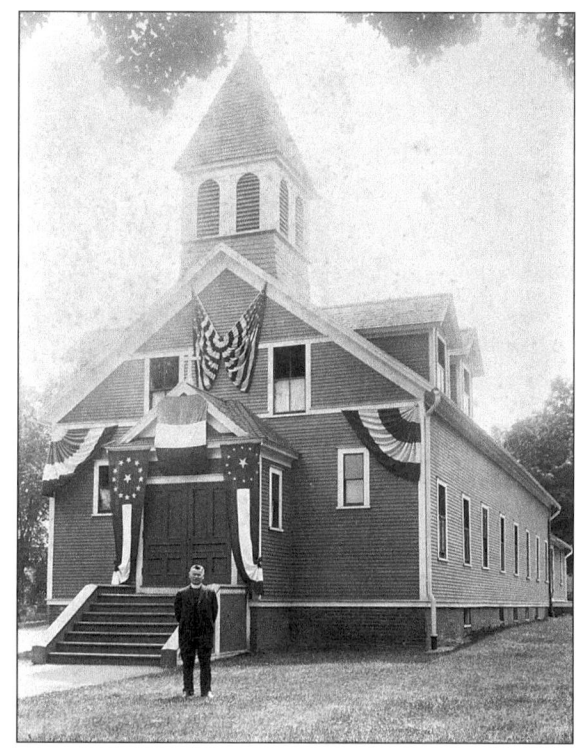

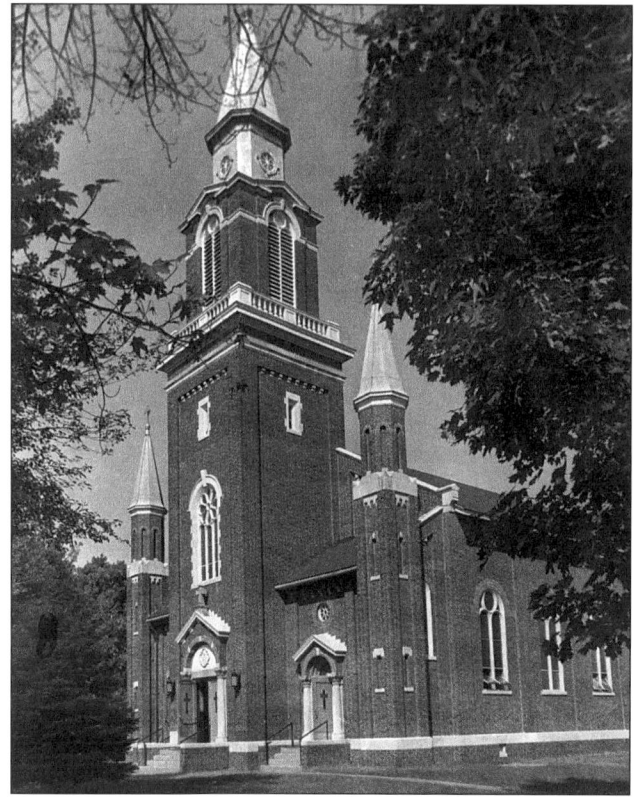

In 1922, the Notre Dame Church purchased a Pleasant Street farm and constructed this new church on the site of the former farm. Still active, the parish—with the Immaculate Conception Church—provides a parochial school.

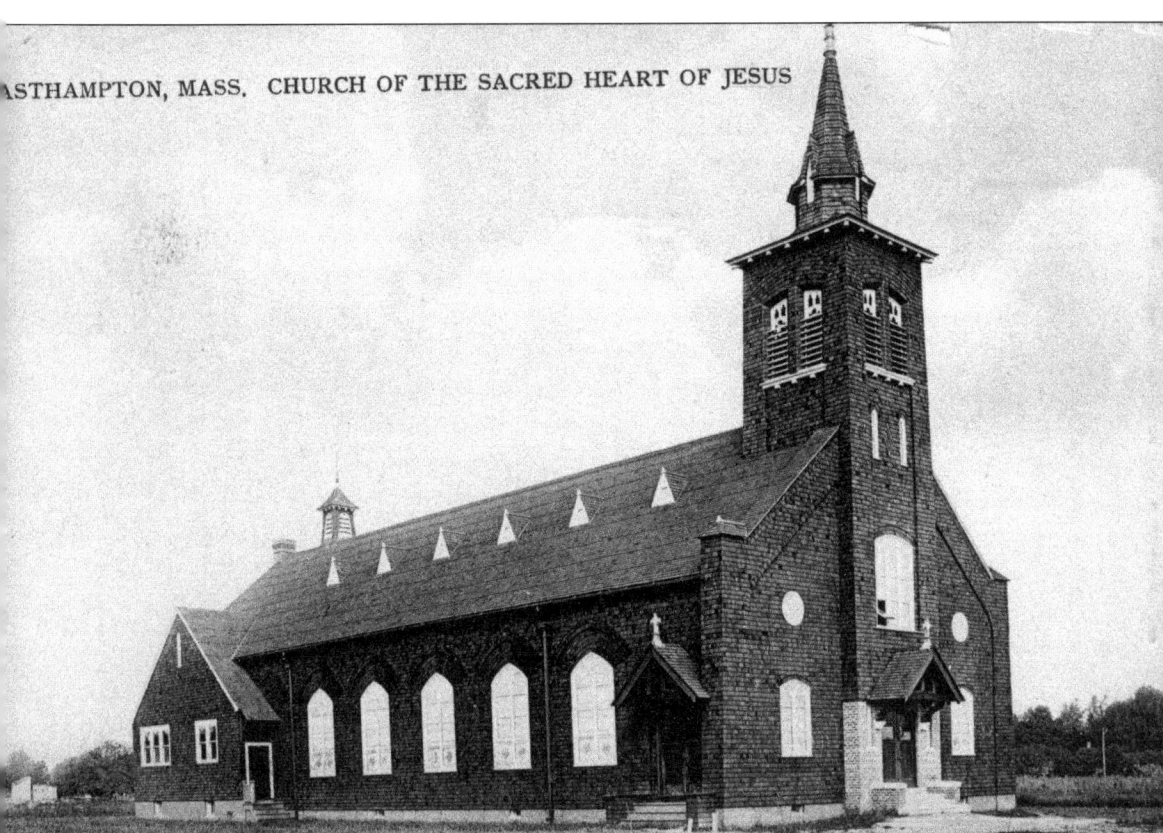

Many Polish immigrants came to town during the early 20th century. By 1909, with some three thousand Polish-speaking Catholics already residing in town, this church was constructed on the corner of Franklin and Knipfer Avenue to serve their spiritual needs.

The first German Lutheran services were held in Knipfer's Hall in 1890. By 1893, the congregation was formally organized as the German Evangelical Lutheran Church with 17 voting members. This building was located on the corner of Maple and Briggs Street. Later, the congregation adopted the name Trinity Lutheran Church.

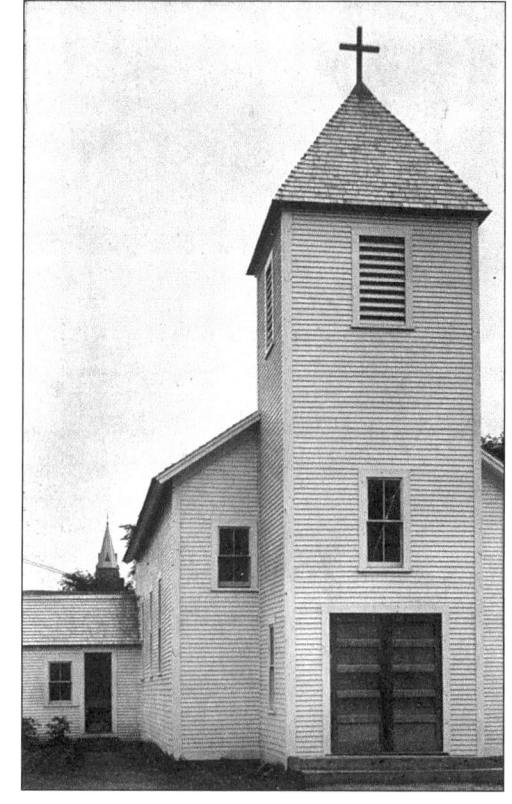

This building, known as Union Chapel, was originally constructed by the Payson Church as a chapel for their German-speaking members. It was used by the Episcopal Church from 1882 to 1886. In 1893, the Lutheran Church purchased it and used it for services until 1949. The church also had a rectory and a church hall next door. Only the rectory stands today.

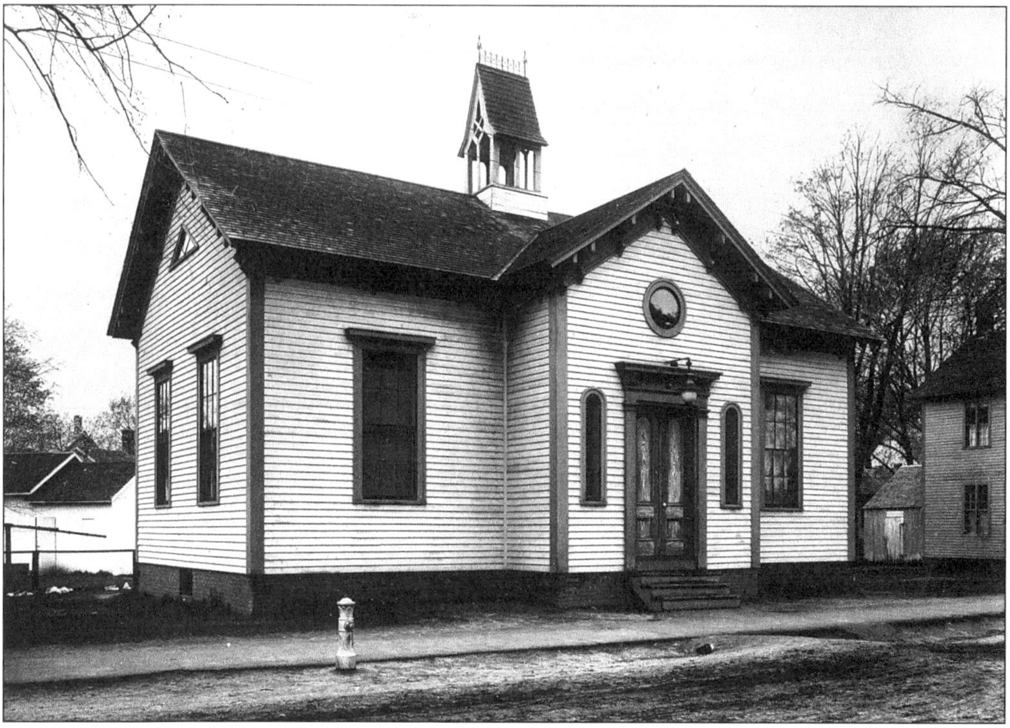

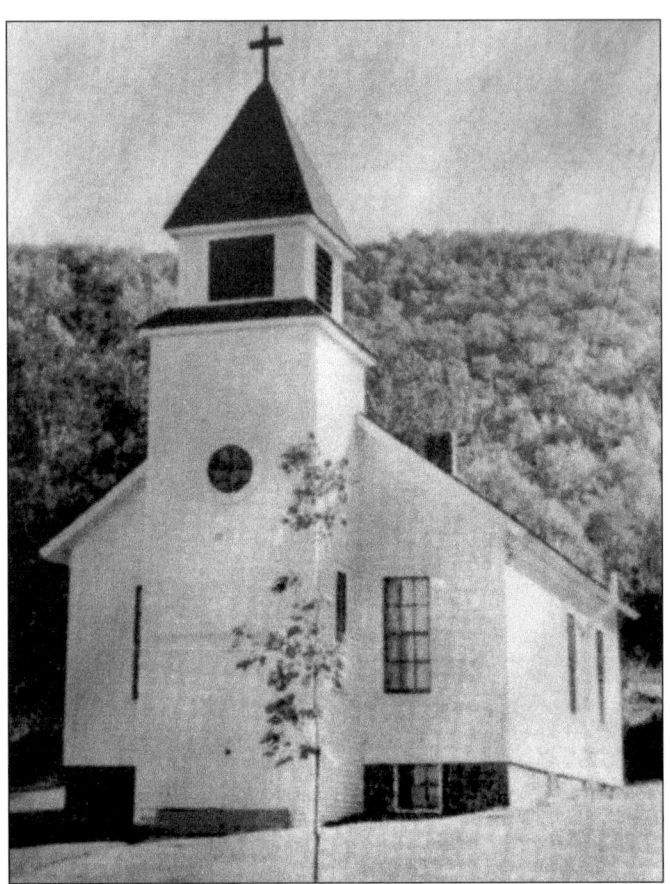

This former school, located in the Mount Tom section of Easthampton, was dedicated in 1916 for Polish-speaking Lutherans. It remained separate from the main Lutheran Church due to language differences. This church, reduced to a handful of members, was closed in 1964.

In 1932, the Trinity Lutheran Church bought an empty lot on the corner of Clark Street and Stonepath Lane. The church was unable to fund a construction project until 1948, when they were able to build this stone edifice. The first services were held September 11, 1949.

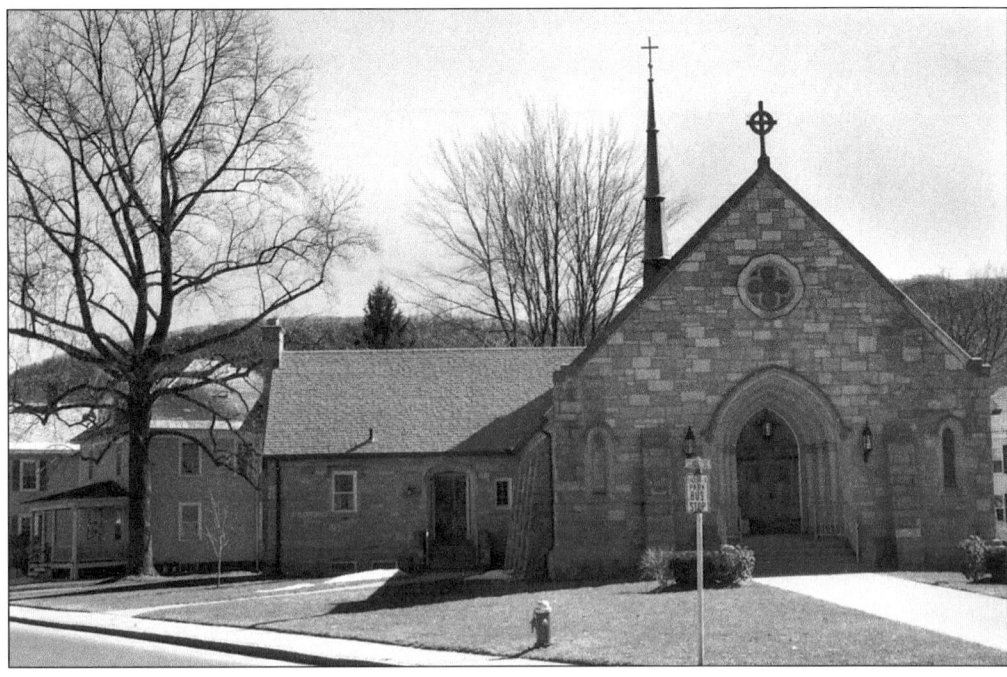

Six

EDUCATION

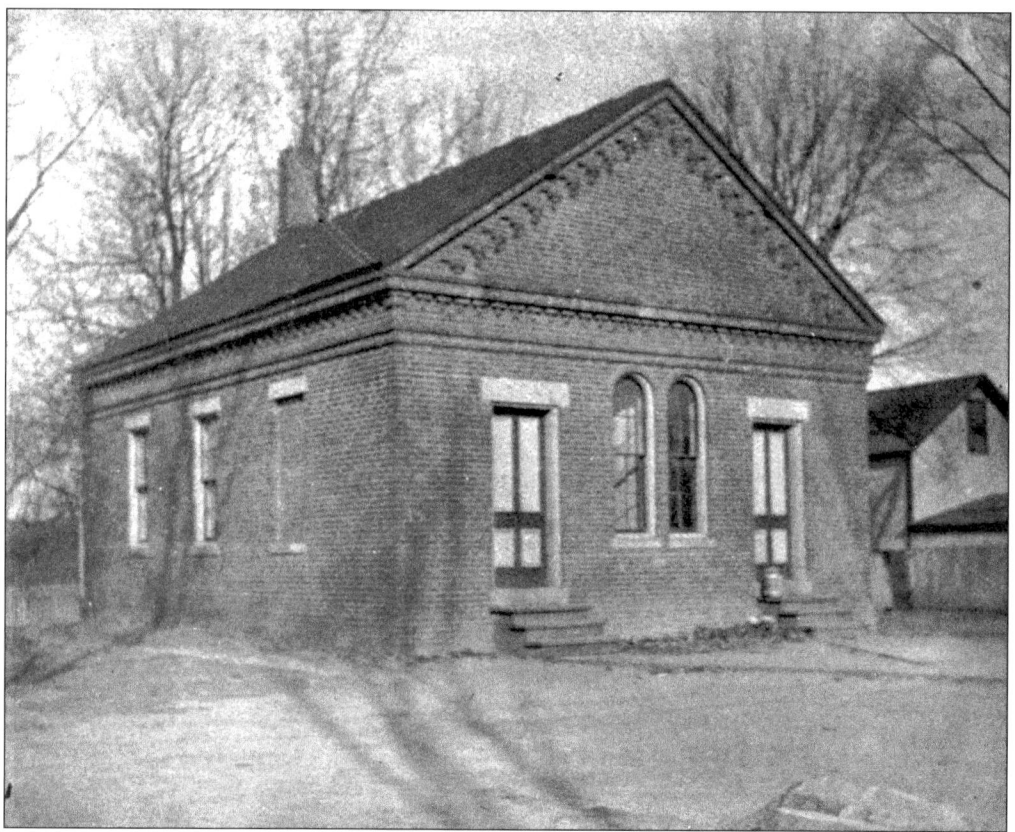

In 1797, the town was divided into four school districts. By the middle of the 19th century, the town offered over 12 small schools, including this building on Lovefield Street. This two-classroom school was used by the town until 1905, when it was taken down.

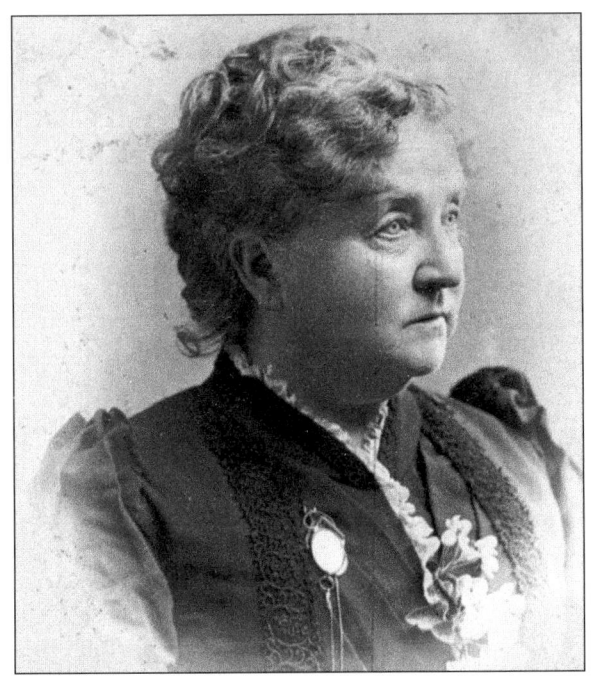

Mount Holyoke College graduate Sarah Chapin, the last principal of girls at Williston Seminary, became the town's first high school principal in 1864. Chapin designed the initial curriculum, and served as principal until ill health forced her to cut back on her duties in 1891. She retired with the class of 1901 and died that summer.

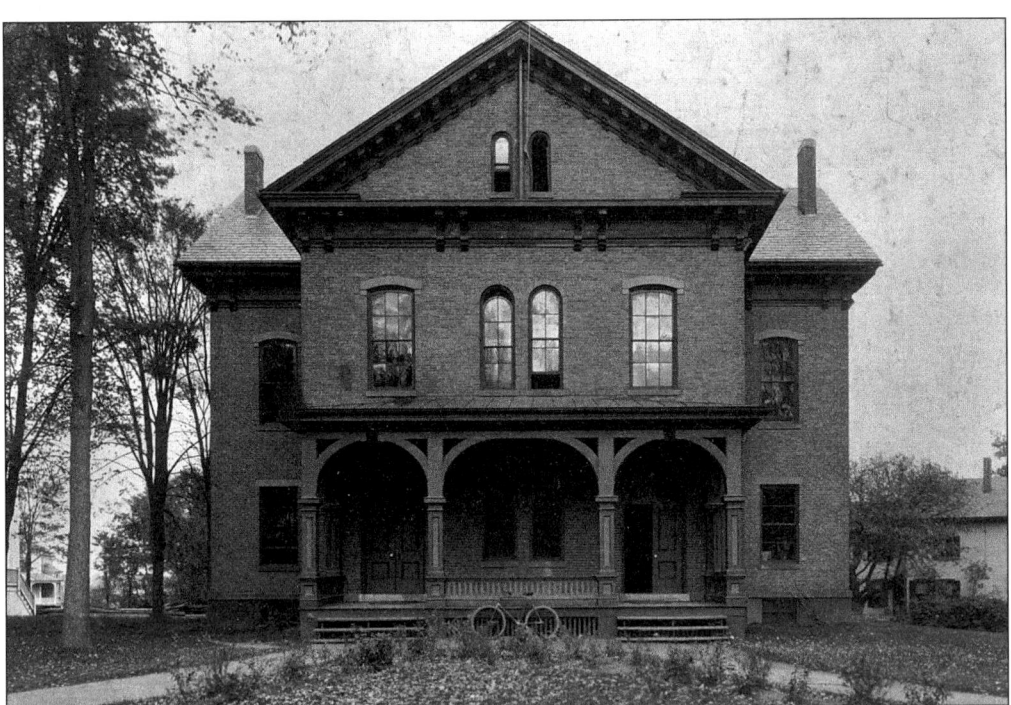

In 1864, Williston Seminary decided to stop offering classes for girls. The town constructed this two-story school for use as the town's first high school. In 1912, the town constructed a new high school and enlarged this building (then called Park Primary School) using brick salvaged from the Center Union School. It was used as an elementary school until 1939 and again in the 1950s and 1960s. The building, now called the Memorial Building, is used as municipal offices.

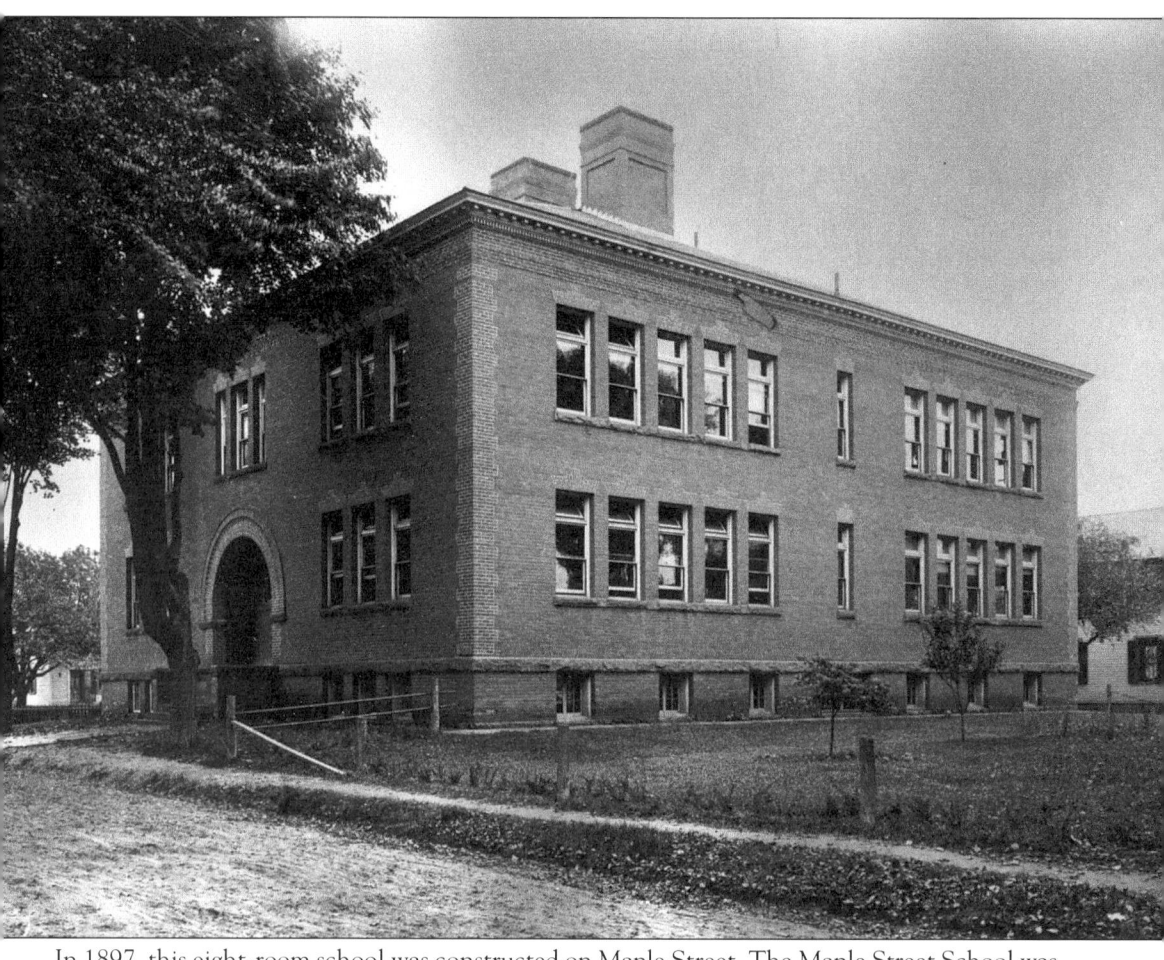

In 1897, this eight-room school was constructed on Maple Street. The Maple Street School was later enlarged to 16 rooms. The junior high school was consolidated here from 1950 to 1962. After 1962, this school was used for elementary classes.

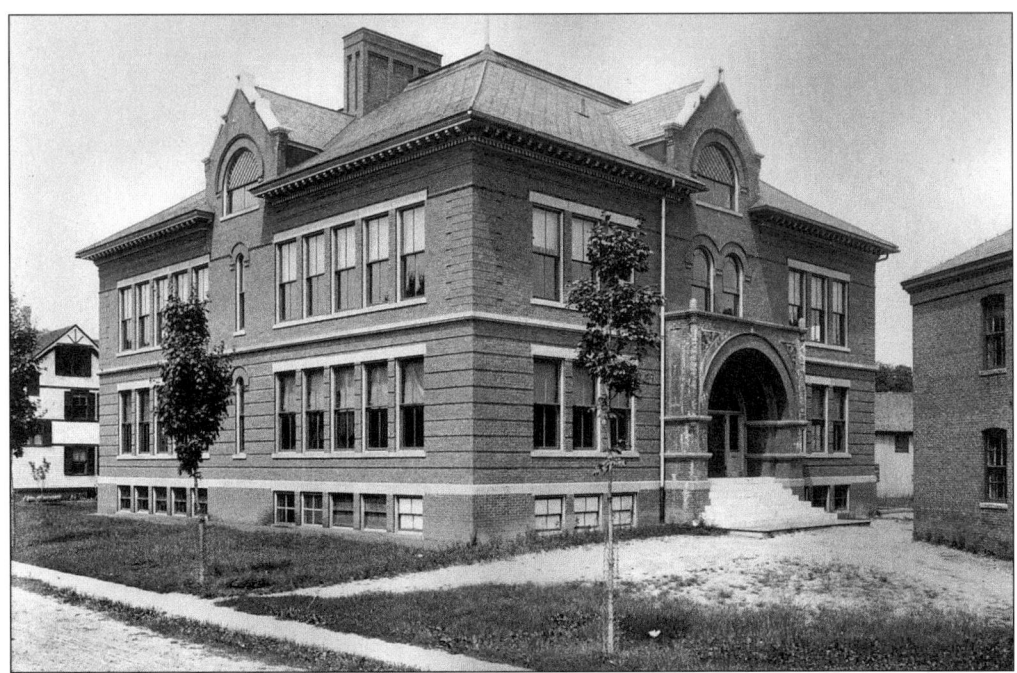

In 1902, the town responded to the population increase from the growth of the West Boylston and Hampton Companies. The Center Street School, an eight-room school, replaced the Center Union School, partly shown to the right. In 1920, the interior of this building was reconfigured as a 12-room school. It has served as a middle school, high school, and grade school.

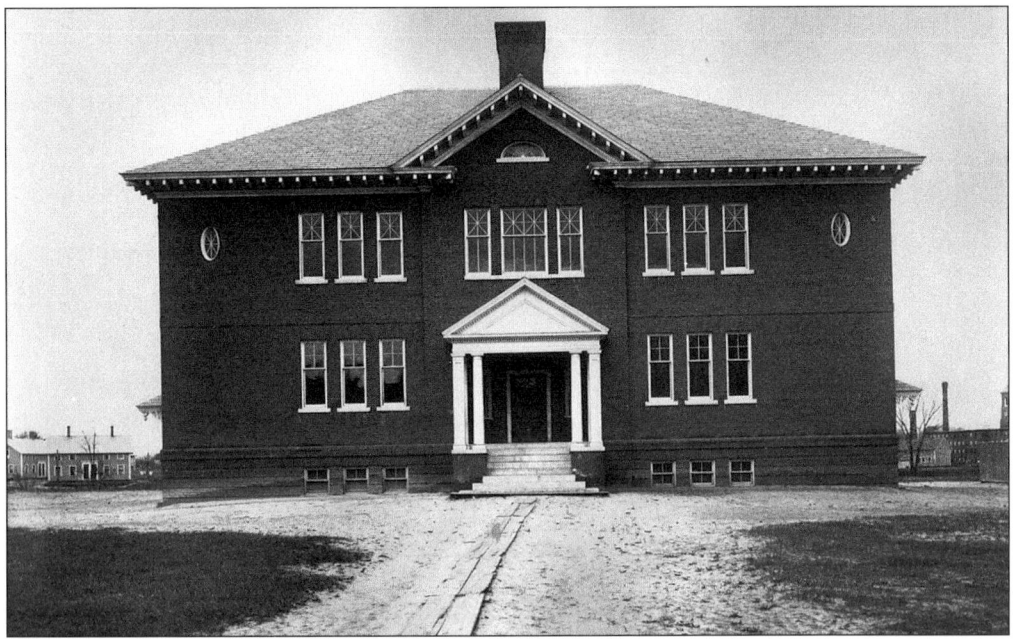

Replacing the Lovefield Street School in 1902, the Parsons Street School was built to serve children in the New City section of town. Enlarged, it is still a grade school today. On the right side of the picture is West Boylston Mill No. 2, with some of New City in the rear.

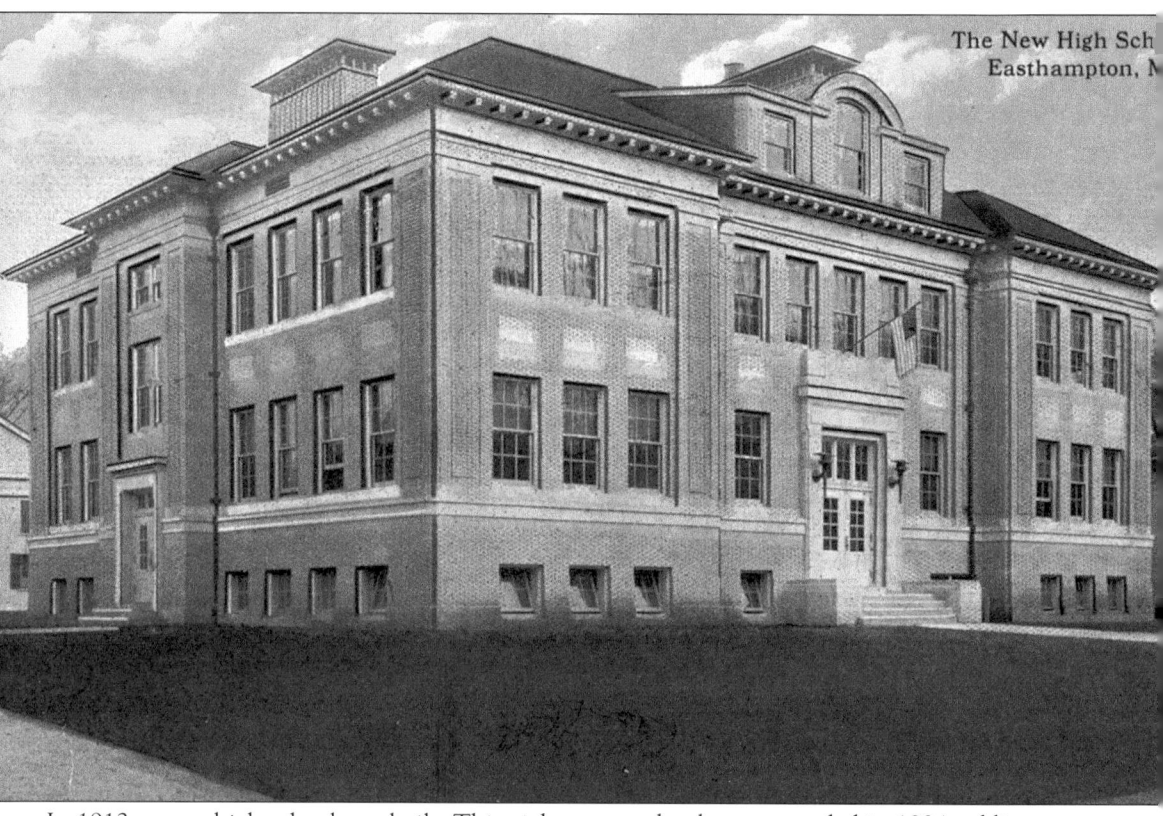

In 1912, a new high school was built. This eight-room school was expanded in 1934, adding a gymnasium and an auditorium. After a new high school was built in 1962, this building was used for a junior high school and middle school. In 1975, it was converted for use as a grade school. Now known as the Neil A. Pepin School, it is still a grammar school.

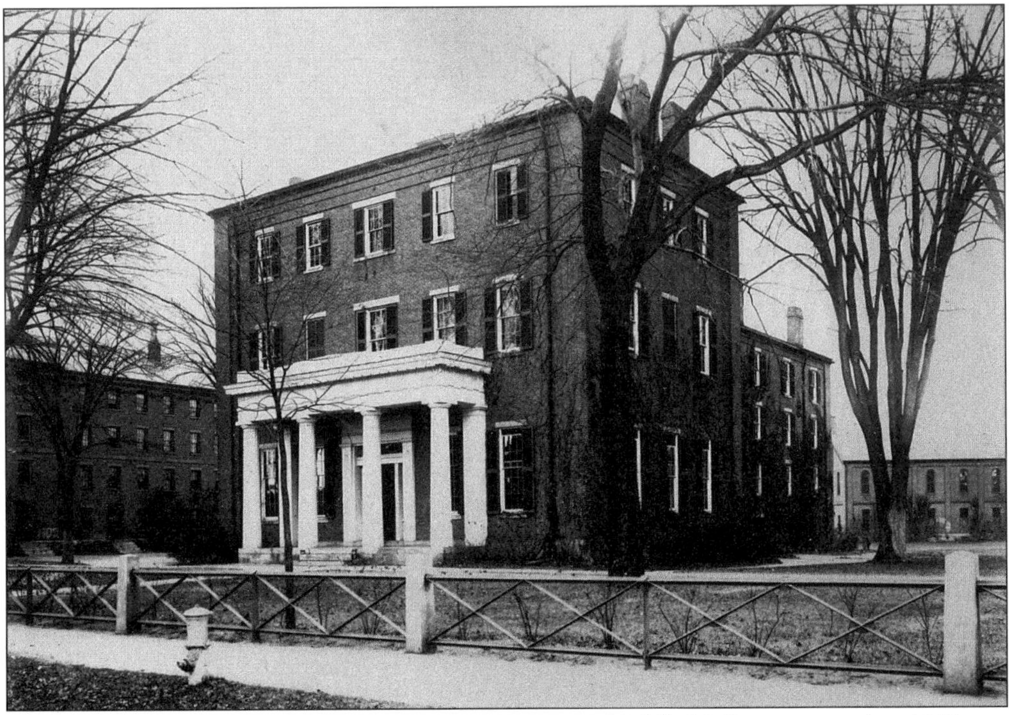

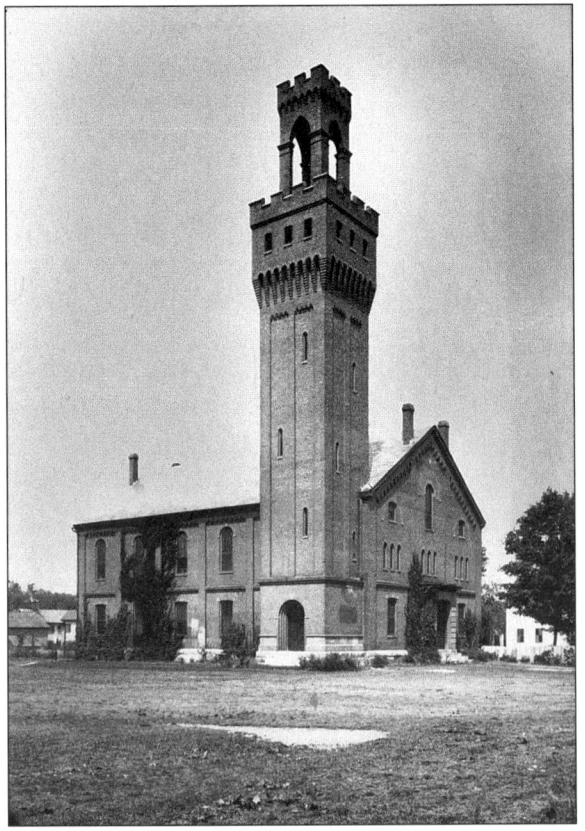

Middle Hall, constructed in 1841, was used for classes and dorm rooms. This building and the other three buildings that made up the Williston Academy Main Street campus were taken down after the academy closed it. The front pillars now grace the Williston-Northampton administrative building.

Built in 1864, the gym became the site of many basketball games for townspeople and students alike. Discontinued after the construction of a new recreation building on the Williston Academy's Park Street campus, the gym was taken down in 1955.

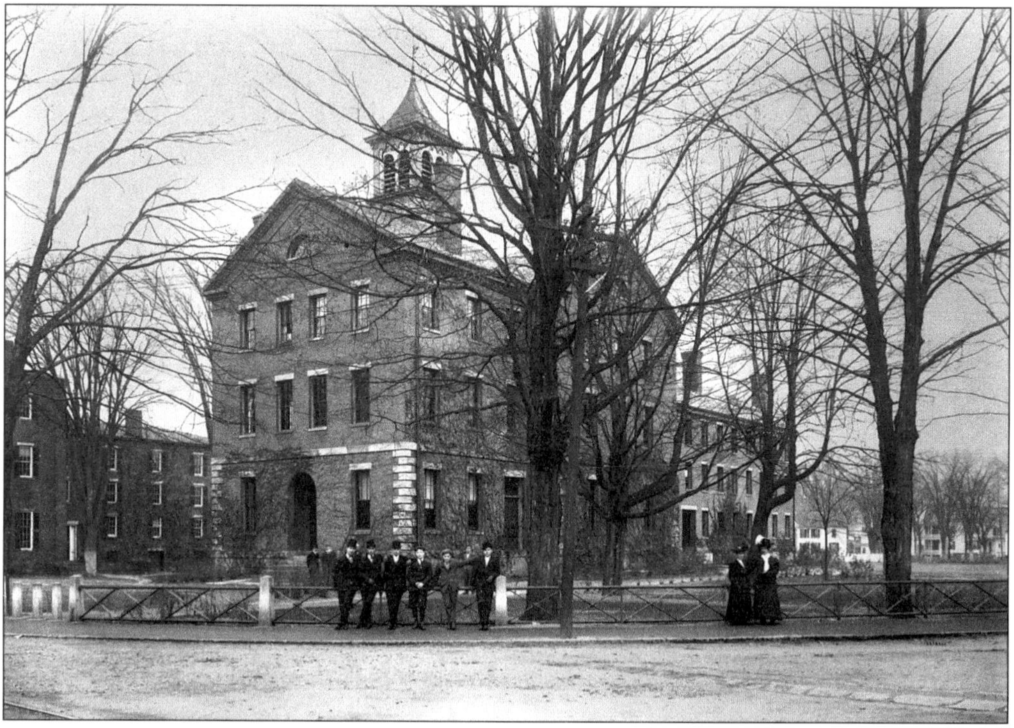

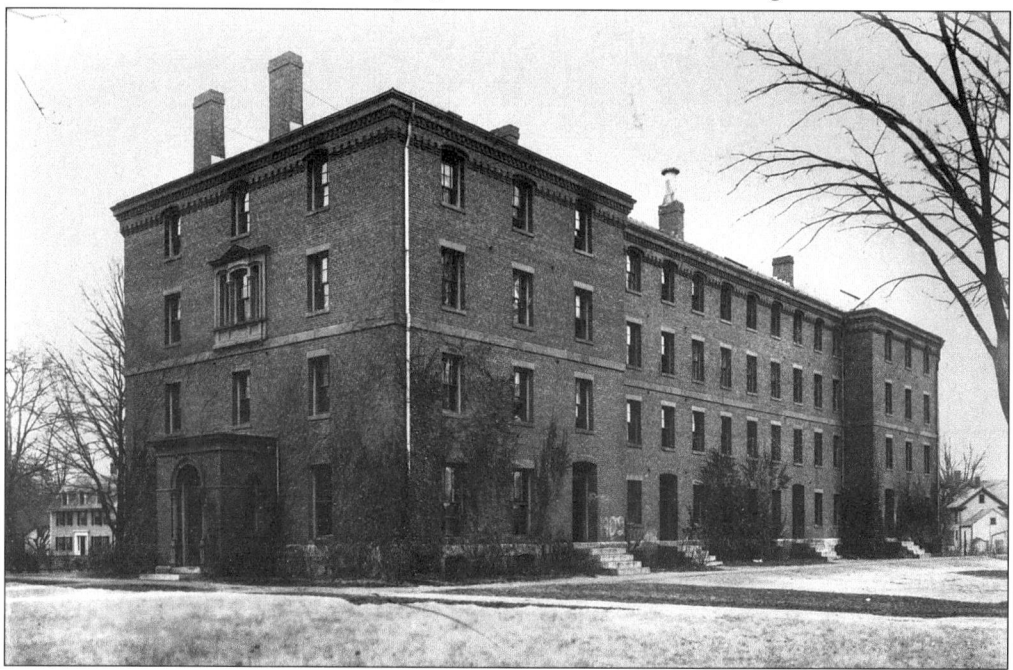

South Hall was built in 1857 and taken down in 1952. The building, which was used for classes and dormitories, was later replaced by a gas station and an office building.

North Hall was built in 1866 and was used as a dormitory. Williston Seminary was originally chartered to educate students for a life of ministry. Gradually, the school stressed secular academics and became Williston Academy in 1925.

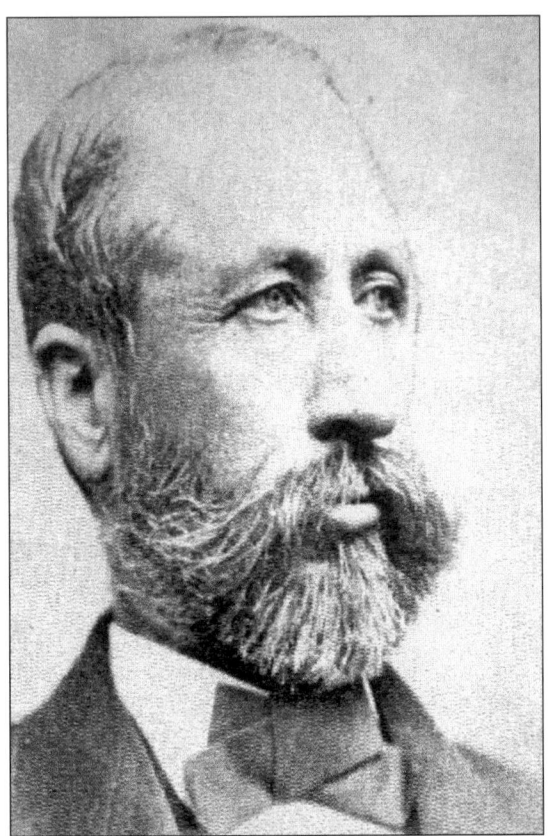

Following the death of Samuel Williston, Col. William Clark—an Amherst College professor and the son-in-law of Samuel Williston—became president of the board of Williston Seminary. Clark was instrumental in establishing the Agricultural College in Sapporo, Japan. He also served as president of the Massachusetts Agricultural College, which is now the University of Massachusetts at Amherst.

Shown in this undated photograph are the members of the F.C. fraternity at Williston Academy. Beginning in 1919, the headmaster Archibald Galbraith updated the curriculum at the school. He also brought the school to a firm financial footing and modernized the school buildings. By 1928, the last two fraternities closed as the school took control of dorms and dining halls.

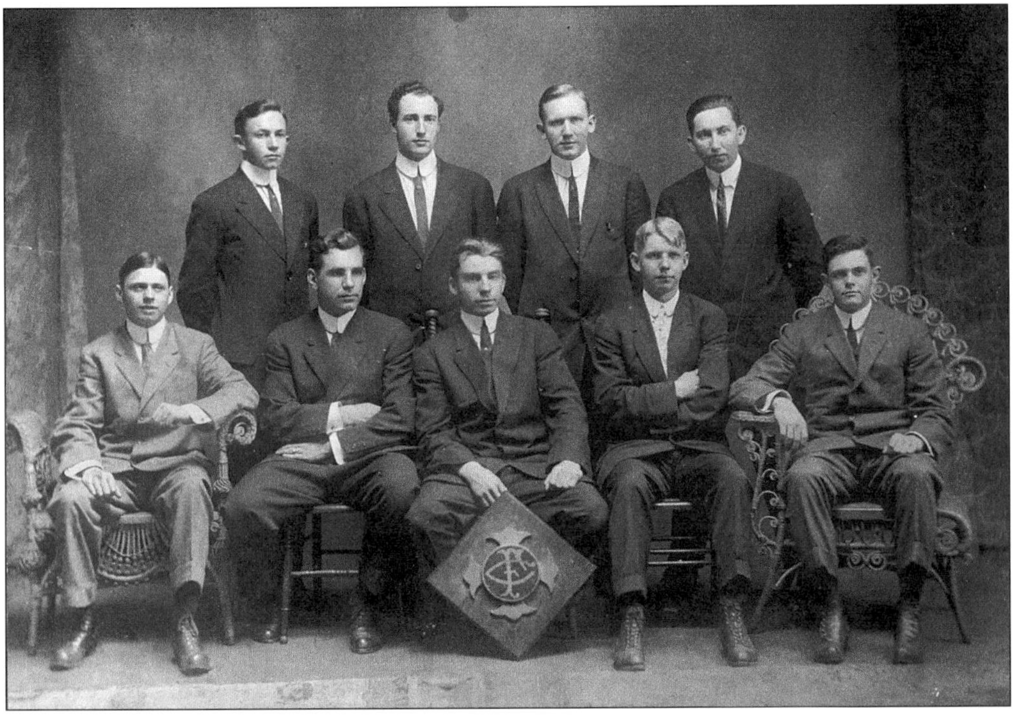

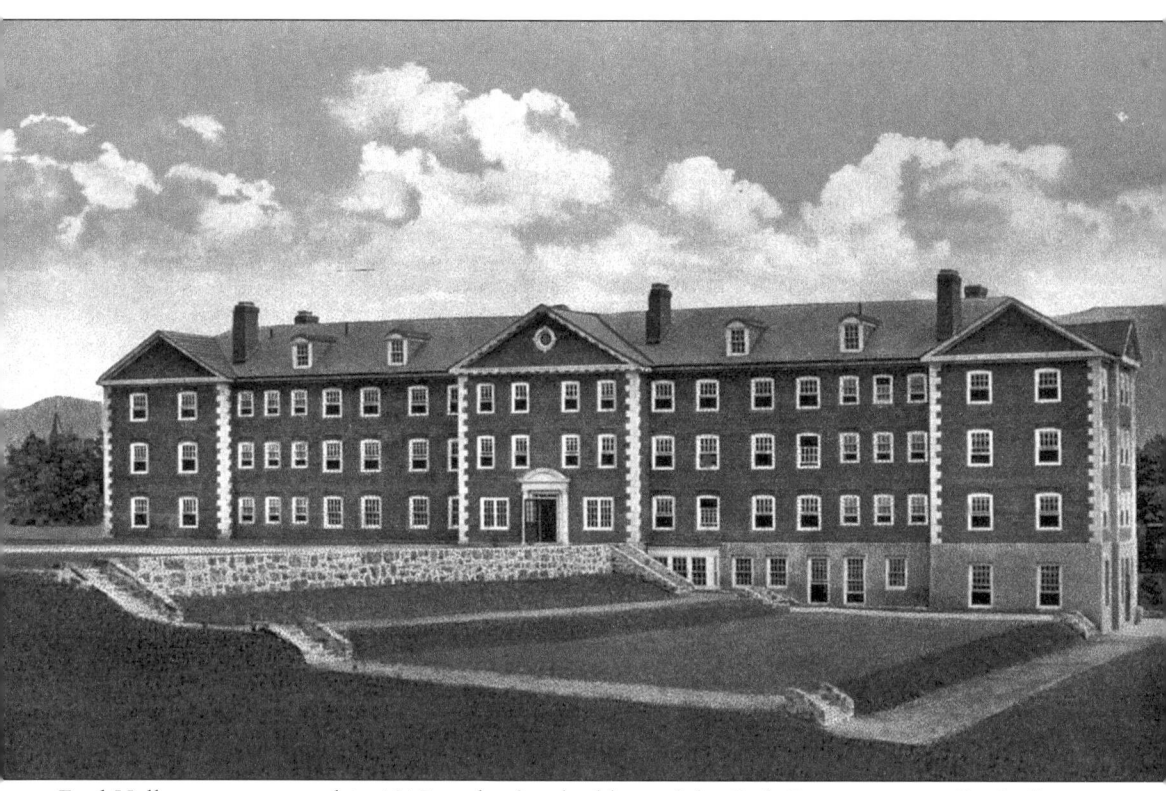

Ford Hall was constructed in 1917 as the first building of the Park Street campus. Gradually, more buildings were constructed at the Park Street campus. Following the retirement of longtime headmaster Archibald Galbraith in 1949, the Main Street campus closed. All school activities took place on this campus, which once was part of the estate of Samuel Williston.

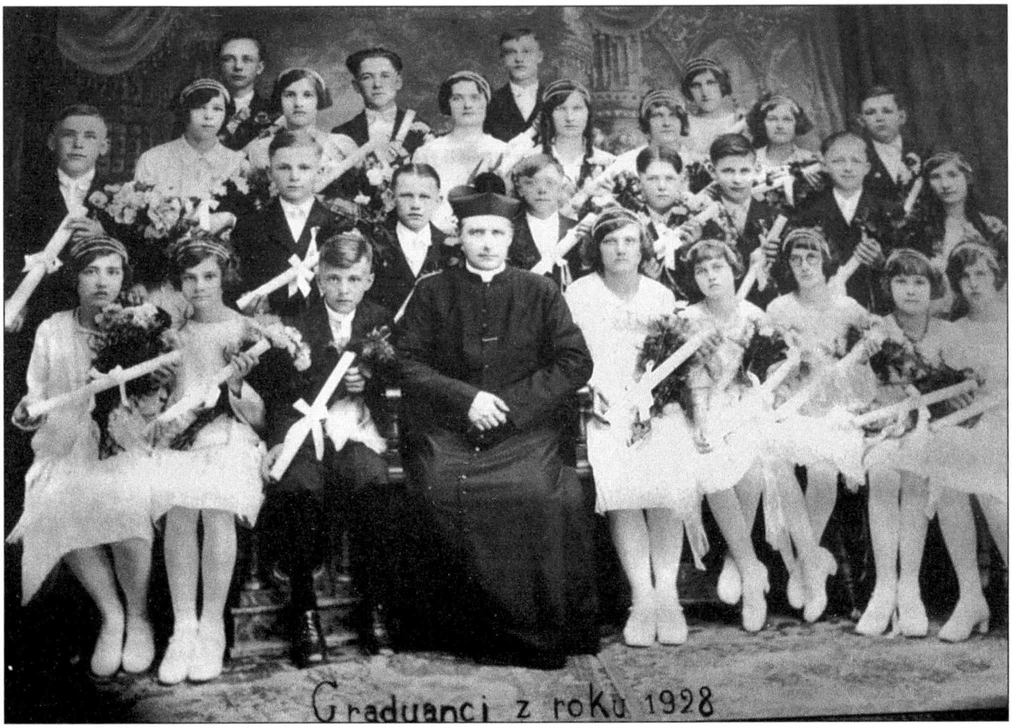

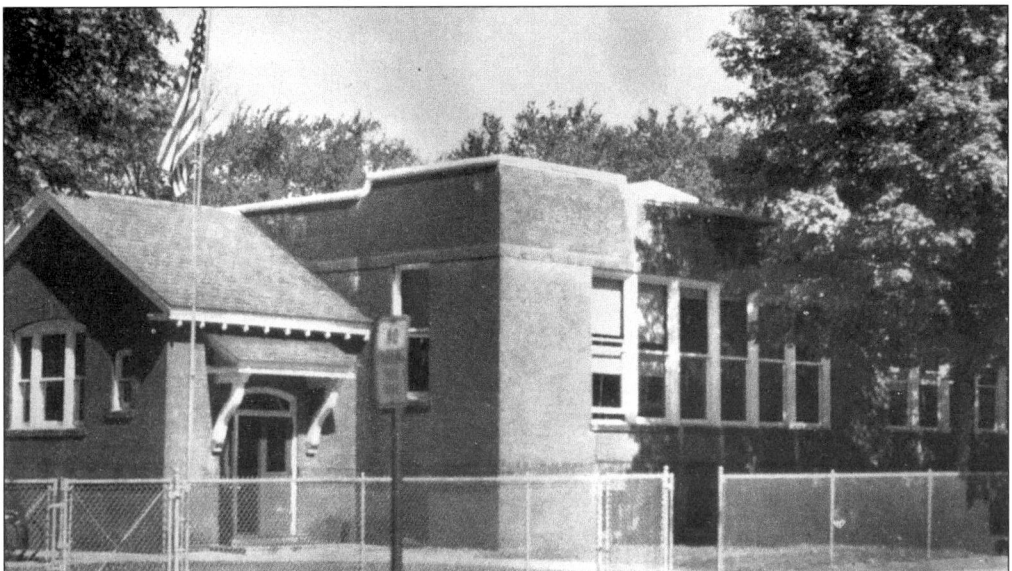

Graduanci z roku 1928

This 1928 photograph shows the eighth-grade graduates of the Sacred Heart parochial school. Until the 1960s, the Catholic Church educated approximately half of the town's children. The church opened a 12-room school to serve the needs of the children in the parish. The school was last used as an alternative high school.

In 1909, the Immaculate Conception school was opened as a four-room building. It was expanded to an eight-room school and is now used as the church education center. This school merged with the Notre Dame school and continues to offer Catholic education from the former Notre Dame school.

Seven
AROUND TOWN

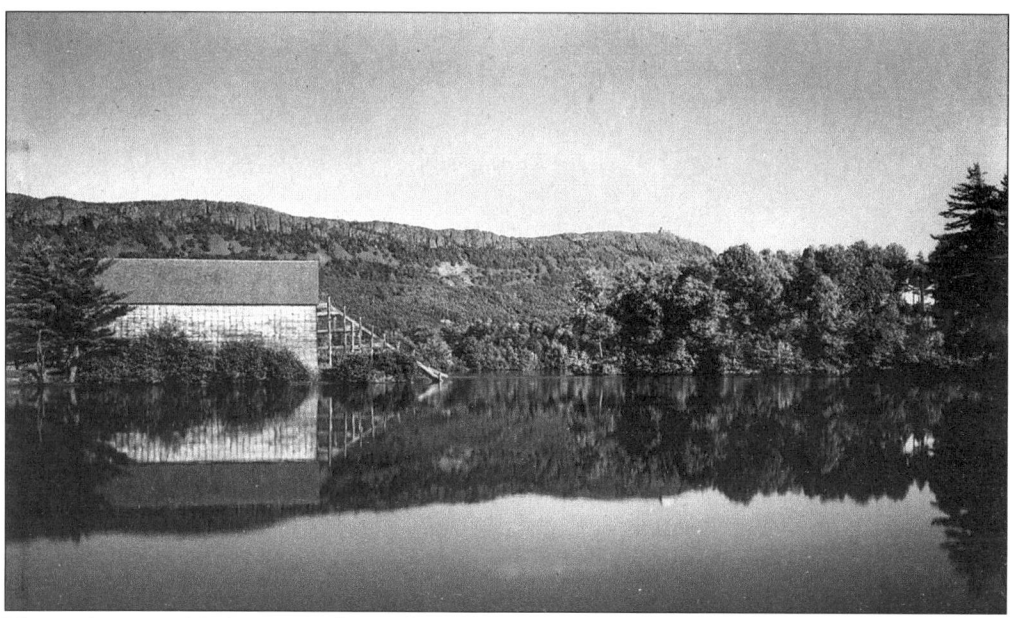

The icehouse at Nashawannuck Pond was used until the last ice dealer closed in the 1940s. Before refrigerators became common appliances, the ice dealer provided an essential service. Ice was harvested and kept in icehouses insulated with sawdust.

Edwin Bosworth was an important building contractor in town during the second half of the 19th century. After learning building trades, Bosworth eventually settled in Amherst. He constructed a building at Amherst College, where Samuel Williston and Horatio Knight served on the board of trustees. They persuaded Bosworth to move to Easthampton to become a building contractor. He built the town hall, the Williston Gym, North Hall, and several mill buildings and houses.

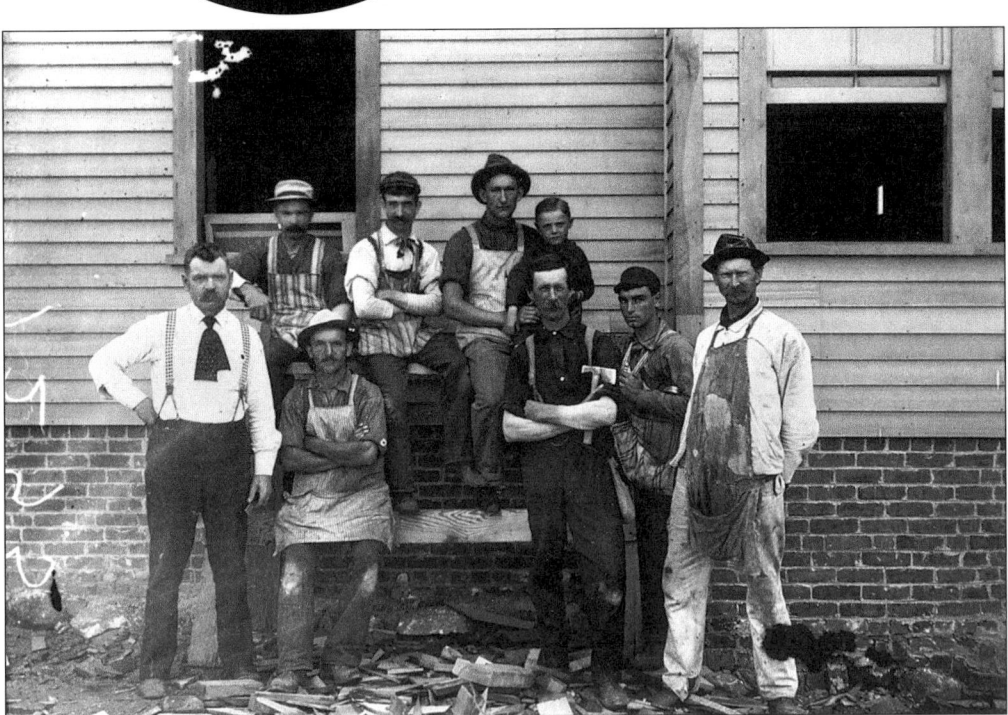

The construction crew of Addison Ferris stops working to pose for this photograph taken by one of the Howes brothers. Ferris (standing at far left) was a house-builder during his professional life. He died at age 72 in 1929. The house he was building in this photograph is unidentified.

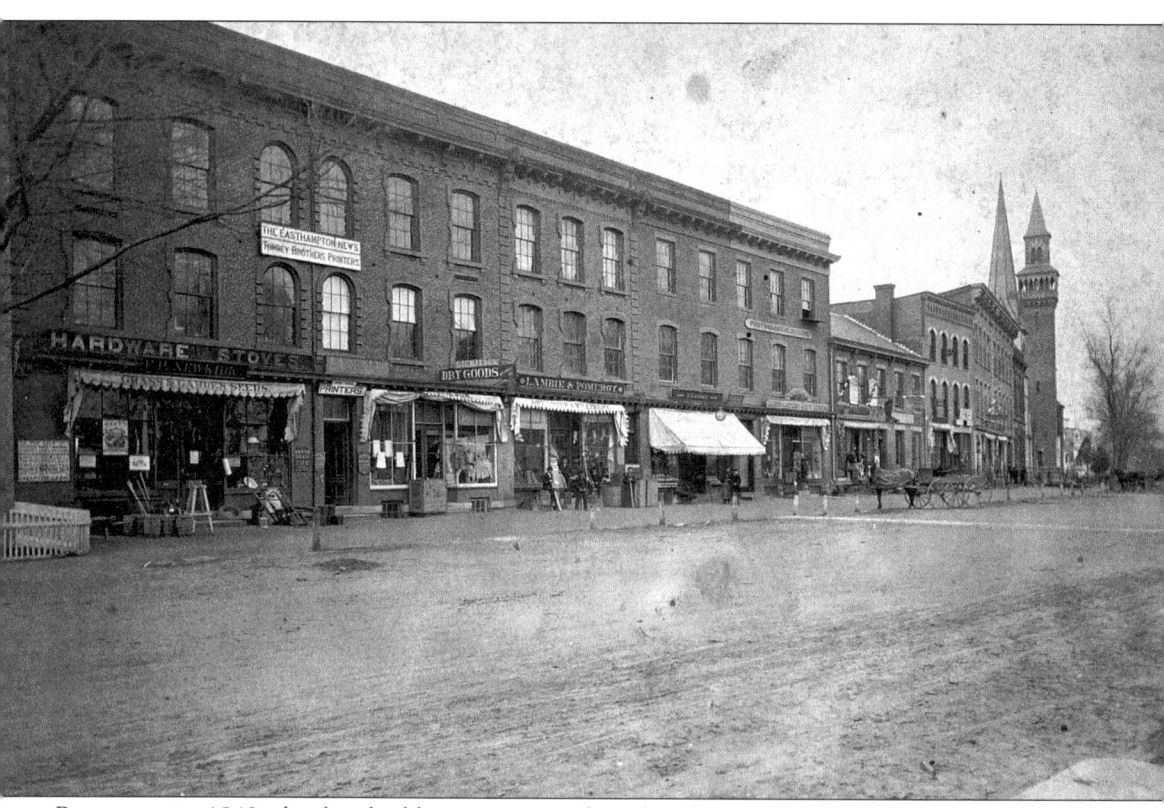

Beginning in 1849, the first building was erected in the cluster of buildings known as Shop Row. Five more buildings were constructed between 1861 and 1868. Then, in 1871, the First National Bank was built. The buildings seen on the left side were later remolded for use by the Easthampton Savings Bank. That building was destroyed by fire in 1971.

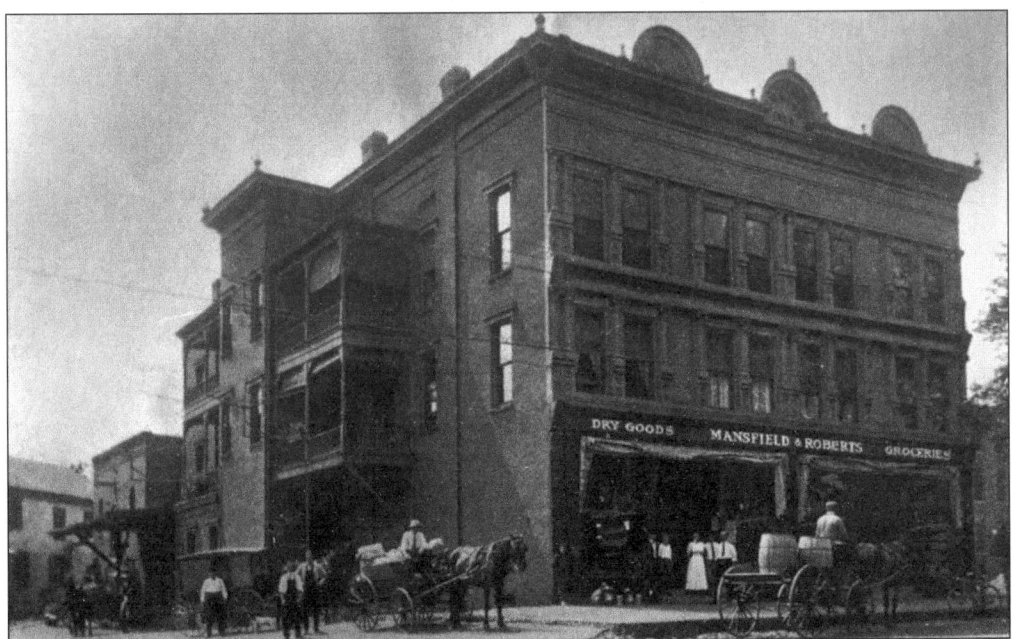

In 1872, E. W. Wood purchased a general store originally owned by Samuel Williston. On November 19, 1896, Wood opened this three-story building, selling it to Mansfield and Roberts in 1899. In 1941, the business closed. A furniture store and restaurant were later tenants. On December 27, 1991, the building was destroyed by fire.

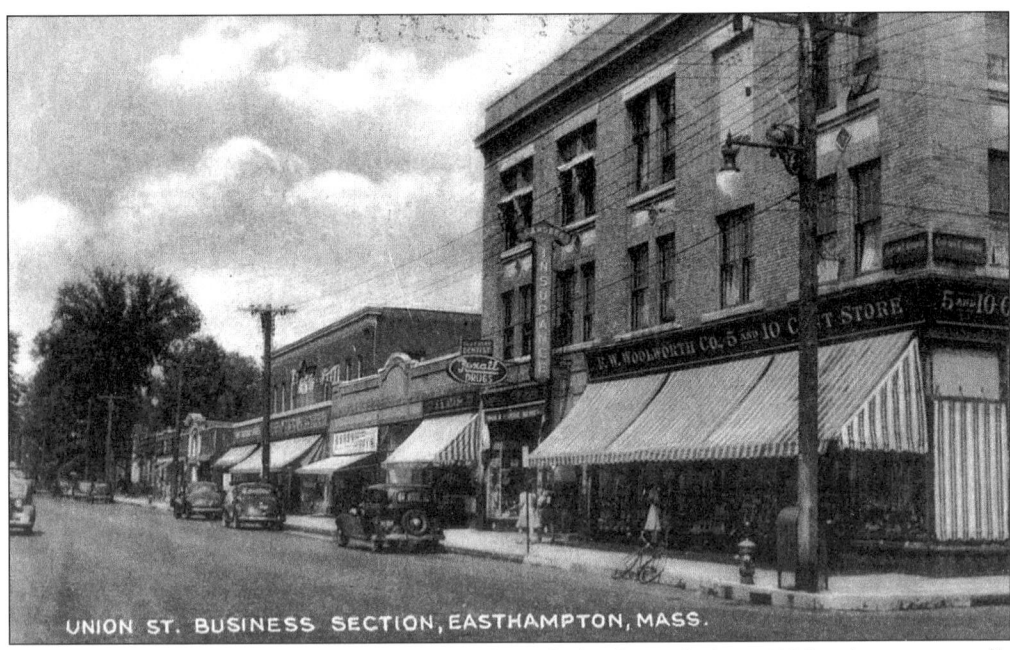

UNION ST. BUSINESS SECTION, EASTHAMPTON, MASS.

Union Street was made up of private residential dwellings before 1900, when new mills introduced a new set of residents to town. Trolleys offered them a way to get to shopping areas quickly. F. W. Woolworth, W. T. Grants, and the First National Grocery Store were some of the national chains with outlets on Union Street.

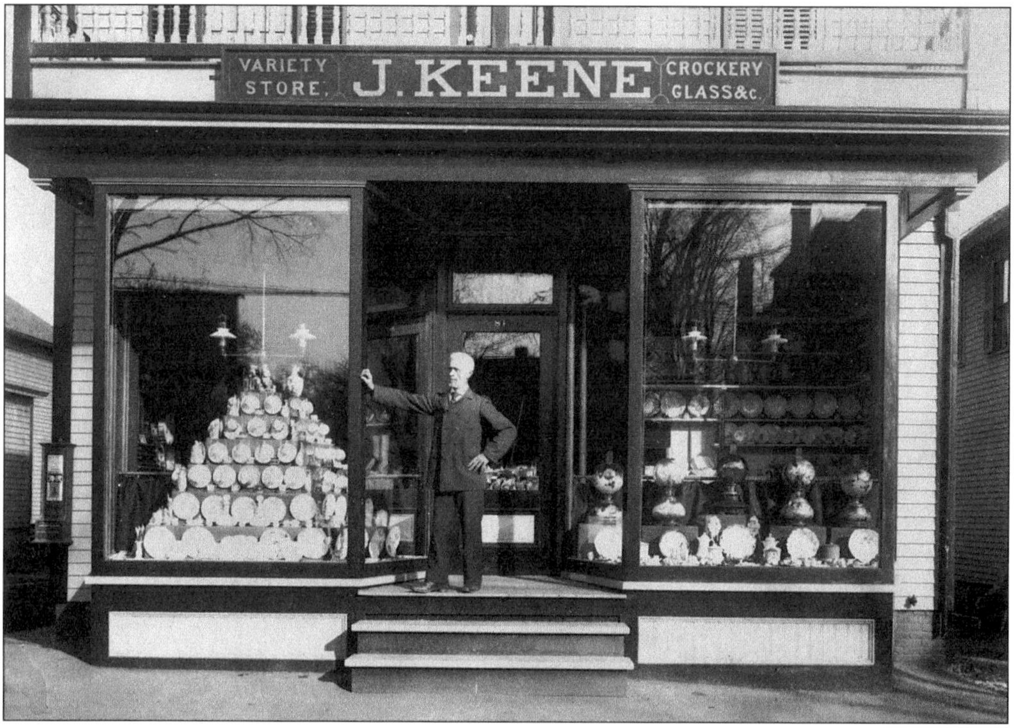

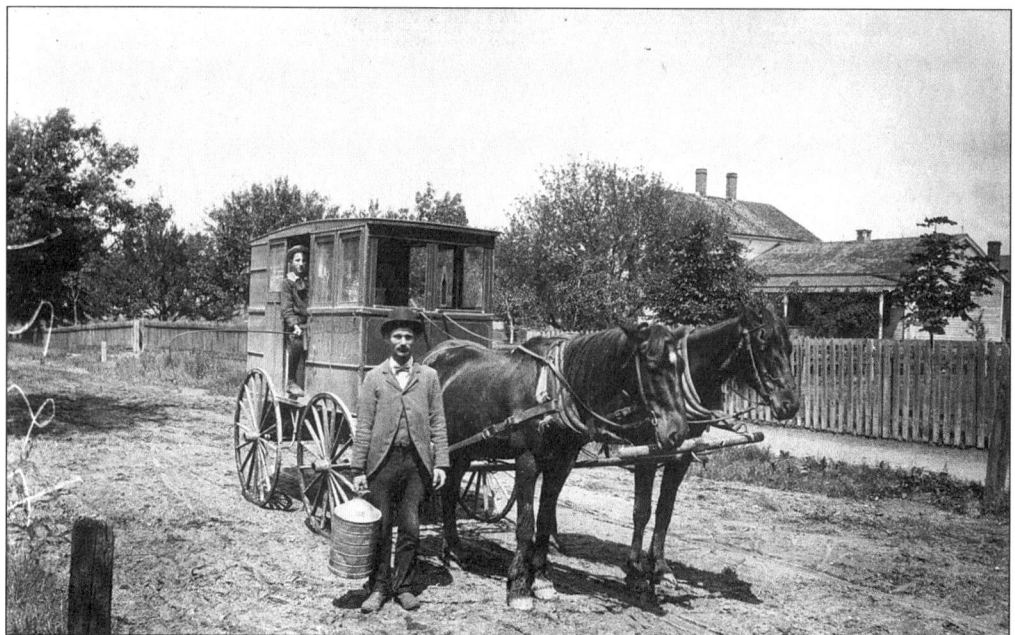

James Keene poses in front of his store. His son, Charles, also sold photography supplies and used his hobby of taking pictures to add another sideline to the business. The photographs that he took of town buildings were sent to England or Germany and made into postcards, which mill workers sent to friends and relatives.

The Howes brothers photographed this delivery man, his team of horses, and the child riding inside of it on Briggs Street.

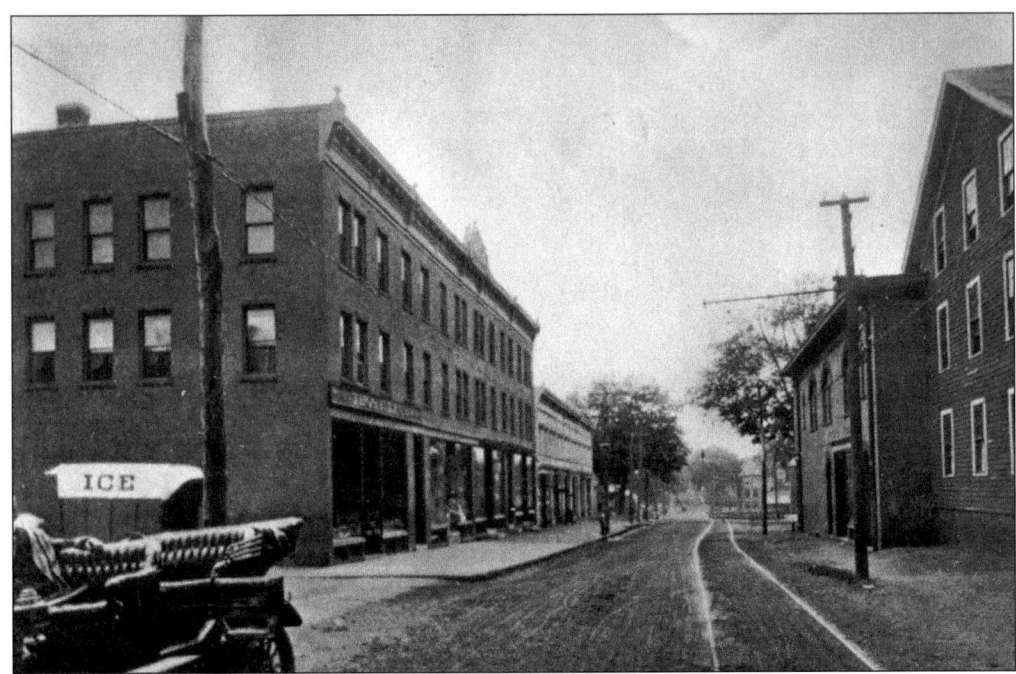

Cottage Street also benefited from the increase in the trolley system and population from 1900. The street became a shopping center. Thomas F. Lynn owned the building on the left, which he used for his package store. The building was sold to a new owner just before Prohibition. In 1923, a fire started by an arsonist destroyed the building and took the life of firefighter Patrick McCarthy. On the right is a bar known as Jamarog's, the present-day location of the Brass Cat.

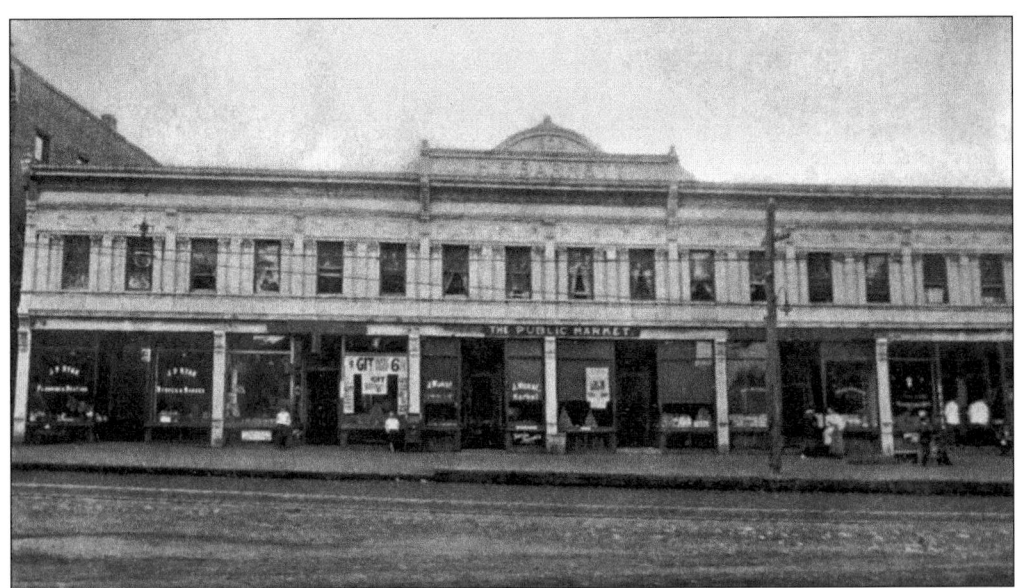

The Barnett Block was made up of six separate buildings on Cottage Street. An embossed-tin front was added to improve the appearance of the buildings and to create a uniform design. W. L. Richard, a clothing store, and DeBarberi's, a confectionery store, were some of the tenants. This building was destroyed by fire in 1932.

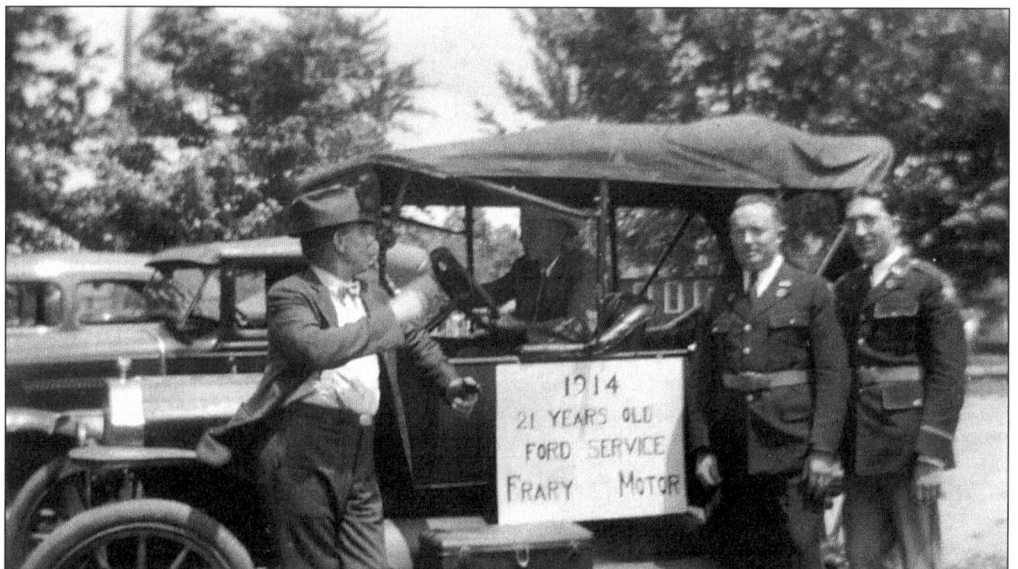

Easthampton offered new car dealers as soon as cars were introduced to the mass market. In 1926, Lang Motors began to sell Ford cars. When Lang Motors began selling Chevrolets in 1932, Ford gave its dealership to Frary Motors.

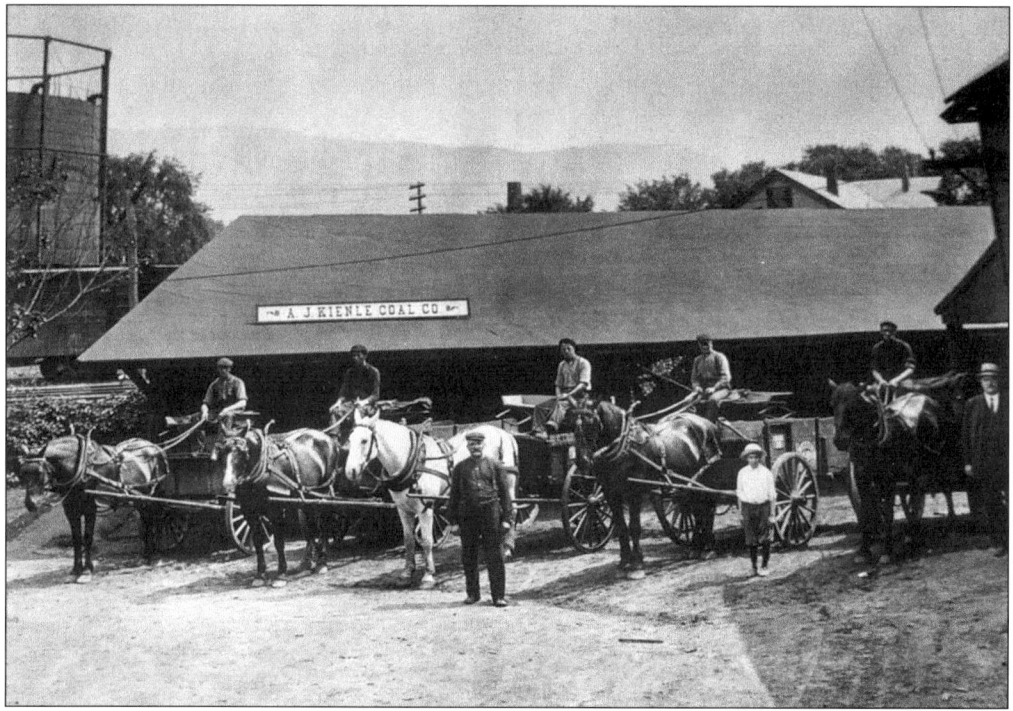

The A. J. Kienle Coal Company, a longtime Union Street business, began as an ice and coal company in 1894. Augustus Kienle was the original owner. The company also sold wood and oil. Marion Kienle, a local music teacher, later operated the Kienle Coal company. The business was sold in 1966.

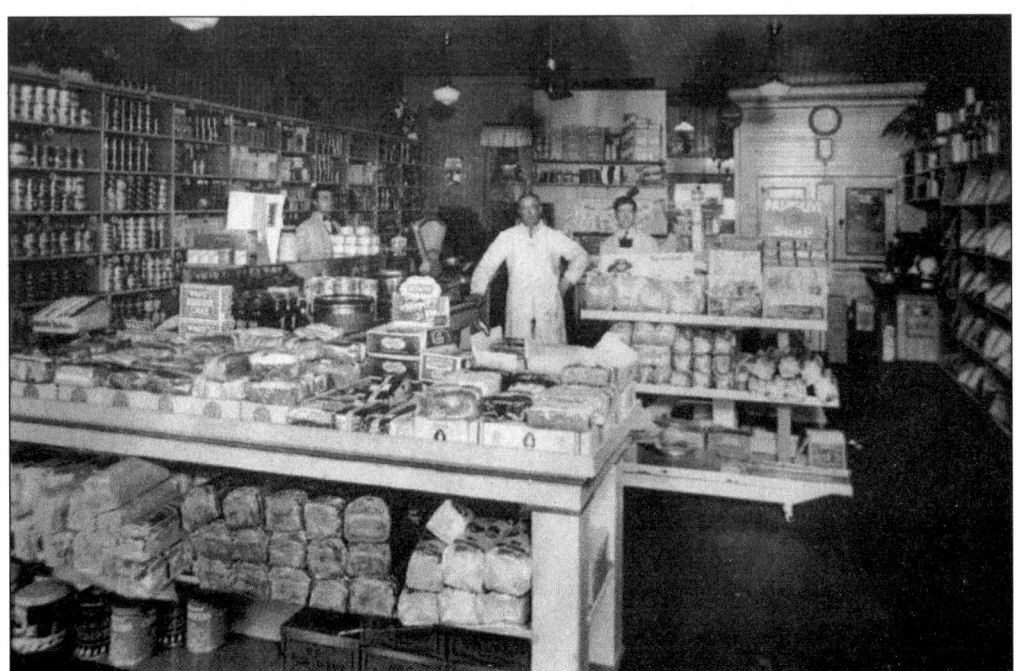

Henry Bernier left Canada in 1891, settling in the town of West Boylston, Massachusetts. When the West Boylston Manufacturing Company was forced to move, Bernier followed the company to Easthampton. After working at the mill and then for another grocer, Bernier opened this Pleasant Street grocery store in 1909. In 1925, Bernier turned the grocery store over to his son Joel, seen above on the left. The store closed in 1953. In 1966, Stanley Home Products razed the store for additional parking.

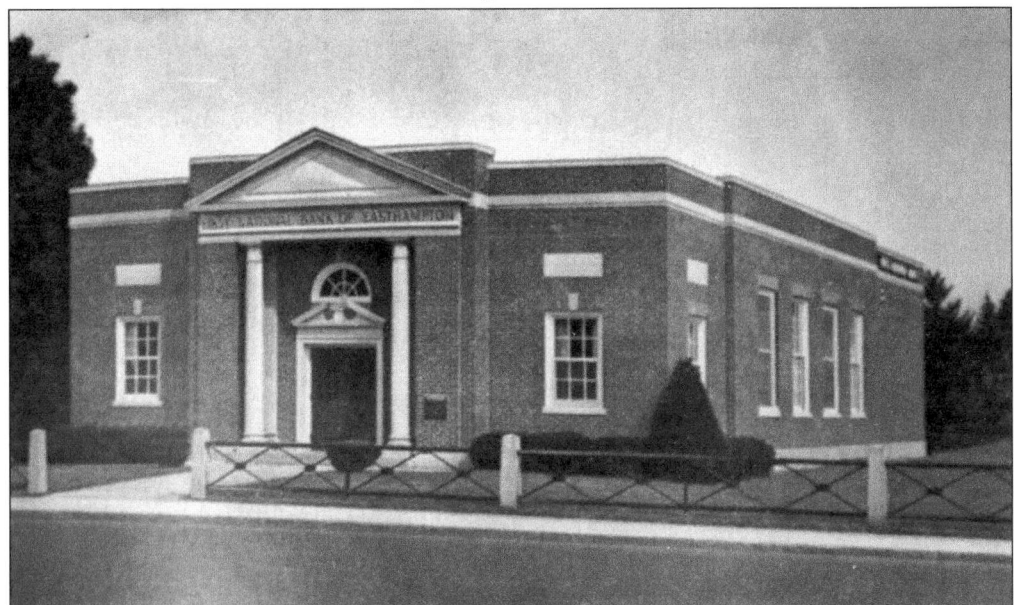

In 1949, Williston Academy closed its Main Street campus and offered it for sale. The old campus was torn down and was replaced by new buildings, one of which was the First National Bank. It was later a branch for BayBank, BankBoston, and now for Fleet Bank.

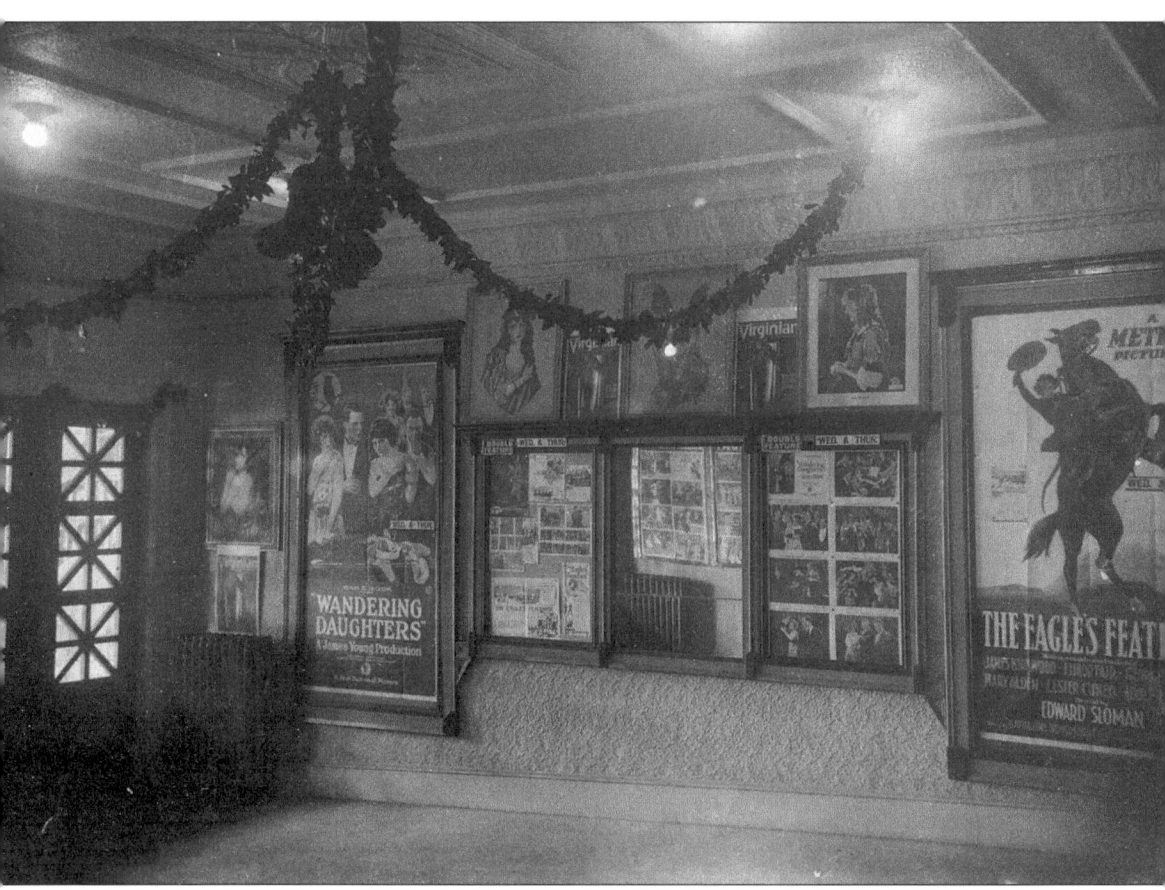

The original Majestic Theater was built in 1910 to serve the growing population of town, showing plays and silent movies. It could seat over 800 customers. In 1922, it was destroyed by fire and replaced by a new theater, which opened February 26, 1923. Shown is the lobby in the early 1920s. In the late 1960s, the cinema's film format turned to an all X-rated line-up. The theater closed and is now awaiting a new owner.

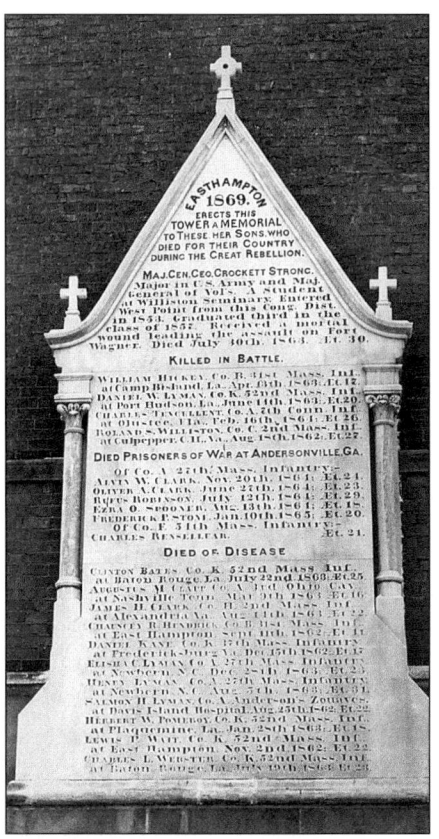

Easthampton lost 22 men to the Civil War, including the 21-year-old blacksmith Charles Rensellear, who was a member of the 54th Regiment, a military unit composed of black men. Rensellear enlisted as a private on November 16, 1863. He was wounded and taken prisoner on December 20, 1864. Brought to the Andersonville prison camp, he died August 8, 1864.

The Grand Army of the Republic was a patriotic organization of Civil War veterans. The post was named in memory of Gen. George Strong, an Easthampton resident and West Point graduate who was killed in battle. The local Grand Army of the Republic was active until it disbanded in 1918. The organization had a meeting room at the rear of town hall.

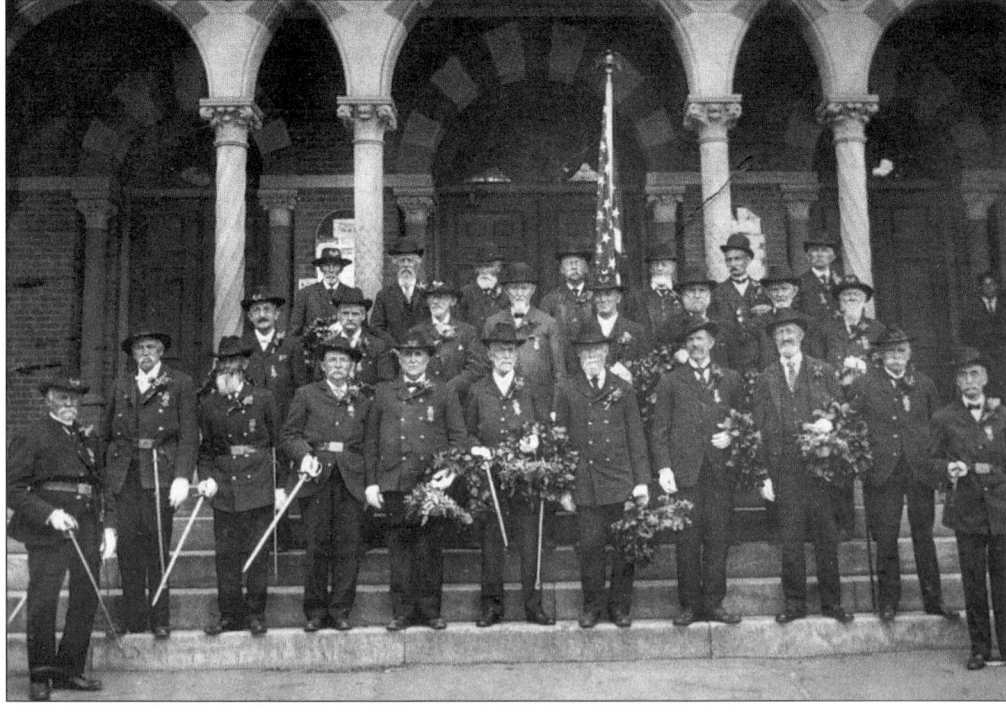

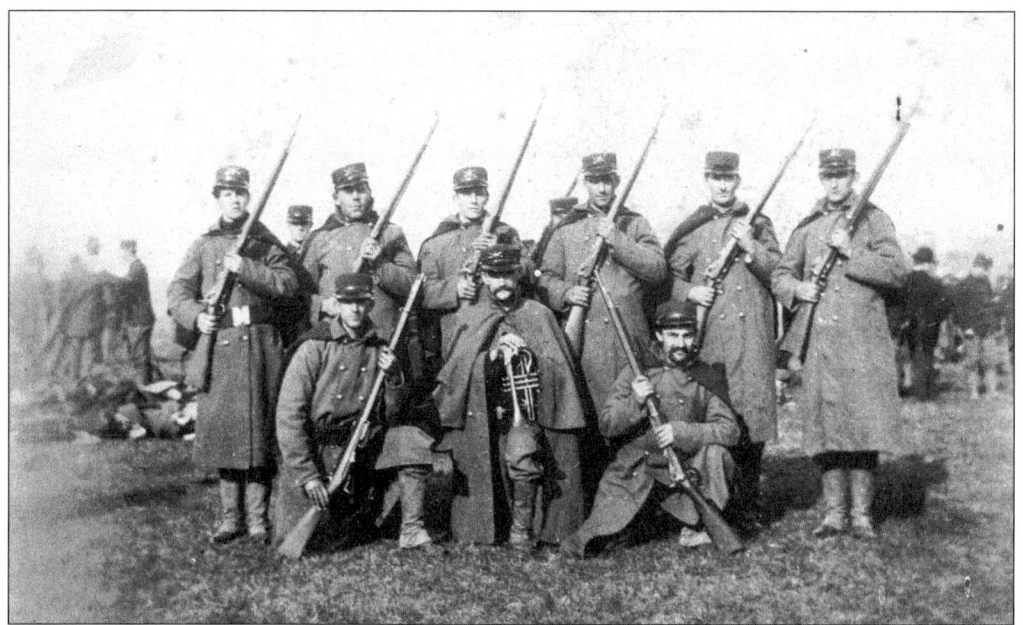

On February 16, 1898, the *Maine* was blown up in Havana Harbor, the incident that began the Spanish American War. Twenty-three Easthampton men enlisted in the armed services, including Wesley Brass, a barber, who represented the town's only casualty. He died in Florida of pneumonia. At the top left of this photograph, Brass can be seen standing.

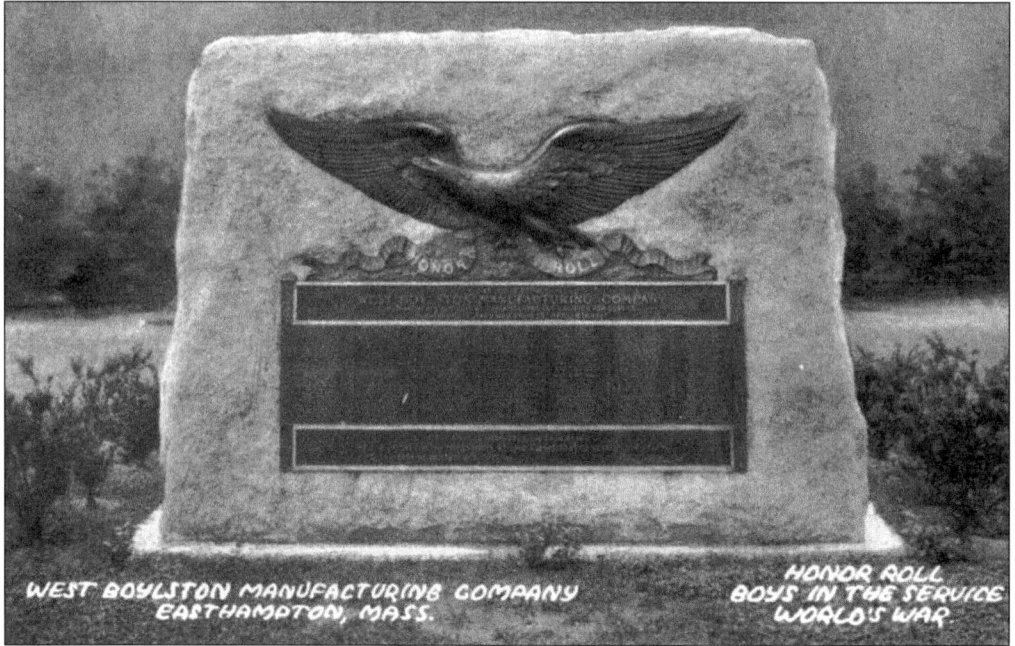

On April 6, 1917, the United States ended its neutral stance and joined the allied forces against Germany, Austria-Hungary, and the Ottoman Empire. Some 687 townspeople enlisted, most joining up with Company I of the 104th Infantry. This photograph dates to 1919, when the West Boylston Manufacturing Company dedicated this stone that listed the names of its employees who had served in the armed services.

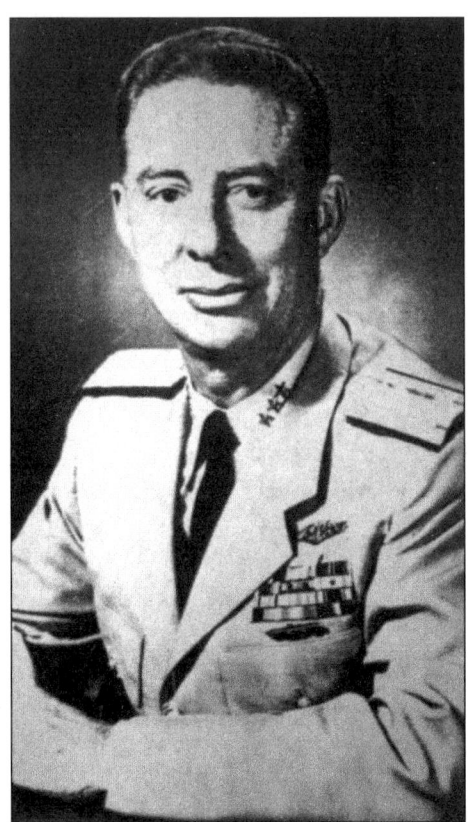

More than 1,500 Easthampton residents enlisted in the armed services during WWII. One former resident, Adm. Lawson Ramage, earned the Congressional Medal of Honor. He lived in Easthampton on two occasions. The first was from 1911 to 1916, when Ramage's father lived in town and managed a Holyoke paper mill. Ramage returned in 1923 and became a student at Williston Academy, where he graduated with the class of 1926. As a submarine commander, Ramage was awarded the Congregational Medal of Honor for tactics in submarine warfare.

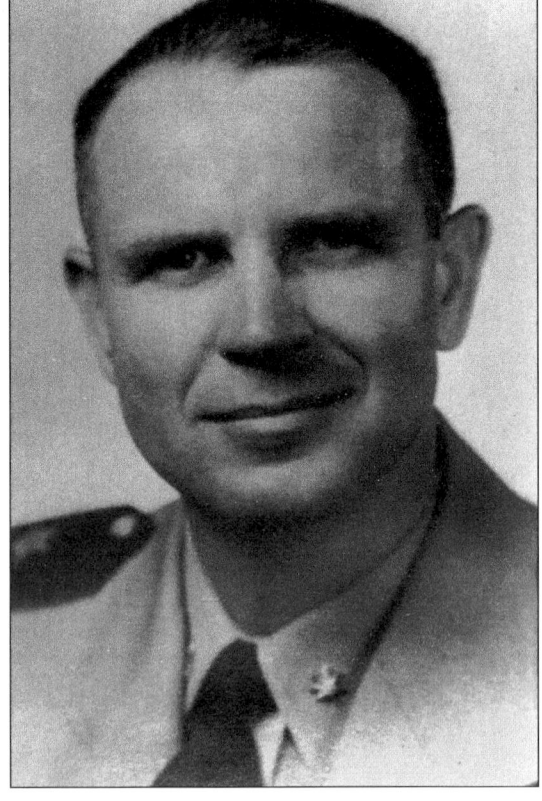

Phillip Allen was born on January 24, 1924. He attended local schools, graduating from Easthampton High School in 1941 and Williston Academy in 1942. In 1946, he graduated from Annapolis. Following his service in WWII, Allen moved to submarine duty. As an assistant superintendent at Portsmouth, New Hampshire, Allen boarded the *Thresher*. The submarine imploded and was destroyed in April 1963.

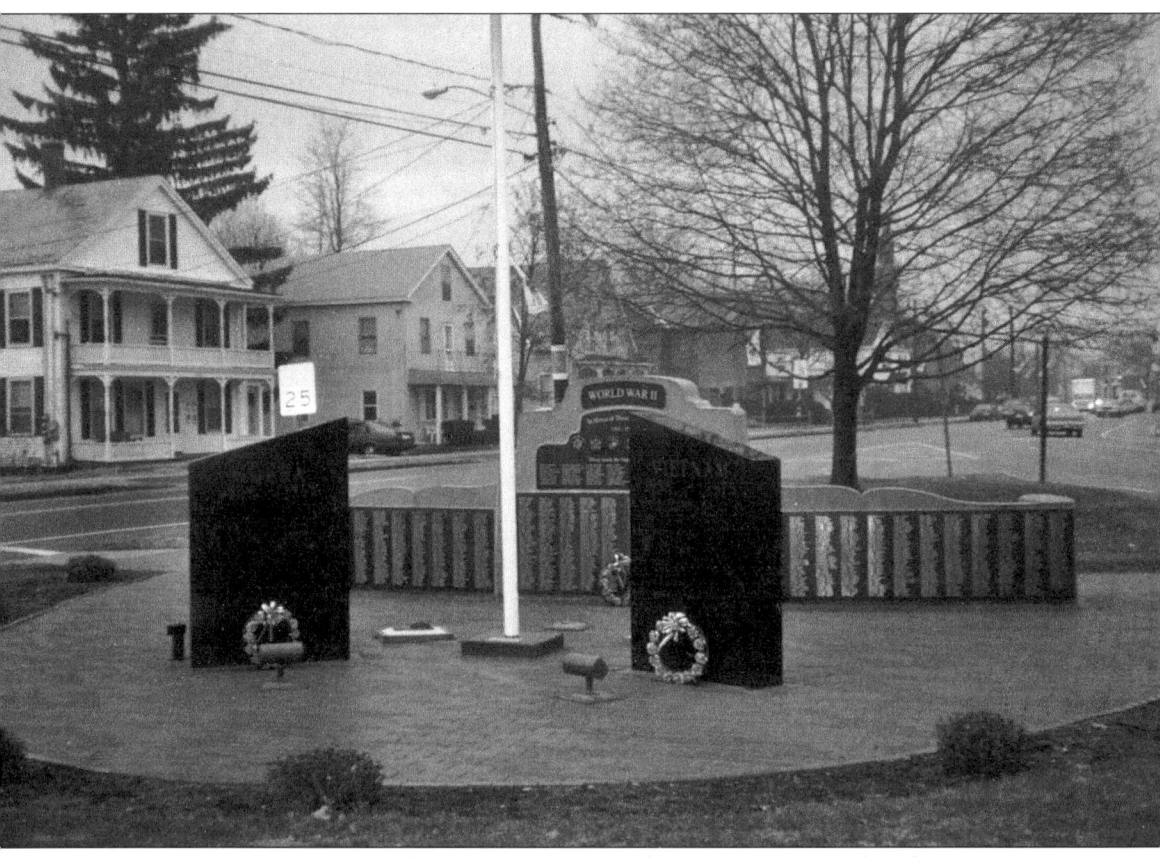

This recent photograph shows the WWII, Korea, and Vietnam Memorials. The monument commemorating WWI stands behind them. Three men from town were killed in the Korean War and five were lost to the Vietnam War.

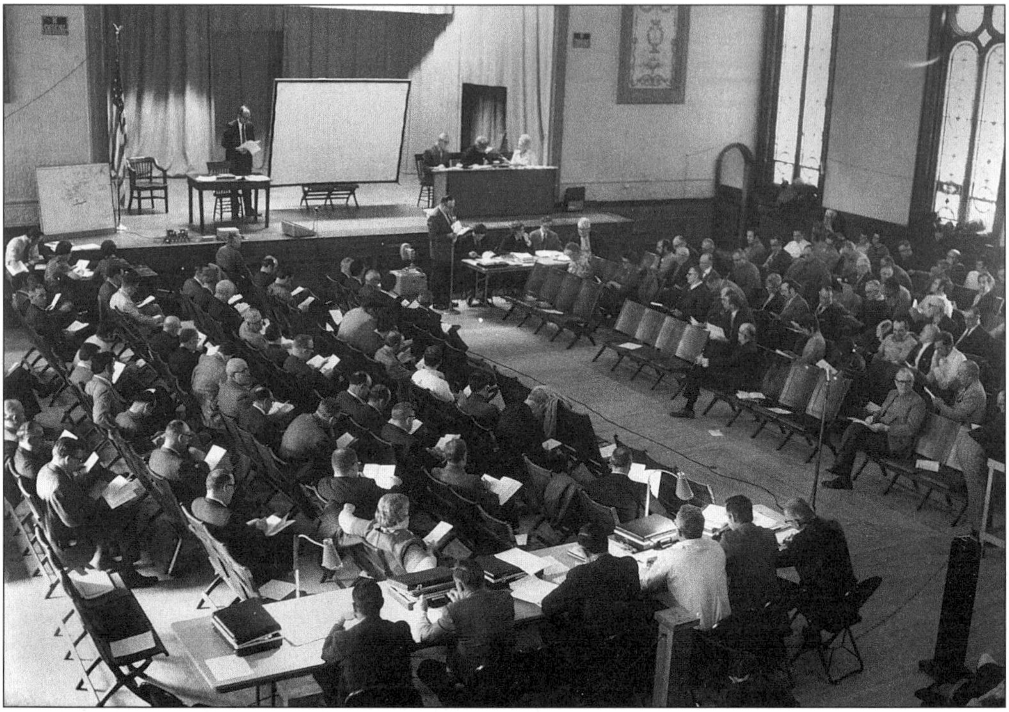

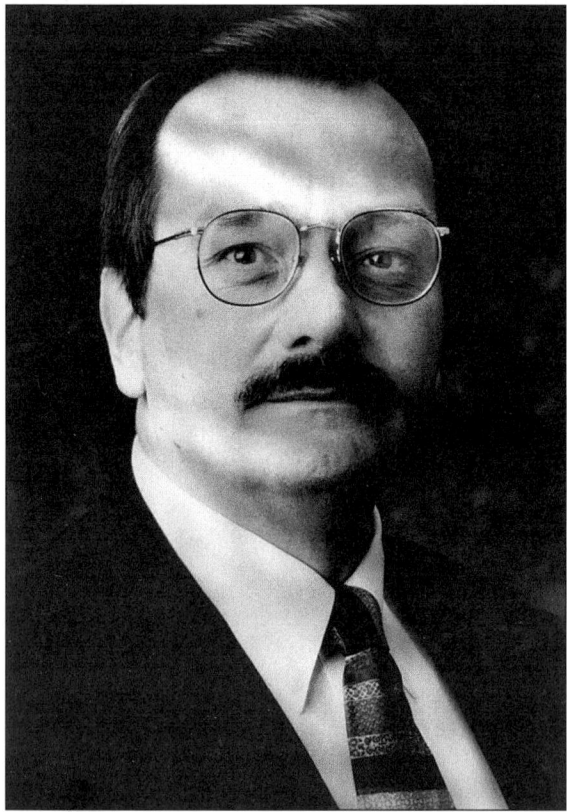

The upper floor of the town hall has been used at various times for elections, games, parties, and—as this 1960s picture shows—town meetings. At first, only male residents could attend town meetings. It was only after the acceptance of the 19th Amendment that all residents could vote. In 1933, a representative town government was adopted. With a new charter in 1996, the practice of town meetings was dissolved in favor of a mayor and city council.

For years, Easthampton relied on a three-member board of selectmen to handle the daily affairs of the town. After a brief try with full-time administrators, a new charter was adopted in 1996. With it came the first mayoral election for mayor. Michael A. Tautznik emerged from a field of seven candidates and won the election. He was reelected in 1999.

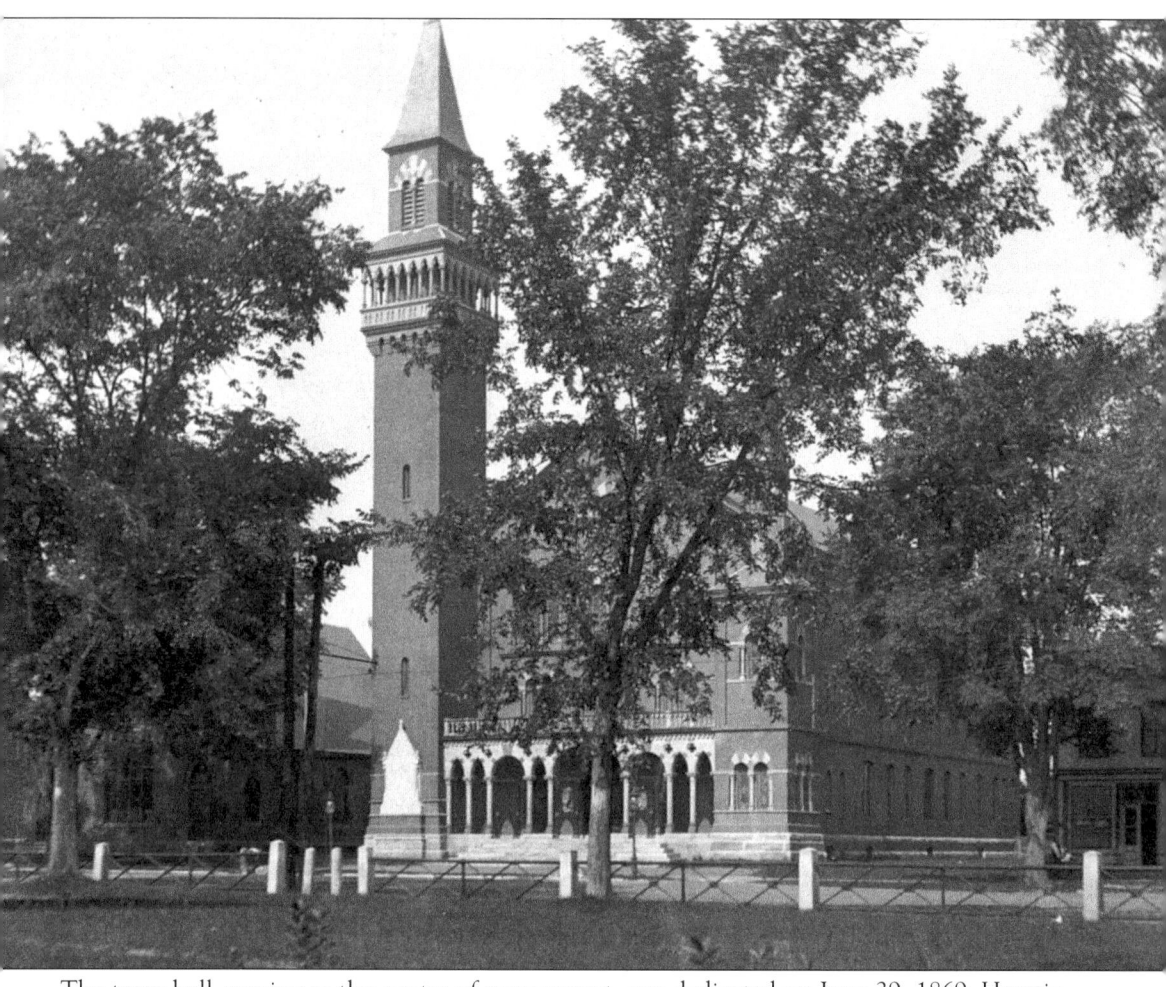

The town hall, serving as the center of government, was dedicated on June 29, 1869. Horatio Knight chaired the building committee. Charles Parker of Boston was the architect, and E. R. Bosworth was the builder. The town hall is listed on the National Register of Historic Places.

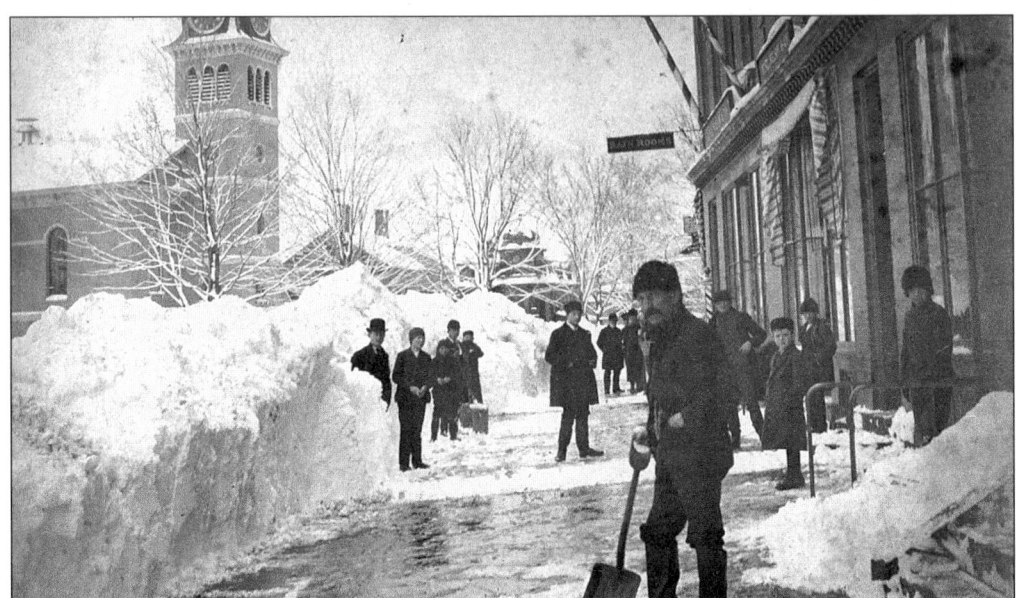

On Sunday March 11, 1888, snow started falling and did not stop until that Wednesday in one of the worst storms of the 19th century. Easthampton, like many East Coast communities, was cut off as telegraph and rail services were interrupted. In this photograph, Shop Row is being dug out. Two elderly men died as a result of the storm, while one boy (future postmaster Edward Diamond) was born.

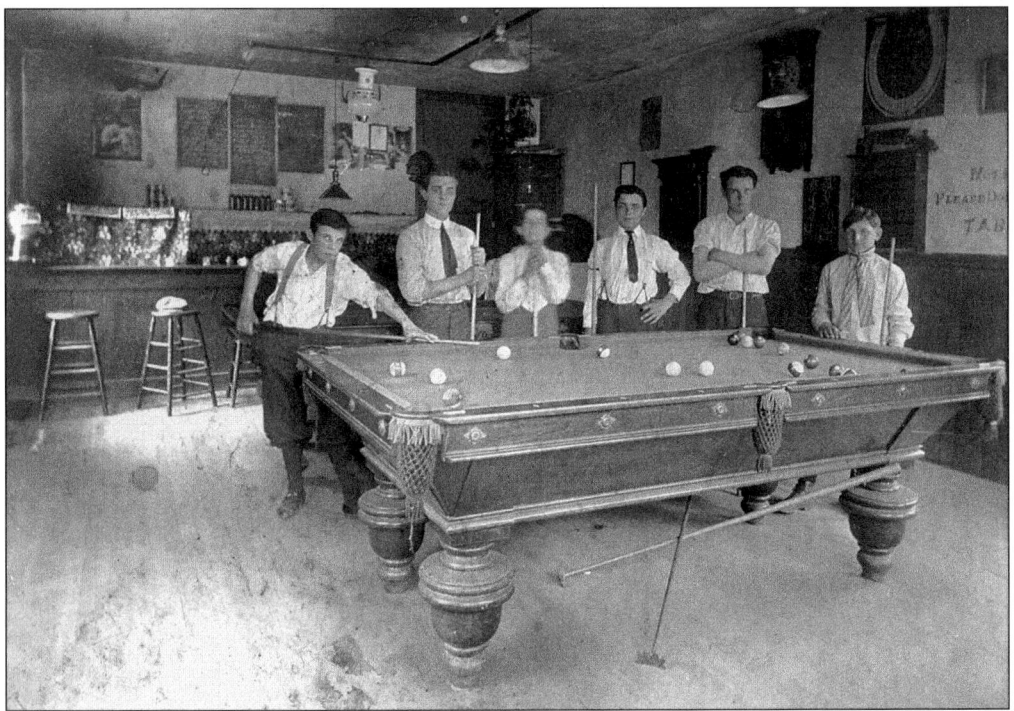

This Cottage Street poolroom and bar was owned by Thomas Lynn and later by Charles Lewandowski, who closed it for Prohibition. Following Prohibition, Thomas Lynn opened a package store that would have a long run on Cottage Street.

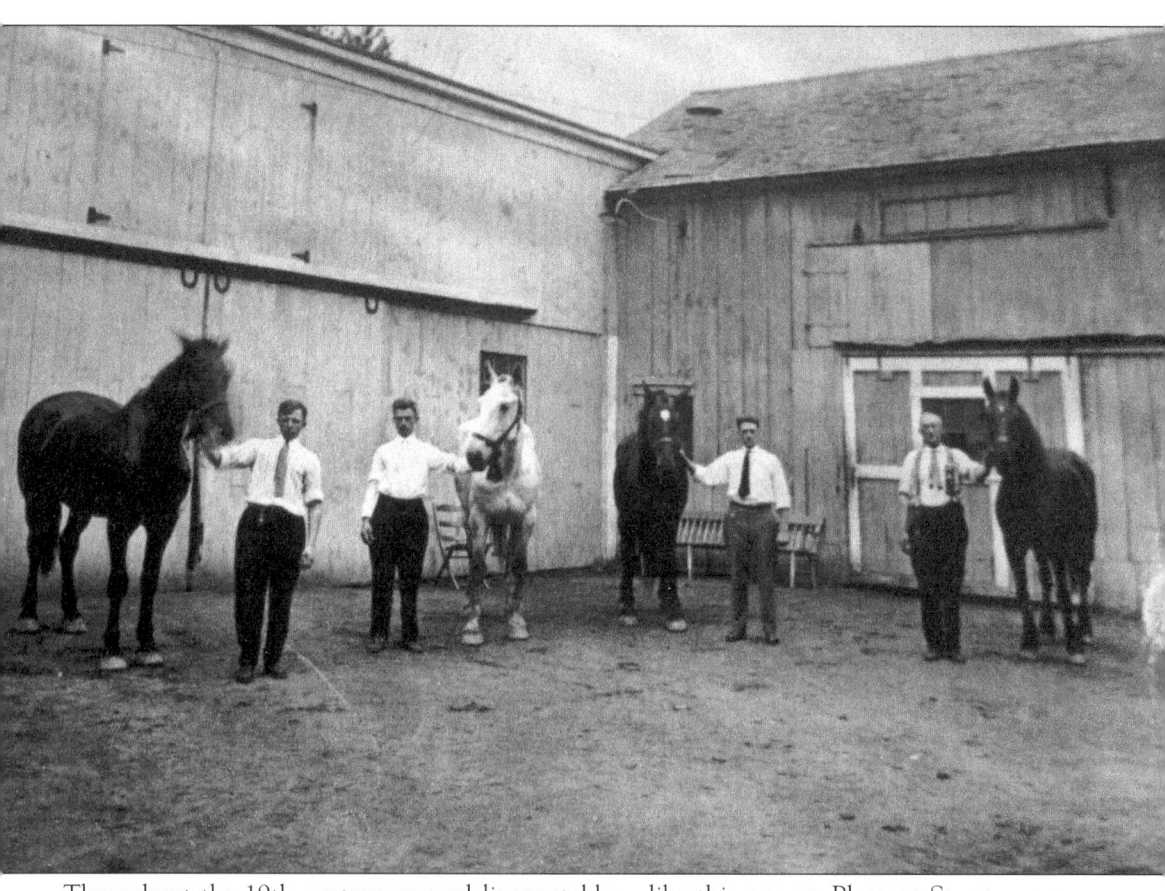

Throughout the 19th century, several livery stables—like this one on Pleasant Street—were located in town. Horses were called on to help people travel and work. The livery stable was a necessity of life.

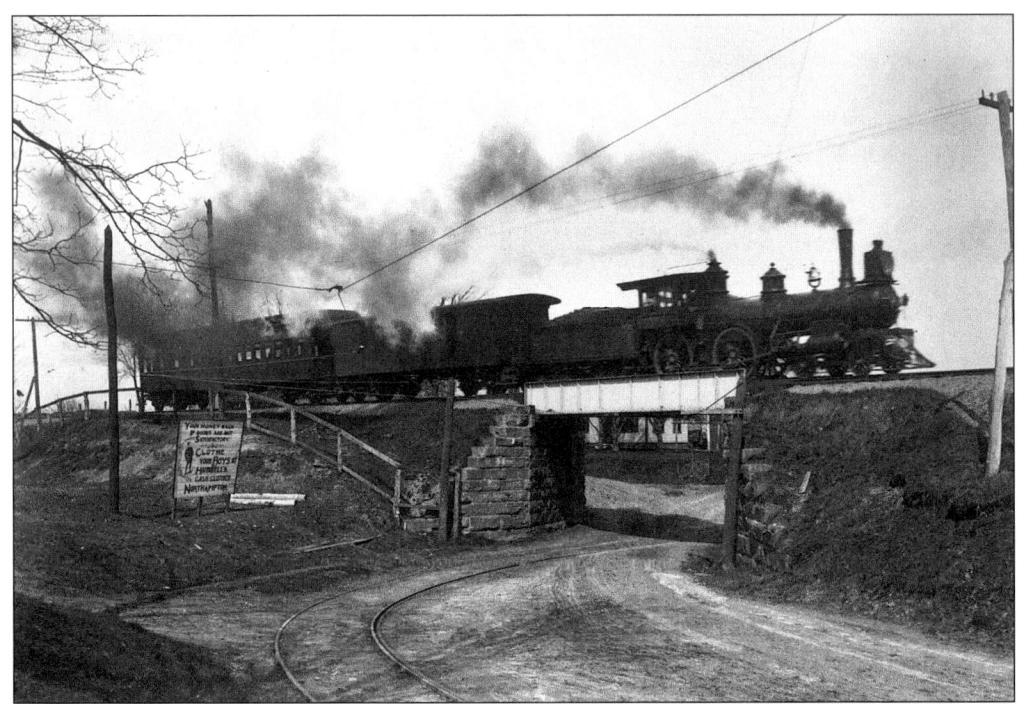

Two railroads served Easthampton. One was the Mount Tom Railroad, which became the Connecticut River Railroad, and still later, part of the Boston and Maine Railroad. The second railroad was the New Haven and Northampton Railroad, which was taken over by the New York–New Haven and Hartford Railroad. Here, a train crosses the overpass at Lovefield Street. Note the trolley track on the street.

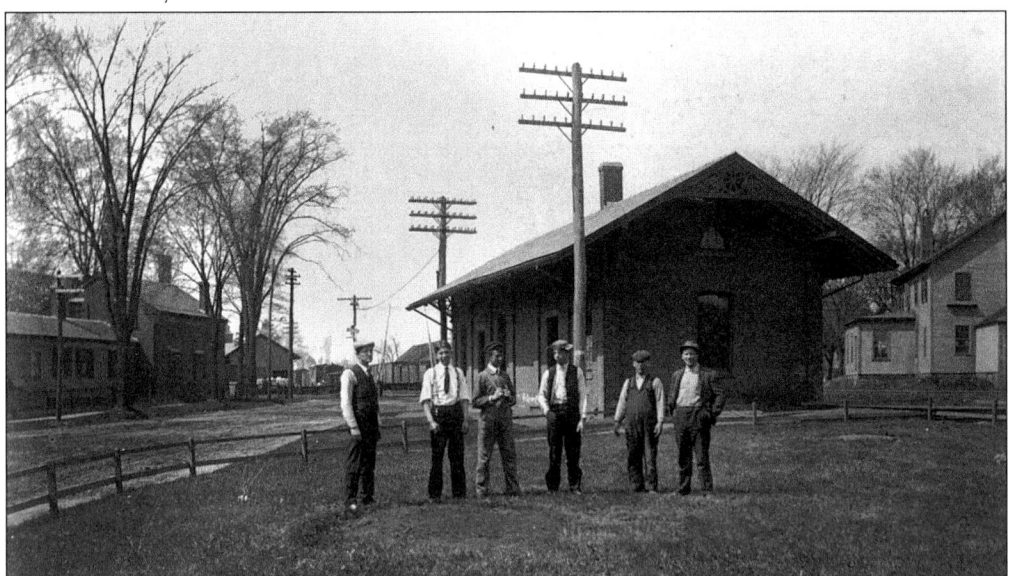

Staff members of the New York–New Haven and Hartford Railroad pose in front of their station. This station and the Boston and Maine station were discontinued in 1914, when a new station was constructed to serve both railroads. The new station was built just a few yards from this station, and is now owned by Williston Academy.

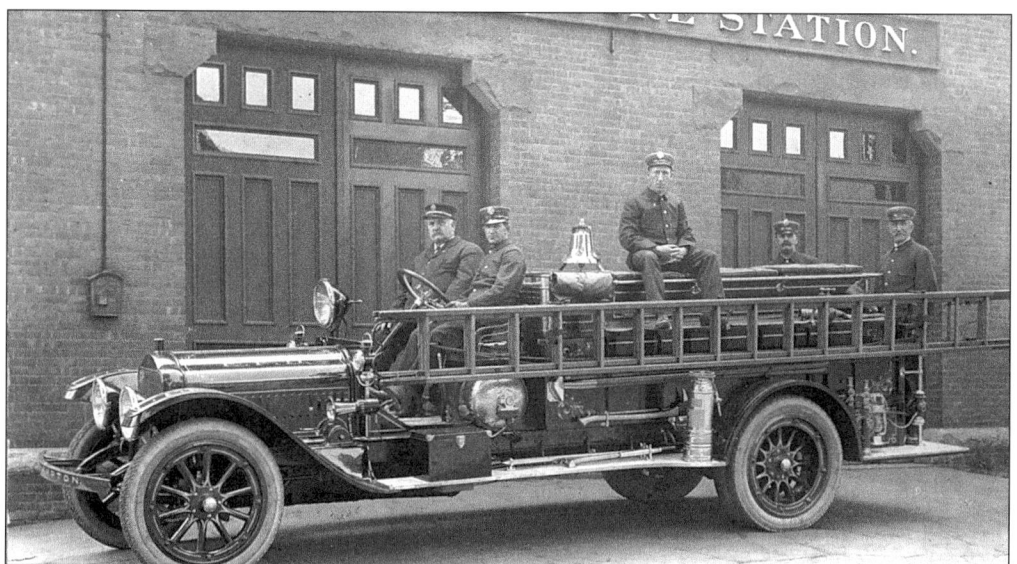

During the 19th century, volunteer fire companies provided fire protection to the town. In 1886, this two-bay building was constructed to house the town's fire equipment. In 1907, the first two full-time firefighters were hired, and the department gradually grew. The fire station was enlarged in 1929, doubling the size of the building and making it a four-bay station. It was decommissioned in December 1999 and now awaits a new use.

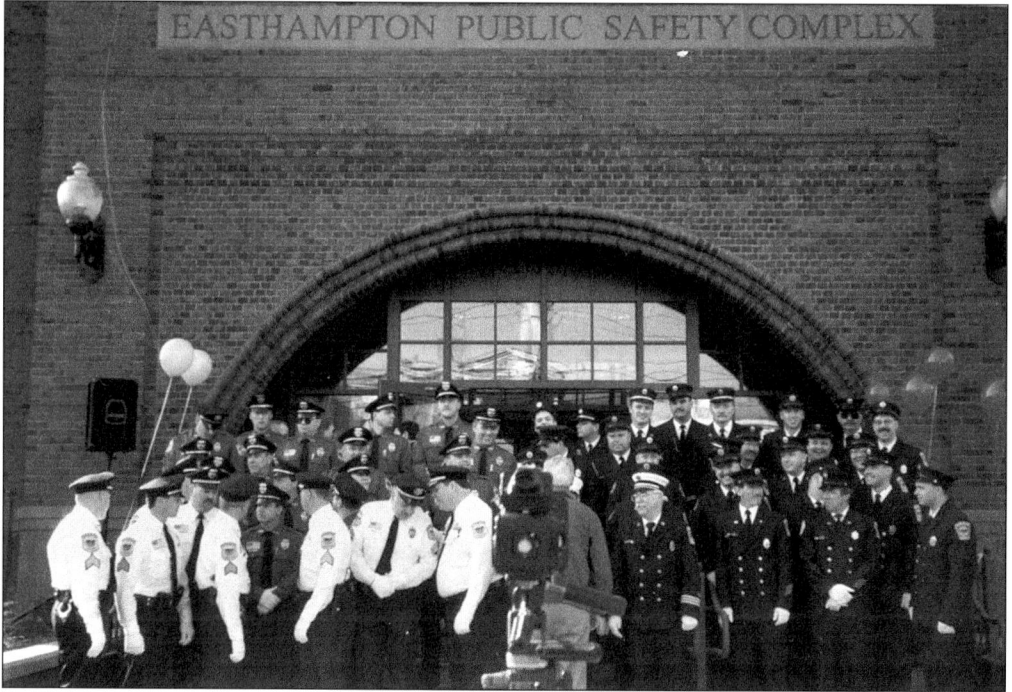

On October 30, 1999, this new public safety complex was dedicated as the new headquarters for the police and fire departments. Members of the two departments post at the front entrance. In December 1999, the complex was officially opened.

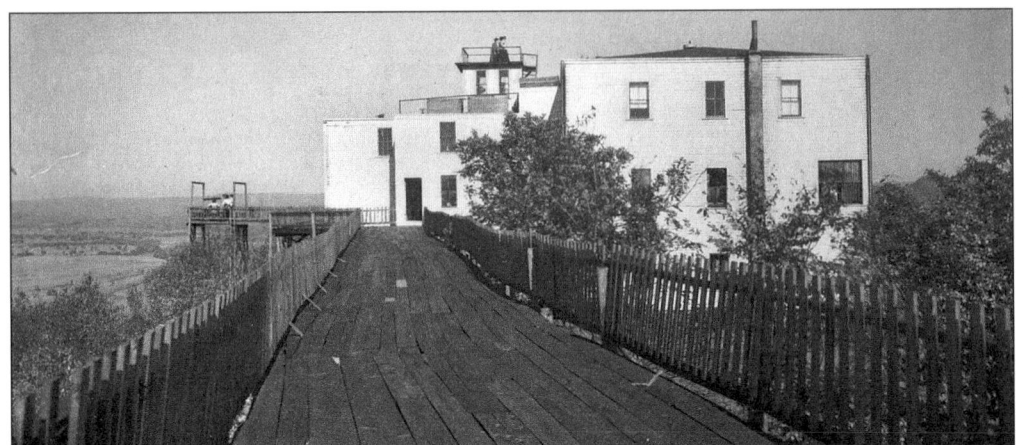

On the summit of Mount Nonotuck stood the Eyrie House, a small hotel for people escaping the summer heat. It served as a summertime hotel, opening in 1861. The hotel boasted 30 rooms, a 200-foot boardwalk, and a spectacular view of Easthampton and surrounding valley. It also offered a variety of animals, including a tame bear. Although it was popular in the 1870s, it gradually fell out of favor with increased use of the trolley, allowing street railway companies to attract people to amusement parks. The Eyrie House was destroyed by fire in 1901 and is now part of the Mount Tom State Reservation.

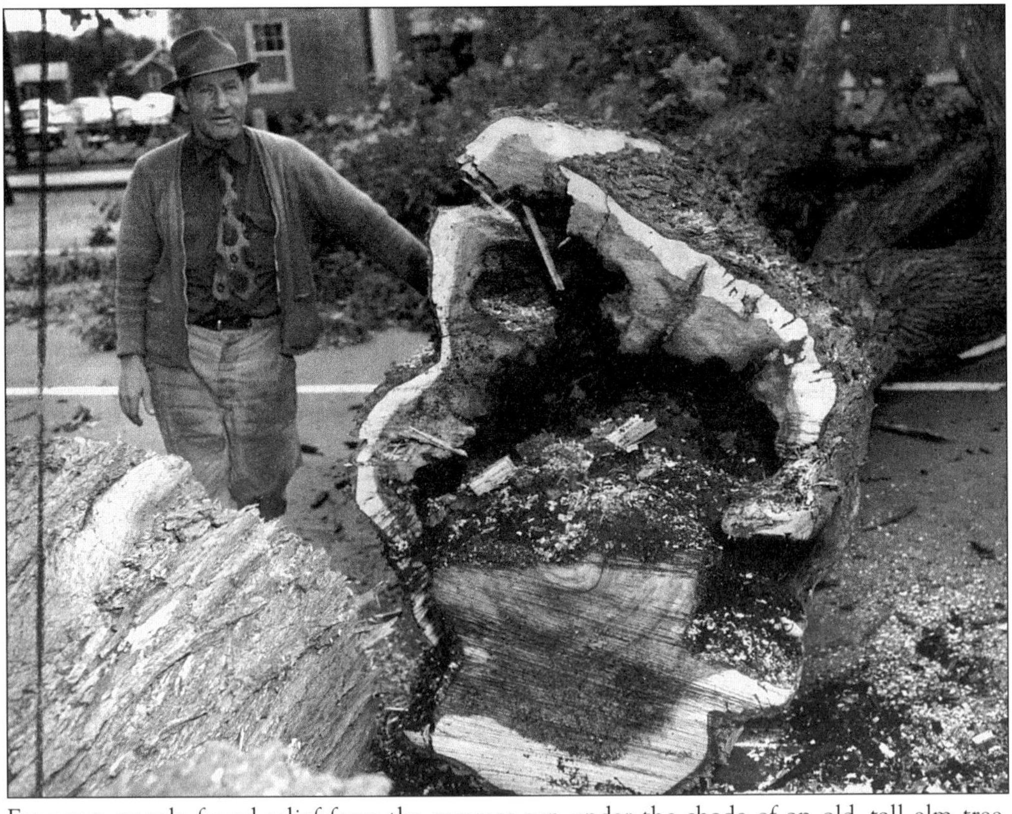

For years, people found relief from the summer sun under the shade of an old, tall elm tree. Dutch elm disease, however, killed many elms beginning in the 1940s. Here, the tree warden Edward Beauregard stands next to an elm that he just downed.

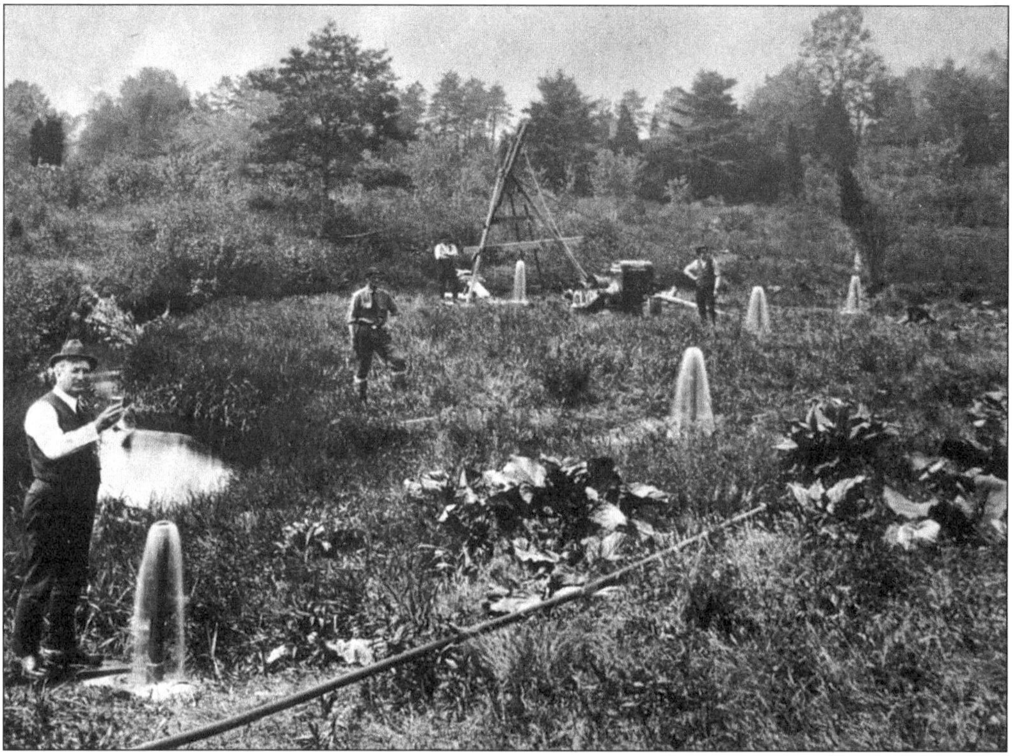

The need for a dependable water source became a top priority for the town in the early 20th century, as it struggled to meet the needs of its growing population. The drilling of artesian wells at Hendrick Street began in 1908. Wells are still the primary source of water for the city.

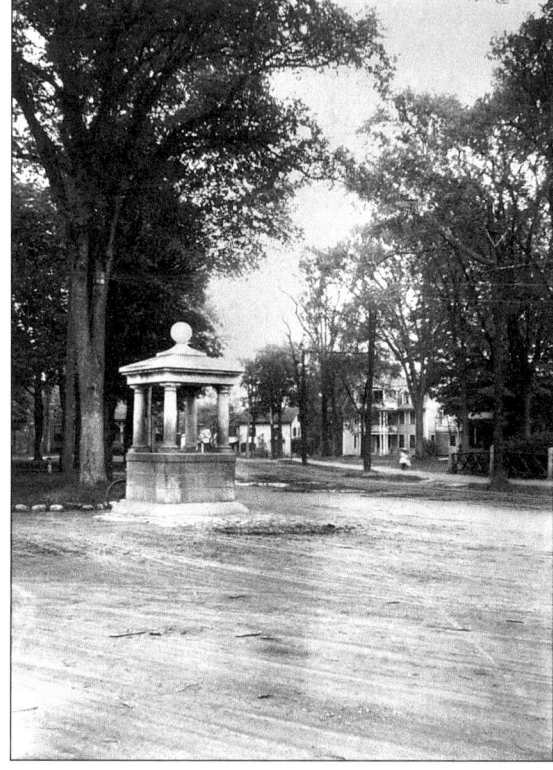

The John Mayer fountain was constructed in 1902 as a place for horses, humans, and dogs to get water. It stands in the town common, which is named Pulaski Park in memory of General Pulaski.

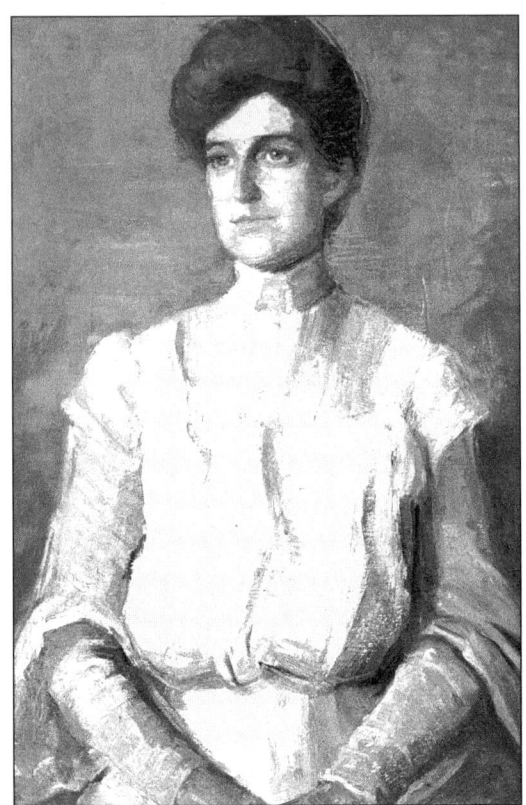

This portrait of Gertrude Clark was painted by Isabelle Ferry, who was born as Isabelle Hermann on September 8, 1852. She moved to town when she married Edward Ferry. Mrs. Ferry was an art teacher for the Holyoke school system and studied art in this country and in France. At various times, she studied under the supervision of Dwight William Tryon and Robert Henri. Her work was displayed in New York City, Hartford, and the Corcoran Gallery in Washington, D.C. One of her students was William Chadwick, who became a noted artist based in Lyme, Connecticut.

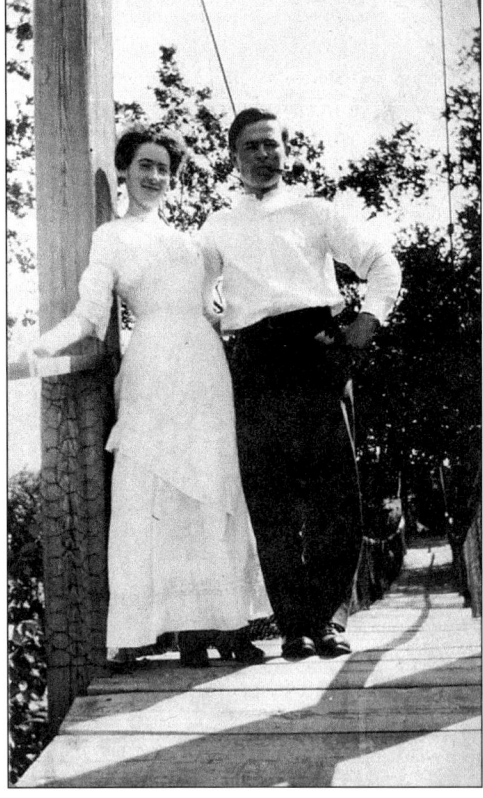

Marie Barcomb and her husband, William Laurion, pose on a swinging bridge over the Manhan River. Marie and her older sister came here to take jobs at the West Boylston Company. The money that they sent to their family in upstate New York gave their parents, four sisters, and two brothers the opportunity to come here also.

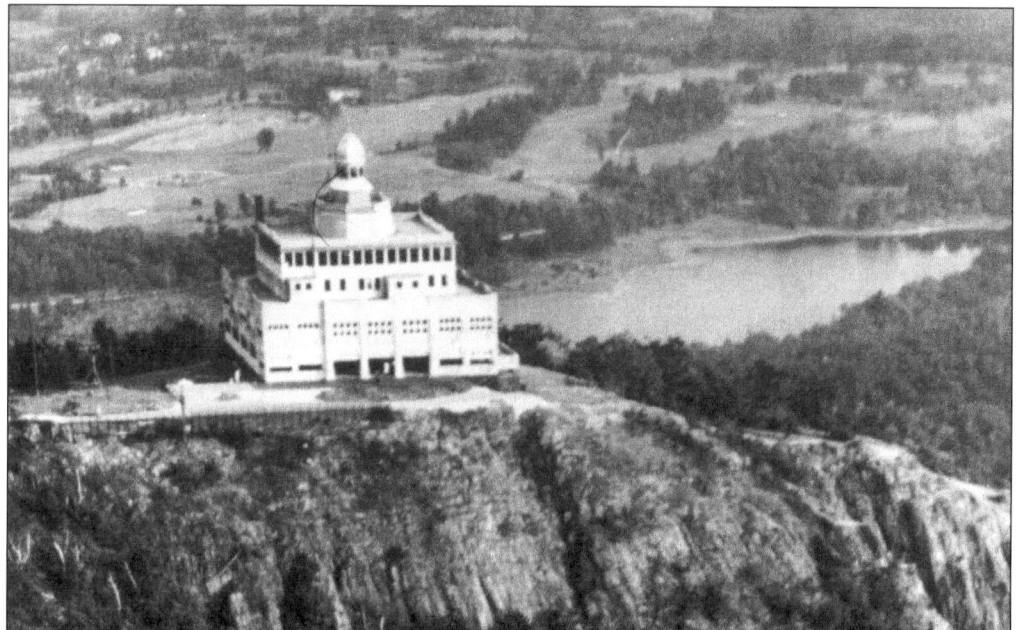

Shown is the second summit house located on Mount Tom, overlooking Easthampton. Summit houses stood on Mount Tom from 1897 until the last one was removed in 1938. The first was destroyed by fire in 1900 and was replaced by the summit house pictured here. It was a popular destination, along with the adjoining Mount Park amusement park. On May 2, 1929, a spectacular fire destroyed the summit house. It was replaced by a steel frame structure, which was sold for scrap iron in 1938.

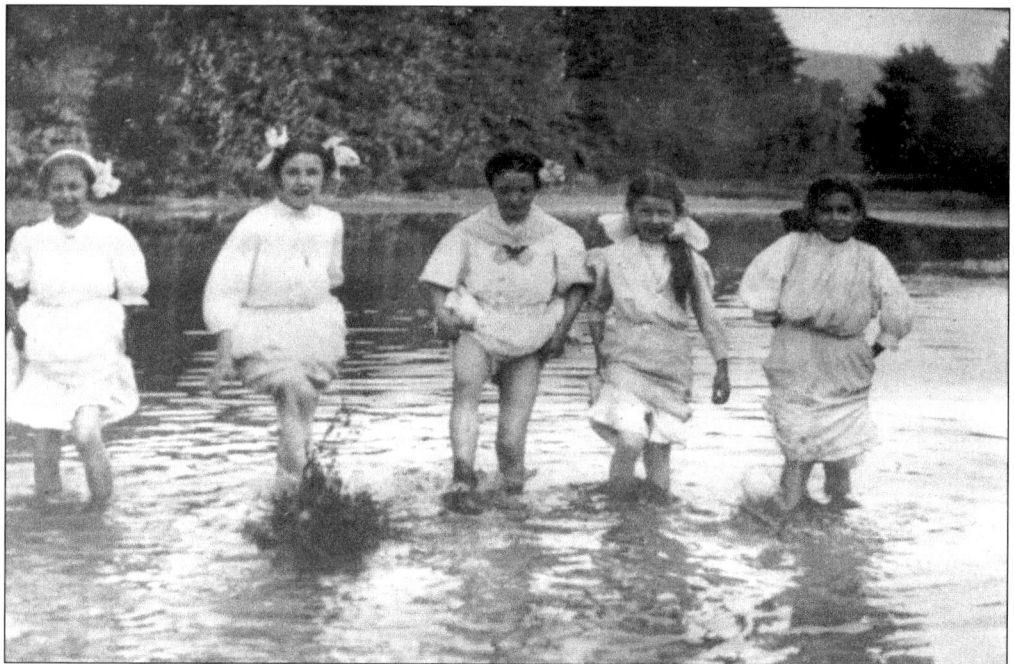

Nellie Dwyer (second from the left) and her four friends look like they are having a great time in the water of Nashawannuck Pond.

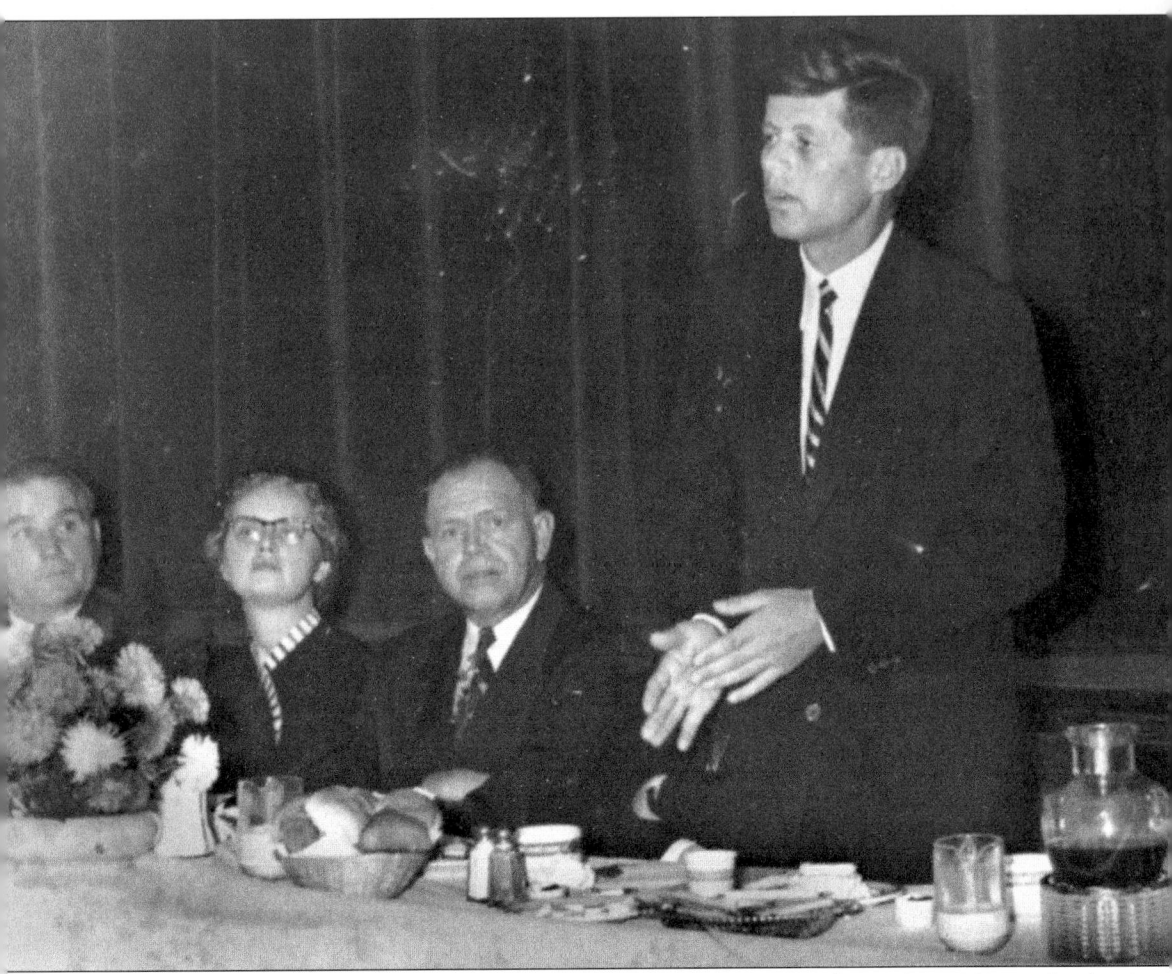

John F. Kennedy made just one trip to Easthampton, and that was during his 1952 run for the U.S. Senate, when he challenged the incumbent Henry Cabot Lodge Jr. Here, Kennedy is speaking at the Pulaski Club while James Flavin, Frank Beltz, and Gertrude Beltz listen.

Eight
WHERE THEY LIVED

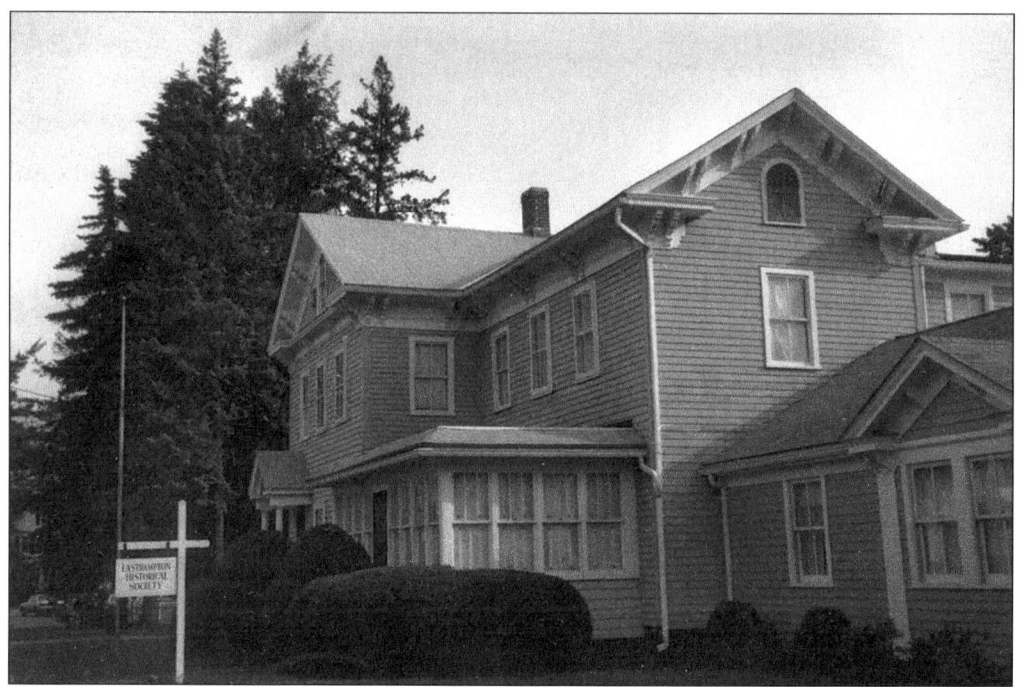

The house at 7 Holyoke Street was originally the home to a grocer and then to the theater-owner Joseph Rapalus, who gave the house to the Easthampton Historical Society. Today, the historical society maintains a museum at this house.

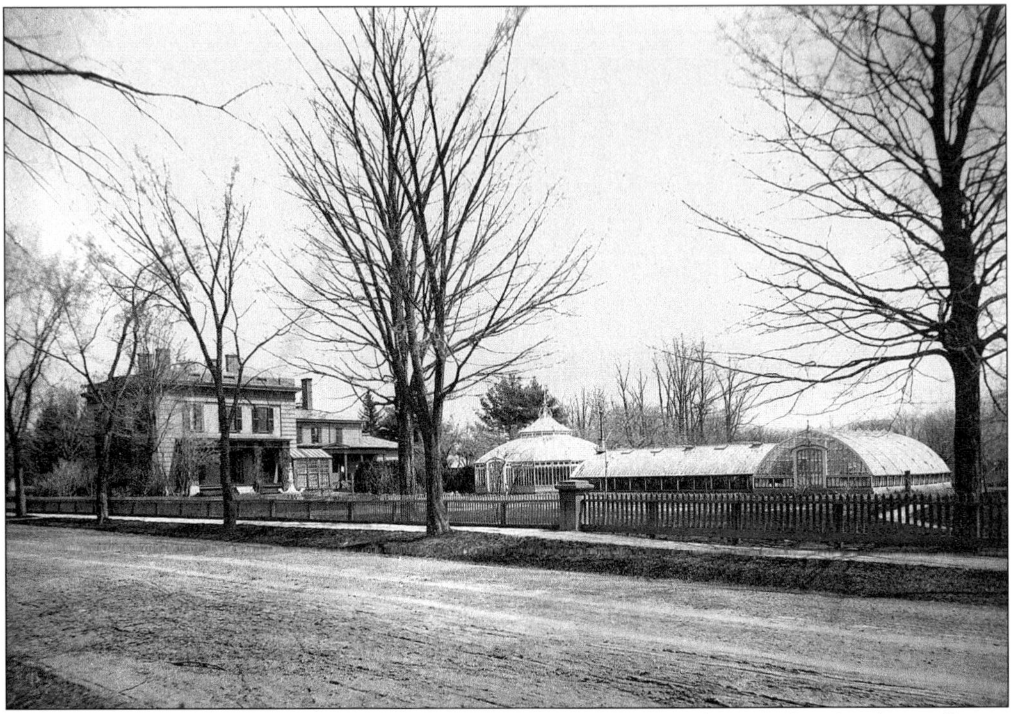

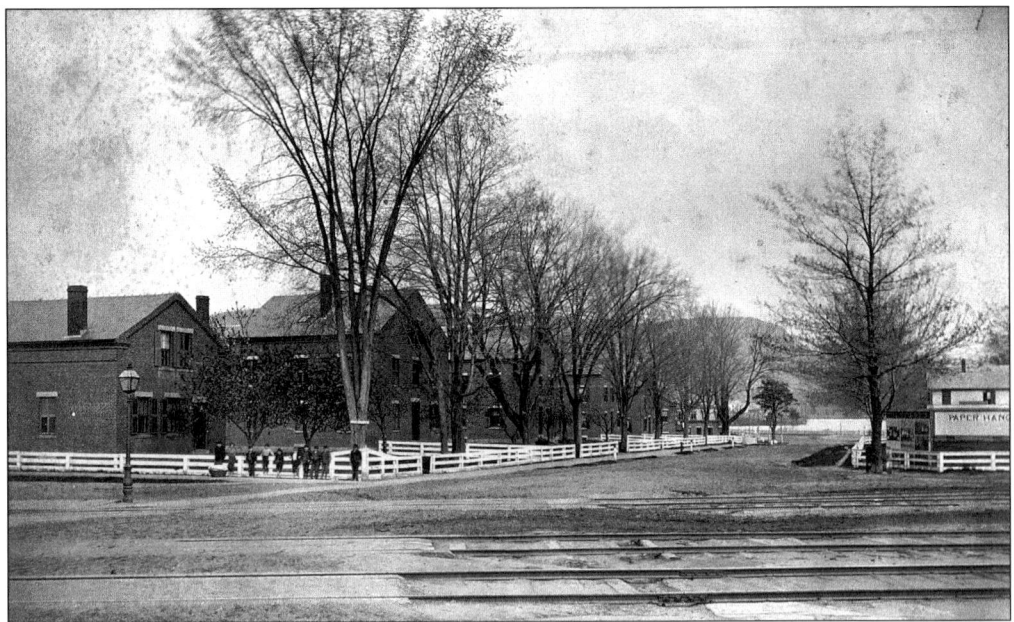

The estate of Samuel Williston on Park Street is now an administrative office for the Williston Northampton School. Williston lived here after he became wealthy and decided to open the button-making plant in Easthampton.

All but one of the Union Street boardinghouses for the Williston-Knight Button Company have been taken down. Five residences were constructed for the women who were hired to tend the machines in the mill. Lieutenant Governor Knight was accused of having an affair with one of the matrons and was expelled from the Payson Church in 1878.

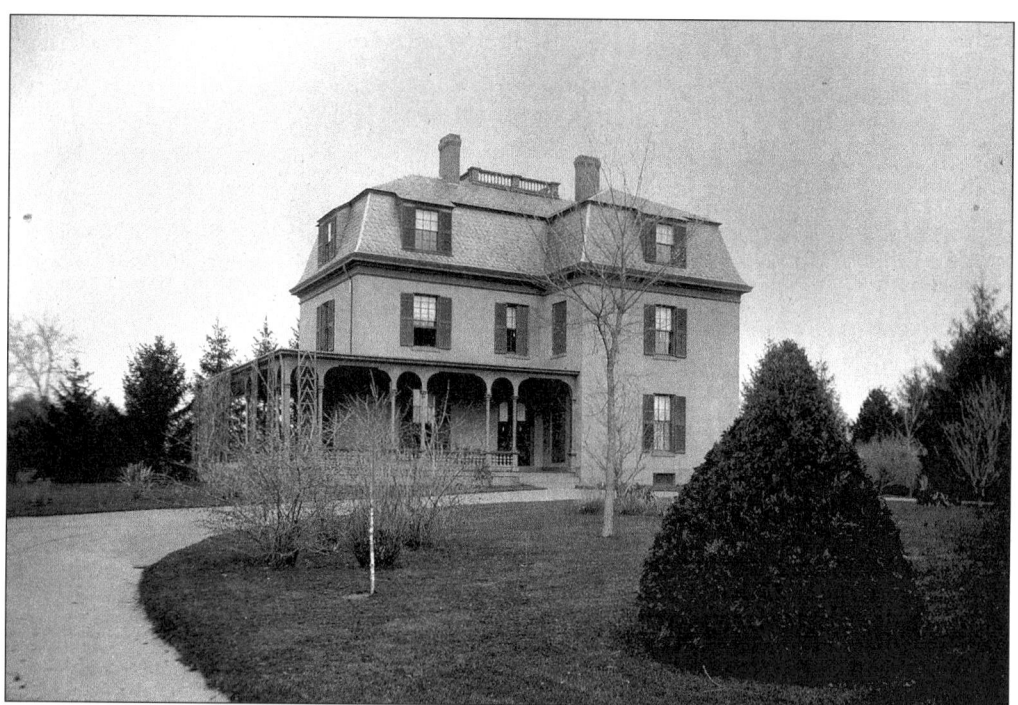

Edmund Sawyer owned this home on Park Street. After Sawyer's death, his estate was carved up, and Brewster Court was cut through it. This house was taken down to make way for a Williston Academy building.

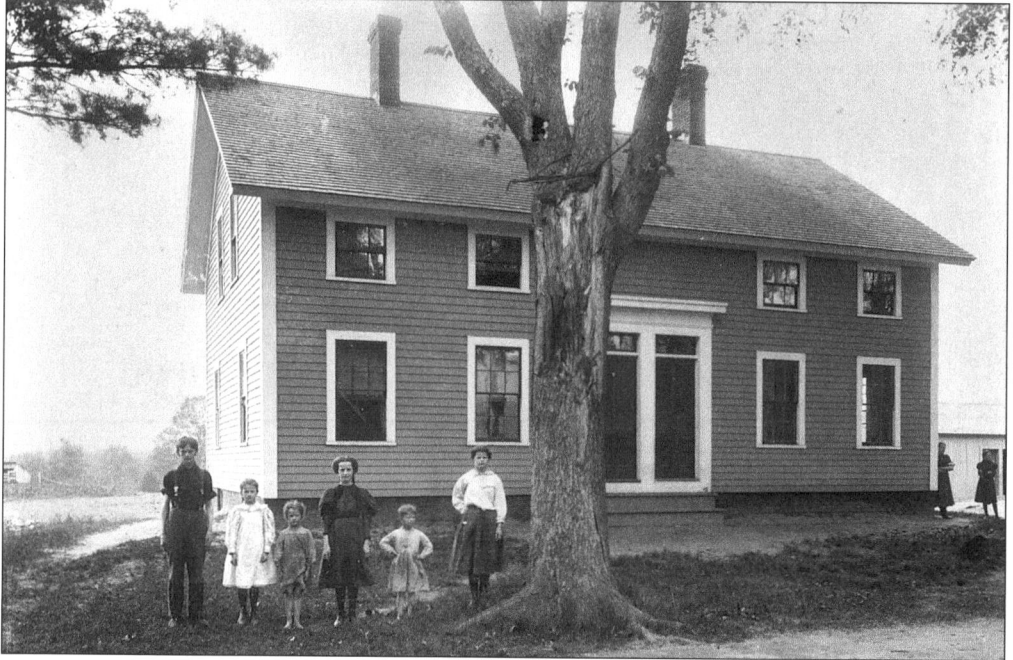

There are some 32 of these Greek Revival–style duplex houses near Pleasant Street and New City. They were constructed by the Williston Mills in the mid-1860s. The West Boylston Manufacturing Company owned them until 1931, when they were sold as private residences.

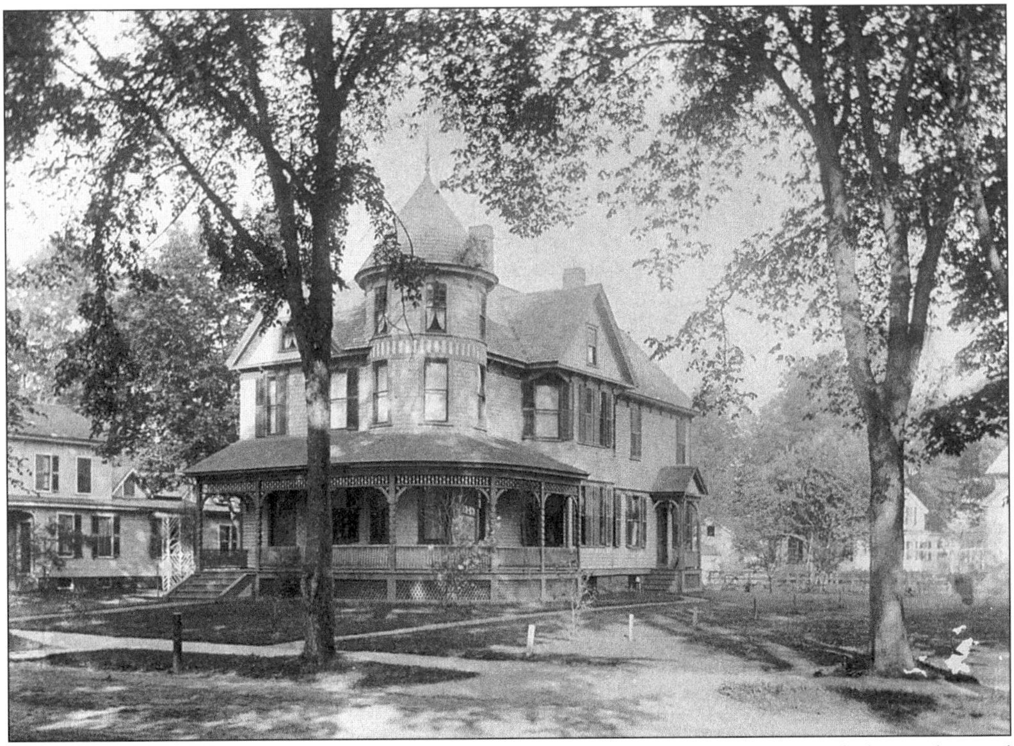

George Colton, owner of the Colton Elastic Mills, owned this Queen Ann–style house located at 21 Park Street. This house was constructed in 1892 and remains a private residence.

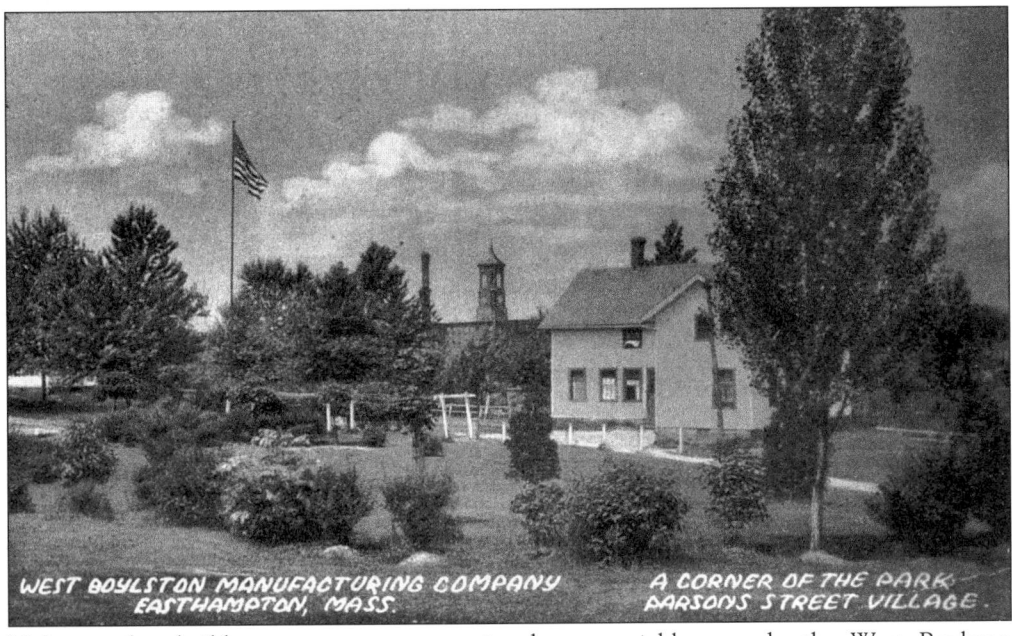

Unhappy that builders were not constructing homes quickly enough, the West Boylston Manufacturing Company constructed the dwellings that made up the New City section of town. Nine streets with over 70 dwellings were built. The company sold them in 1931 as private residences.

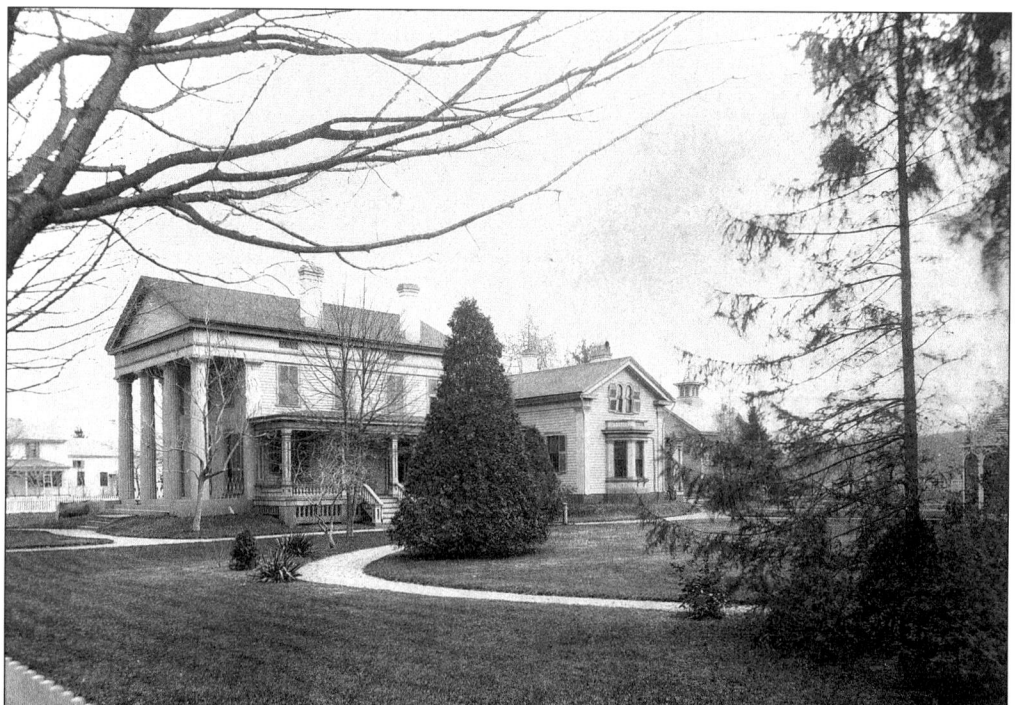

This Greek Colonial–style house was built for Horatio Knight. The house now stands on a greatly reduced parcel of land and has been converted to apartments

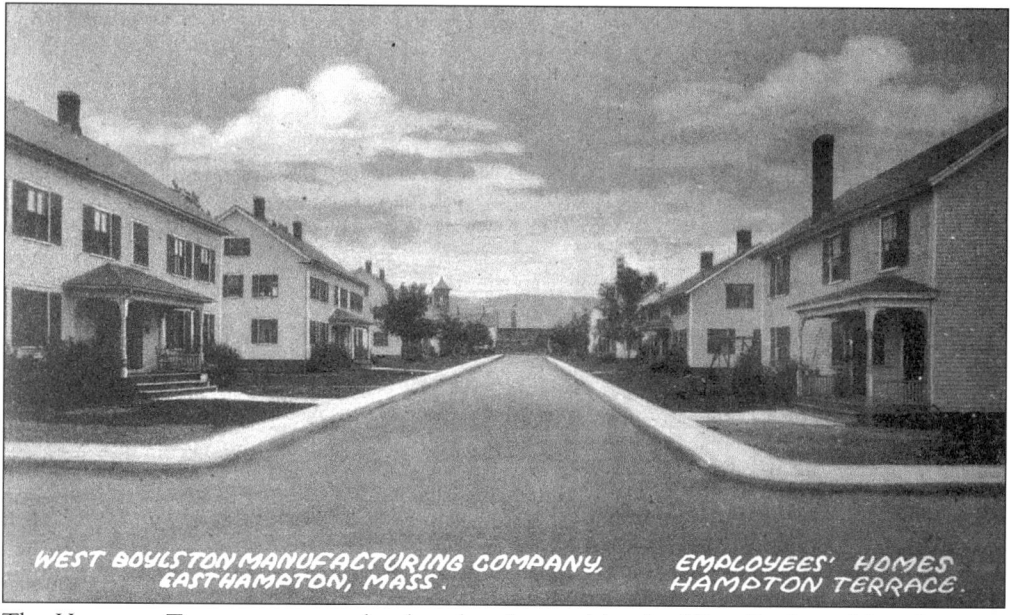

The Hampton Terrace area was developed and owned by the West Boylston Manufacturing Company. The company built the dwellings along seven streets, including Pleasant Street, Hampton Terrace, Terrace View, Berkley Street, Arlington Street, Pleasant Green, and Ridgewood Terrace. The crown jewel of this area was the company's recreation hall, which was built in 1919.

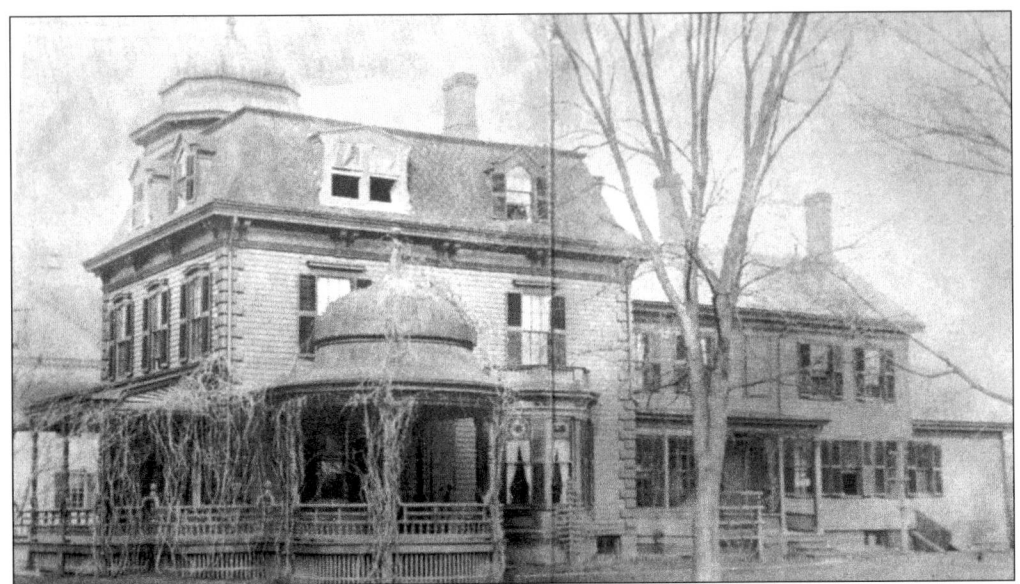

E. Thomas Sawyer, the general manager of the Easthampton Rubber Thread Company, built this mansion in 1867. Sawyer died in 1897, when he accidentally swallowed a false tooth that had broken off his plate. The St. Phillip's Episcopal Church used the building as a rectory for many years.

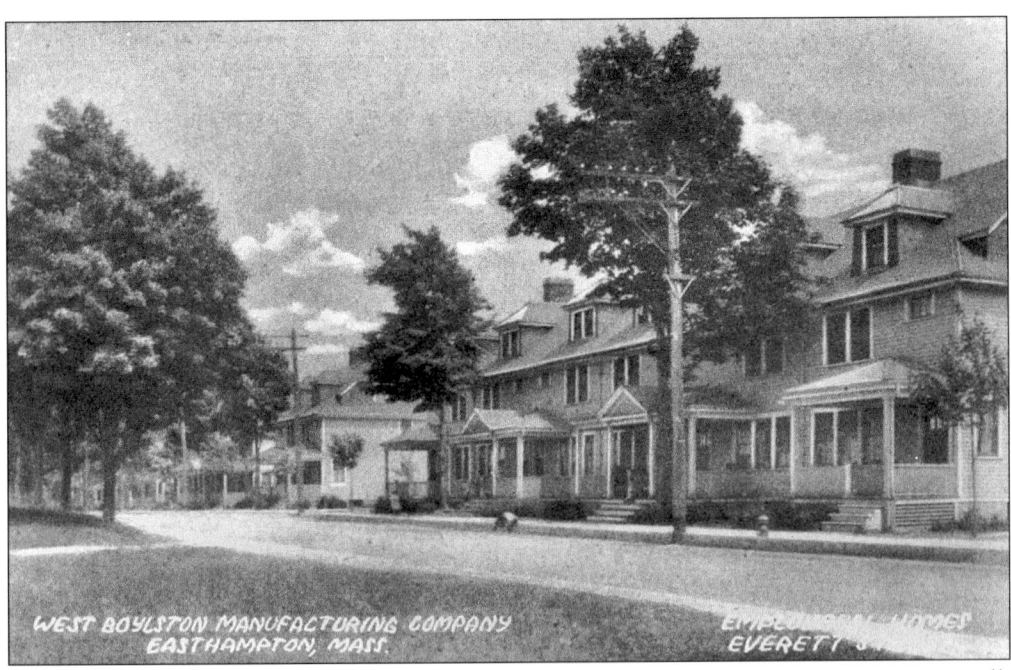

The West Boylston Manufacturing Company built these row houses along Everett, Lovell, Grant, Irving and Hudson Streets. Employees used a footbridge for easy access to the rear of Mill No. 6. The company owned some 94 individual dwellings.

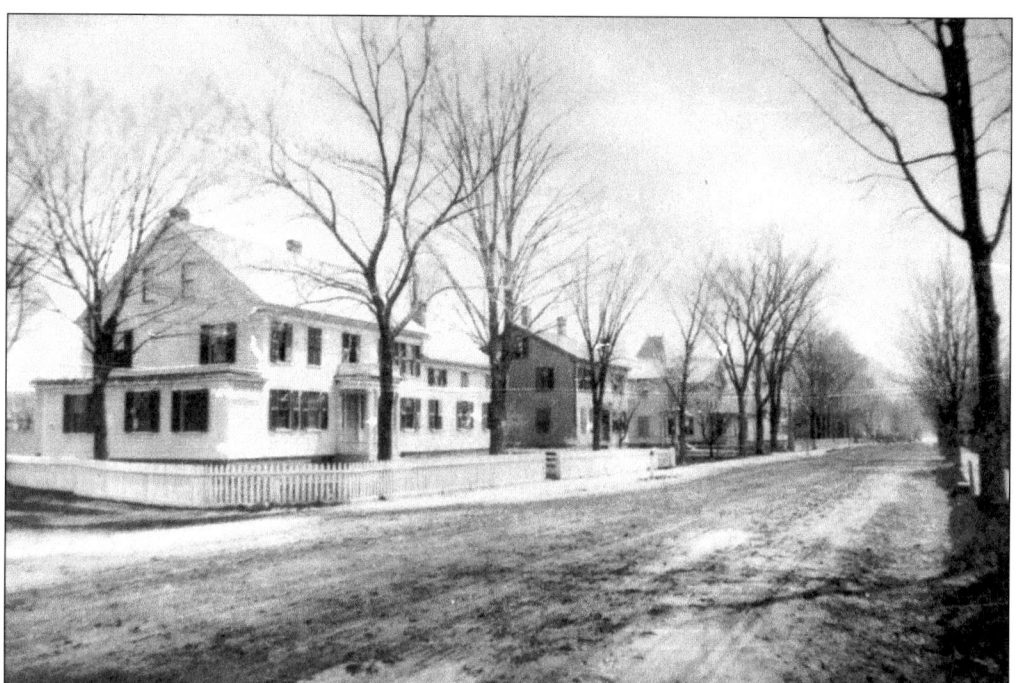

Located on the corner of Union and High Streets was a piece of land, a Williston Academy boardinghouse, and a home owned by Dr. Edward Williams. In 1932, the federal government purchased both houses. The Union Street post office was later constructed on this site.

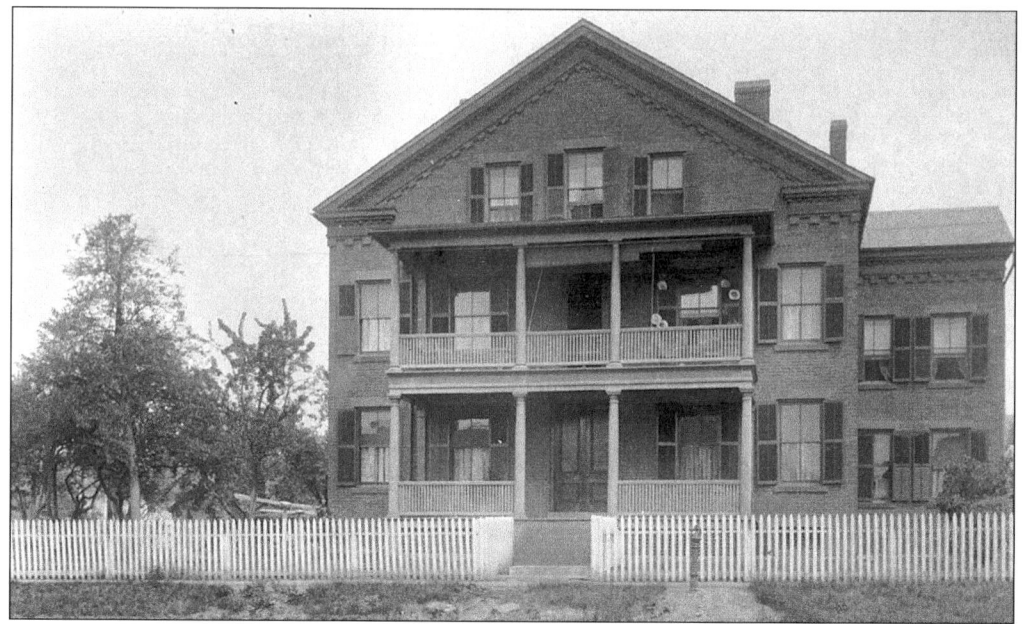

Herman Hupfer, an employee of the Glendale Company, owned this house at 21 Adams Street. It was sold in 1913 to the Sisters of Saint Joseph for use as a convent serving the Immaculate Conception Parish. It is now an apartment building.

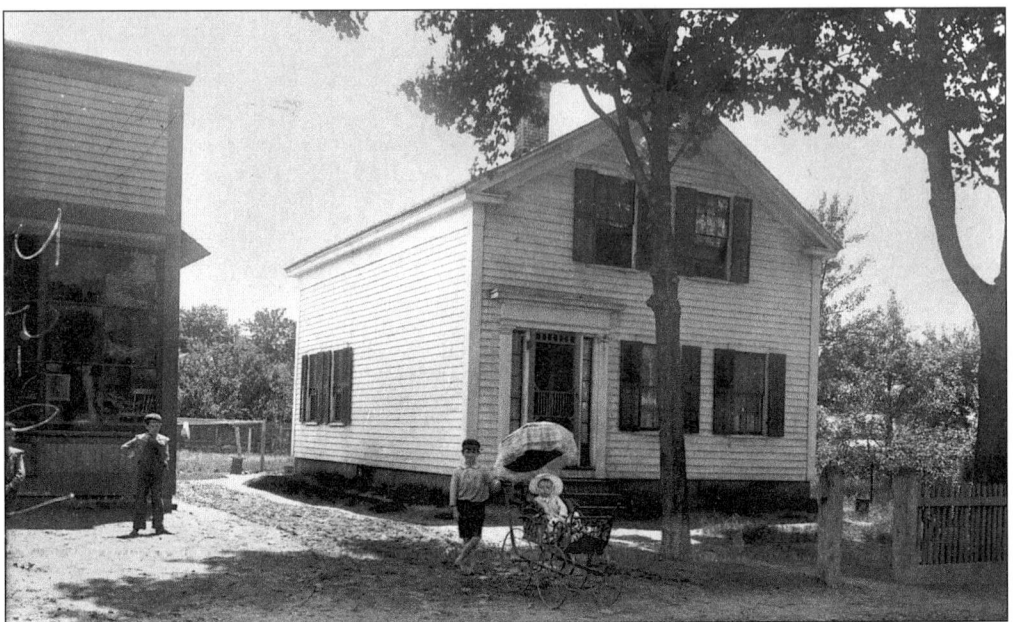

At the turn of the 19th century, this Cottage Street house was moved to the rear of its lot in order to sell its frontage to a commercial development. This house is now located behind 98 Cottage Street.

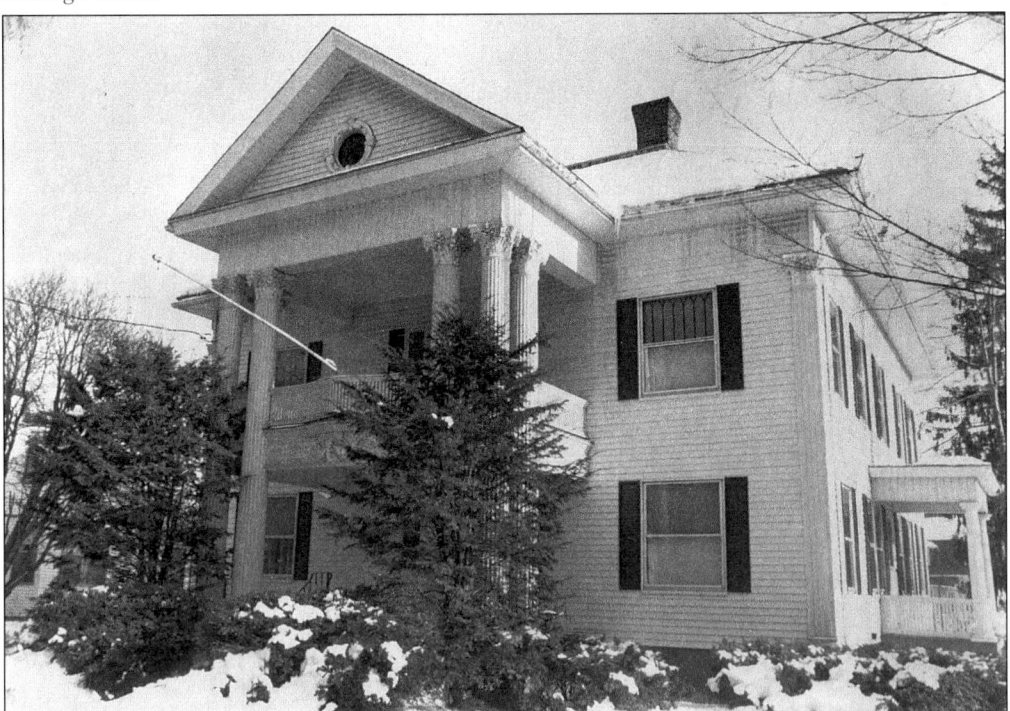

Built in 1904 by local builder Delos Pepin, this house at 216 Main Street is of neo-classical design. It is located on a portion of Edmund Sawyer's former estate. It was first owned by an attorney named Winslow Edwards. Franklin Pitcher purchased the house in 1915. In 1920, he donated it to the Helping Hand Society, the organization that maintains the house today.

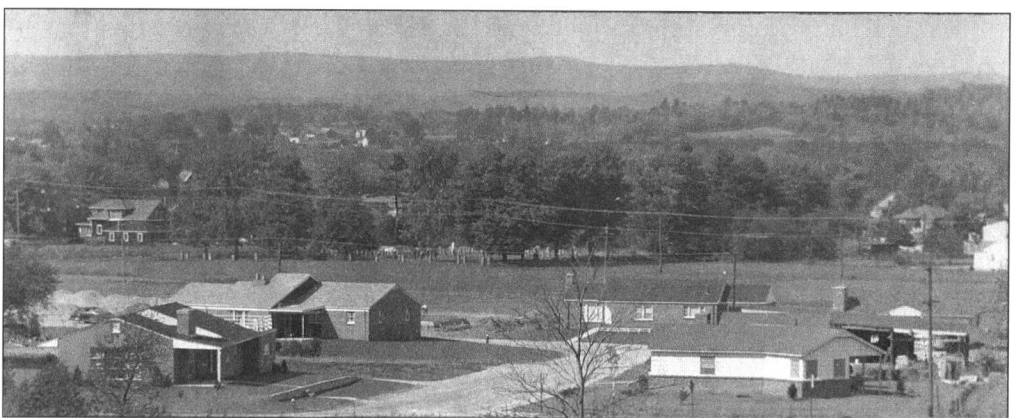

An example of post-WWII housing is the Keddy Vadnais development, which is located between Holyoke and East Streets. These types of houses were built on smaller lots for a single family.

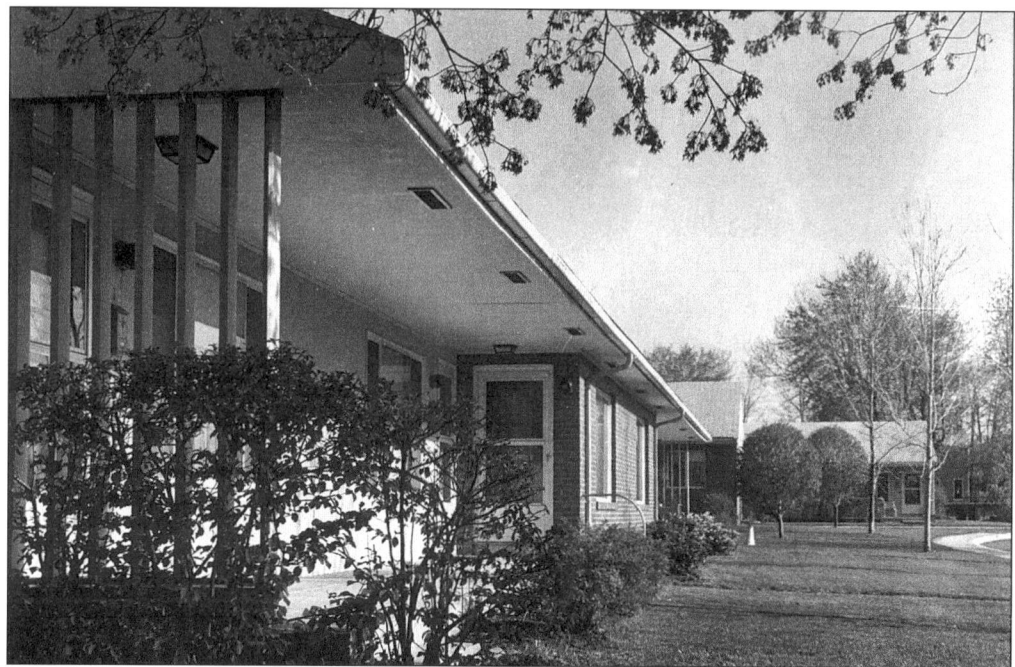

In 1948, the Easthampton Housing Authority was created to help provide housing for families, low-income individuals, and the elderly. On November 11, 1958, ground was broken for Sunrise Manor, a 30-unit facility for the elderly.

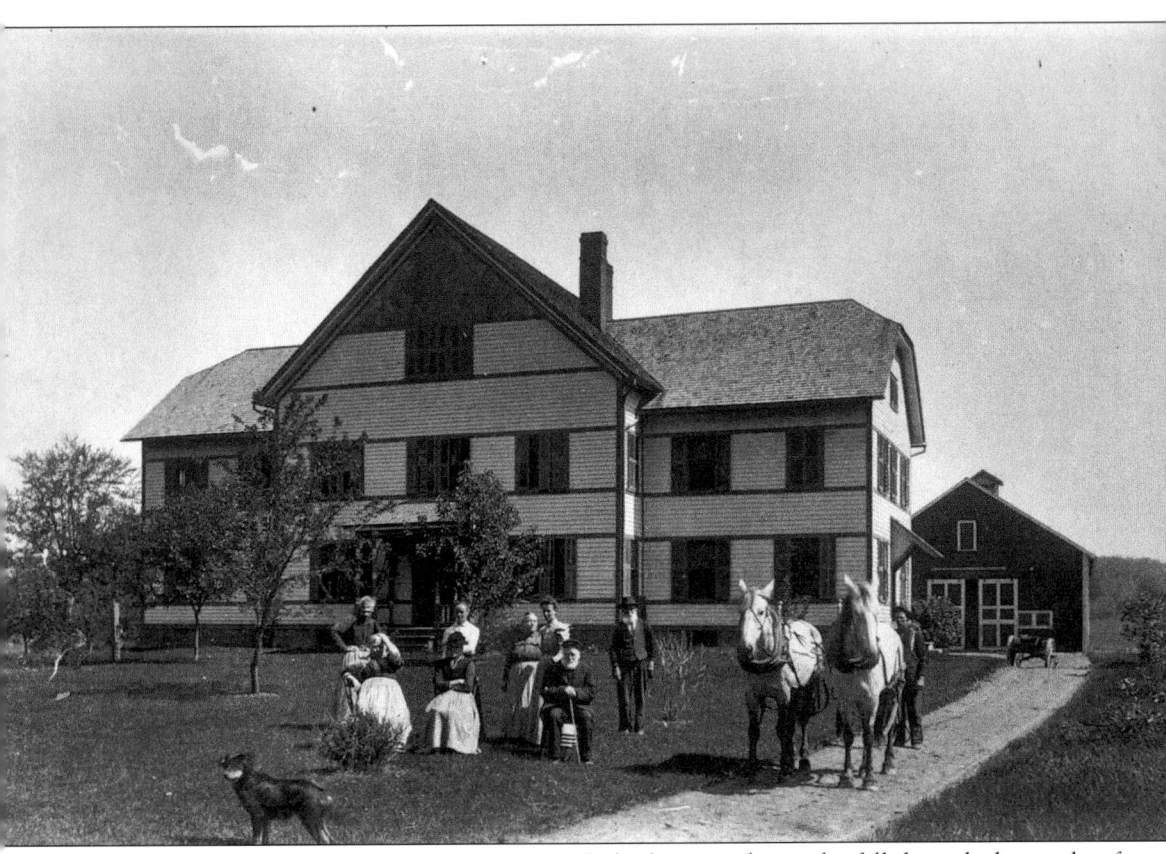

Easthampton built the town farm in 1890 to help those residents who fell through the cracks of the new industrial economy of the late 19th century. The Oliver Street house was enlarged during the Depression to house more residents. Now called the Town Lodging House, it is still in use as a home for indigent residents of the town. The town farm is listed on the National Register of Historic Places.